Experts in Court

The LAW AND PUBLIC POLICY: PSYCHOLOGY AND THE SOCIAL SCIENCES series includes books in three domains:

Legal Studies—writings by legal scholars about issues of relevance to psychology and the other social sciences, or that employ social science information to advance the legal analysis;

Social Science Studies—writings by scientists from psychology and the other social sciences about issues of relevance to law and public policy; and

Forensic Studies—writings by psychologists and other mental health scientists and professionals about issues relevant to forensic mental health science and practice.

The series is guided by its editor, Bruce D. Sales, PhD, JD, ScD(hc), University of Arizona; and coeditors, Bruce J. Winick, JD, University of Miami; Norman J. Finkel, PhD, Georgetown University; and Valerie P. Hans, PhD, University of Delaware.

* * *

Experts in Court

Reconciling Law, Science,
and Professional Knowledge

Bruce D. Sales
Daniel W. Shuman

AMERICAN PSYCHOLOGICAL ASSOCIATION

WASHINGTON, DC

Published by
American Psychological Association
750 First Street, NE
Washington, DC 20002
www.apa.org

To order
APA Order Department
P.O. Box 92984
Washington, DC 20090-2984
Tel: (800) 374-2721
Direct: (202) 336-5510
Fax: (202) 336-5502
TDD/TTY: (202) 336-6123
Online: www.apa.org/books/
E-mail: order@apa.org

In the U.K., Europe, Africa, and the Middle East, copies may be ordered from
American Psychological Association
3 Henrietta Street
Covent Garden, London
WC2E 8LU England

Typeset in Goudy by by World Composition Services, Inc., Sterling, VA

Printer: Edwards Brothers, Inc., Ann Arbor, MI
Cover Designer: Berg Design, Albany, NY
Technical/Production Editor: Gail B. Munroe

The opinions and statements published are the responsibility of the authors, and such opinions and statements do not necessarily represent the policies of the American Psychological Association.

Library of Congress Cataloging-in-Publication Data

Sales, Bruce Dennis.
    Experts in court : reconciling law, science, and professional knowledge / Bruce D. Sales and Daniel W. Shuman.—1st ed.
        p. cm.—(Law and public policy : psychology and the social sciences)
    Includes bibliographical references.
    ISBN 1-59147-246-6
    1. Forensic psychology—United States.   2. Forensic psychiatry—United States. 3. Evidence, Expert—United States. I. Shuman, Daniel W. II. Title. III. Series: Law and public policy.

KF8965.S25 2005
347.73'67—dc22
                                        2004024365

British Library Cataloguing-in-Publication Data
A CIP record is available from the British Library.

Printed in the United States of America
First Edition

For our wives, Betsy and Emily

CONTENTS

Experts in Court

1

INTRODUCTION:
WHY EXPERT WITNESSES?

Evaluating the propriety of the conduct of trials is critical not only to individual litigants but also to society as a whole. Our courts regularly decide matters that affect life, liberty, and property and that address the character of relations between individuals (e.g., child custody), between individuals and the state (e.g., school prayer), and between states (e.g., water resources). The decisions that courts render often transcend the individual cases, reverberate throughout society, and have an extraordinary impact on all of our lives.

To evaluate trials, we need to recognize that they involve arguments about the relevant law and the relevant facts. The factual disputes revolve around the accuracy of descriptions of the event (i.e., what actually happened, where it happened, when it happened, and why it happened), as well as the actor's intentions (the person's mental state at the time of the event). Consider the following example from the case of *Aga v. Hundahl*.[1] A 32-year-old female patient, Nancy Aga, diagnosed with *leiomyosarcoma*, a malignant, fleshy tumor in the wall of her rectum, underwent surgery on April 20, 1989. After successful completion of the operation, Ms. Aga was given Tagamet, a drug to decrease stomach acid during recovery. Six days

---

[1] 891 P.2d 1022 (Haw. 1995).

3

later she began to hallucinate and her doctors briefly administered Haldol, an antipsychotic medication, and then discharged her from the hospital. They then admitted her to another hospital for *brachytherapy*, a form of radiation therapy. At around 8:00 p.m. that same day, Nancy began hallucinating. While one nurse returned her to her room, another went to secure physical restraints for her. Nancy then quickly broke the window in her room with a heavy container used to hold radiation ribbons and fell seven floors to her death.[2] Was her death a suicide for which the hospital should not be held accountable, or was it the result of medical malpractice for which they should be held accountable? The deceased's family argued that the physician was negligent in managing the Tagamet and Haldol. The hospital responded that the patient's decision to jump was a suicide independent of the effect of the drugs.[3] To prove its interpretation of the facts, the hospital offered the testimony of an expert witness, a psychiatrist who testified that the fall was a suicide and not the result of a drug-induced hallucination. Without expert testimony, how could the fact finder determine who should be responsible for the death?

In our adversarial system of justice, it is the responsibility of the lawyers, in representing their clients, to find and present evidence that favors their client's view of the facts relevant to the case.[4] To convince the fact finder (the jury when there is one, and the judge in a nonjury trial) of the correctness of each side's view of the facts, the opposing lawyers are permitted to present lay and expert witnesses, as well as real evidence (e.g., documents or objects).

Lay witnesses typically present evidence about their sensory impressions (i.e., what they saw, heard, tasted, felt, or smelled) and are limited by the rules of evidence in their presentation of opinion testimony. According to Federal Rule of Evidence 701, which also reflects the law as it exists in the states, lay witnesses can only offer opinions that are rationally based on their personal perceptions; provide a clear understanding to the jury of the witness's testimony or the determination of a factual issue in question; are not based on scientific, technical, or other specialized knowledge; and are not within the province of expert testimony.

In some instances lay and expert testimony may both be admissible to address the same issue, and the presentation of lay or expert testimony

---

[2] *Id.* at 1025–1027.
[3] *Id.* at 1030–1031.
[4] Fleming James, Jr., et al., Civil Procedure (4th ed. 1992). "The adversarial model assumes we are more likely to uncover the truth about a contested event as the result of the efforts of the parties who have a self-interest in the discovery of proof and exposing the frailties of an opponent's proof than from the efforts of a judge charged only with an official duty to investigate the case." Daniel W. Shuman, *Expertise in Law, Medicine, and Health Care,* 26 J. Health Politics, Pol'y & L. 267, 269 (2001).

is then a strategic choice. For example, a criminal defendant who invokes an insanity defense may, but is not required to, prove the defense through the use of psychological or psychiatric expert witnesses. The defendant may also prove an insanity defense through the testimony of lay witnesses who observed his particularly bizarre behavior just before or at the time of the crime. Similarly, the state that seeks to disprove that defense may offer rebuttal lay or expert testimony.[5] In other instances, the use of expert testimony will not be optional. It will be essential to proving the case. For example, in *Aga v. Hundahl*, discussed earlier, to prove that a mental health service provider mismanaged a drug interaction resulting in the patient's deadly fall, expert testimony addressing the standard of care and its violation was necessary to avoid a dismissal without jury consideration.[6]

Experts typically address the court in one of three ways. Experts can be presented to provide facts and opinion that will be necessary to help resolve a disputed factual issue in a case. For example, is the plaintiff's depression the result of a prior incident of sexual abuse or did it result from an injury caused by the defendant's negligent driving? In this context the expert is being asked to assist the fact finder to resolve the kinds of questions on which the adjudication of most cases turn (e.g., Was the defendant intoxicated while driving? Would the defendant be dangerous to himself or others?). In a variation of this approach, the expert witnesses might testify as to disputed facts that are essential to assist the court in resolving questions different from those presented in the ordinary civil or criminal case. These questions typically revolve around the constitutionality of a law.[7] For example, would a state law allowing only one state-supported military academy that admitted only males violate the Equal Protection Clause of the United States Constitution's Fourteenth Amendment? Expert testimony that addresses whether the admission of women to a state-supported all-male military academy would substantially diminish the ability of the school to train its male students will assist a court in deciding whether the state violated the Constitution. Expert witnesses also can educate jurors about scientific or other technical or specialized information that is unlikely to be known by jurors and that will help them decide a case more fairly, but that does not by itself directly determine whether a claim is valid or a defense justified. In this type of testimony, the expert is not specifically addressing whether a litigant did or did not do something or was injured, but rather educating the jury about the expert knowledge relevant to the disputed facts so that

---

[5] *See, e.g.*, Cate v. State, 644 N.E.2d 546, 547–48 (Ind. 1994).
[6] *See, e.g.*, Connors v. Univ. Assoc. in Obstetrics & Gynecology, 769 F. Supp. 578, 582 (D. Vt. 1991).
[7] Kenneth Culp Davis, *An Approach to Problems in Evidence in the Administrative Process*, 55 HARV. L. REV. 364 (1942).

the jury will be more informed in judging the testimony in the case. For example, without mentioning anything about the credibility of a victim-witness's eyewitness identification, an expert witness might offer testimony about the conditions under which eyewitness testimony in like situations is likely to be substantially flawed.[8]

Although the existence and number of lay witnesses who might have perceived an event relevant to the litigation is limited and will not expand over time, the number of experts who exist in the field and could provide an opinion relevant to a factual issue in question in the litigation is potentially far more plentiful. Indeed, many commentators have observed that lawyers often have a sufficient number of available expert witnesses to allow them to select one that will best represent a client's partisan interests. It is not surprising that the use of expert witnesses has been controversial because of the role that lawyers play in selecting them and because of the substantial dilemmas that experts pose for the courts.[9] For instance, because lawyers select their own experts, there has long been concern that experts are partisan.[10] This criticism is made salient by the fact that experts are often paid substantial fees to provide their testimony, with these fees constituting an important source of income for the expert. Thus, there is an inducement for these experts to tailor their testimony in such a way that the hiring lawyer will want to use them in the future. In addition, because expert witnesses presenting testimony are being judged not by their professional peers but by those who lack experience in their sphere of expertise, experts may not face the same incentive to adhere to their profession's standards. Thus, these experts may provide less than expert testimony.

It should not be surprising then that the use of expert witnesses is the subject of significant controversy.

> There is a great deal of skepticism about expert evidence. It is well known that expert witnesses are often paid very handsome fees, and common sense suggests that a financial stake can influence an expert's testimony, especially when it is technical and esoteric and hence difficult

---

[8] PETER W. ENGLISH & BRUCE D. SALES, MORE THAN THE LAW: BEHAVIORAL AND SOCIAL FACTS IN LEGAL DECISION MAKING (2005).

[9] Daniel W. Shuman & Anthony Champagne, *Removing the People From the Legal Process: The Rhetoric and Research on Judicial Selection and Juries*, 3 PSYCHOL. PUB. POL'Y & L. 242, 252 (1997). The dilemmas posed by the use of experts are not unique to privately retained experts and may also be present with court-appointed experts. See, Leslie Eaton, *For Arbiters in Custody Battles, Wide Power and Little Scrutiny*, http://www.nytimes.com/2004/05/23/nyregion/23CUST.html?ex= 1086260920&ei=1&en=c919a3a04f044776, last visited May 23, 2004; Anthony Champagne et al., *Are Court-Appointed Experts the Solution to the Problems of Expert Testimony: A Pilot Study*, 84 JUDICATURE 178 (2001).

[10] *See, e.g.*, William L. Foster, *Expert Testimony—Prevalent Complaints and Proposed Remedies*, 11 HARV. L. REV. 169 (1897).

to refute in terms intelligible to judges and jurors. More policing of expert witnessing is required, not less.[11]

As one protection against admitting invalid or unreliable expert testimony, the judge is responsible for ruling on objections made by a lawyer to the admissibility of a proposed expert's testimony. This responsibility poses unique problems for the courts addressing the admissibility of scientific expert testimony. Whereas scientists are focused on the validity of research, courts must attend to concerns of procedural fairness and perceived legitimacy of the process, as well. The temporal framework for scientific and legal decisions also differs.

> [I]n a scientific setting . . . the decision makers are professionals; there is no need to come to a definitive conclusion; the decision making process comports with certain rules established by the professional scientific community. In the courtroom . . . there is a need to come to a definitive conclusion; the decision making process has to satisfy norms of due process and fairness. In our tradition, for example, the adversary system and party examination and cross examination are central. The issue then, is not only how objectively reliable the evidence is, but also the legitimacy of the process by which it is generated. It is not just how valid the data is, but how well the jury can understand it after direct and cross examination, and legal instructions.[12]

More than one commentator has noticed this tension. "The relationship between science and law [is] . . . a marriage of opposites, . . . a conflict between rival systems, . . . a clash of cultures."[13]

PURPOSE OF THIS BOOK

Given these concerns, what proffered expert testimony should be accepted or rejected by the courts? And by what standard should these decisions be made? The purpose of this book is to answer these questions. Although we address the use of expert testimony across the legal system, we devote special, but by no means exclusive, attention to the use of mental health professionals as experts. Mental health professionals (e.g., psychologists, psychiatrists, social workers, counselors; henceforth referred to as *mental health professionals* or *MHPs*) exemplify the issues raised for all experts and

---

[11] Austin v. American Ass'n. of Neurological Surgeons, 253 F.3d 967 (7th Cir. 2001), *cert. denied* 534 U.S. 1078 (2002).
[12] United States v. Hines, 55 F. Supp. 2d 62, 65 (D. Mass. 1999).
[13] Mike Redmayne, *Expert Evidence and Scientific Disagreement*, 30 U.C. Davis L. Rev. 1027, 1035 (1997).

many that are unique. MHPs are asked to offer opinions about intangibles (e.g., a litigant's mental status) for which MHPs may lack consensus about etiology, treatment, and prognosis. To make matters more complex, lawyers and judges will ask MHPs to reach conclusions about past, present, and future mental states.[14] For example, mental health professionals may be called to make judgments about a defendant's mental state at the time of the crime (e.g., Was the defendant insane at the time of the crime?), current mental status (e.g., Is the defendant competent to stand trial?), or future mental status (e.g., Is the defendant likely to be dangerous to another in the near future?). Lawyers and judges often fear that MHPs have no objective criteria that govern their opinions and predictions, and that the inferences they draw from observations of a person may be purely experientially based, without a demonstrable scientific foundation.[15] These concerns are fueled by multiple prestigious mental health professional experts testifying to fundamentally inconsistent opinions in the same case.[16]

To some of these critics, the solution is to reduce or eliminate MHP testimony. For example, such critics recommend the elimination of the insanity defense or the elimination of allowing mental health professionals to testify as to the ultimate issue on the insanity defense (i.e., whether the person was insane at the time of the crime).[17] To other critics of MHP expert testimony, the answer to this concern is to raise the bar for the admissibility of this testimony in an effort to screen out testimony that is less reliable. These critics have found common cause with scientists who have been concerned with the negative impact on the perception of the discipline that nonscientific testimony creates.[18]

---

[14] Retrospective Assessments of Mental States in Litigation: Predicting the Past (Robert I. Simon & Daniel W. Shuman, eds. 2002).

[15] Daniel W. Shuman & Bruce D. Sales, *The Admissibility of Expert Testimony Based Upon Clinical Judgment and Scientific Research*, 4 Psychol. Pub. Pol'y & L. 1226 (1998).

[16] Peter W. Low et al., The Trial of John W. Hinckley Jr.: A Case Study in the Insanity Defense (1986).

[17] Because of this concern, the drafters of the Federal Rules of Evidence amended the rules to prohibit mental health professionals from offering a conclusion about whether a defendant was insane at the time of the crime. *See* Fed. R. Evid. 704(b) Adv. Comm. Note. ("The purpose of this amendment is to eliminate the confusing spectacle of competing expert witnesses testifying to directly contradictory conclusions . . . .").

[18] William M. Grove & R. Christopher Barden, *Protecting the Integrity of Legal System: The Admissibility of Testimony from Mental Health Experts Under Daubert/Kumho Analyses*, 5 Psychol. Pub. Pol'y & L. 224, 238 (1999); Michael Lavin & Bruce D. Sales, *Moral Justifications for Limits on Expert Testimony*, in Expert Witnesses in Child Abuse Cases 59, 60–61 (Stephen J. Ceci & Helene Hembrooke, eds. 1998).

For purposes of this book, unless explicitly noted otherwise in the text, we use the phrase *nonscientific* to refer to all testimony that partially or completely fails to meet the definition of science. This broad umbrella includes most testimony offered by plumbers, accountants, and automobile mechanics, for example. It also includes testimony by medical practitioners and clinical psychologists who base their opinions on an unspecified combination of scientific tests and experiential judgment.

To the critics, addressing the problem posed by MHP testimony is particularly important because these experts often assume that their approach to clinical practice will also constitute an appropriate approach to forensic practice. For a myriad of reasons, this is not necessarily so. Unlike prescription medication, clinical practice is not regulated by an agency similar to the Food and Drug Administration that is charged with assessing the safety and efficacy of a treatment.[19] Clinicians are not required to prove to anyone that they have grounded their practices in scientific research findings, nor are they required to change their practices in light of evolving research.[20] In addition, whereas diagnosis in clinical settings is an evolving phenomenon that the clinician can modify as therapy proceeds, forensic assessment, in most instances, is a snapshot described on the witness stand.[21] Finally, although the questions sought to be answered in clinical settings are defined by the clinician and patient, the questions raised in the forensic setting are defined by the law without regard to their grounding in constructs that respond to clinical or scientific knowledge.[22] Thus, MHPs who participate in the judicial process must reexamine their methods and procedures according to the different norms that exist in the forensic realm. The importance of MHPs' engaging in this reformulation is heightened by the fact that litigants do not have the right to refuse to consent to an opposing expert who uses unreliable or invalid techniques or methods to form the basis for subsequent testimony. They can only object to the admission into evidence of this testimony or, if the testimony is admitted, attempt to convince the trier of fact to ascribe it little credibility.

ORGANIZATION OF THIS BOOK

To address the concerns posed by MHPs and other expert witness, our approach in this book differs dramatically from other attempts to evaluate

---

[19] 21 U.S.C.S. §§ 301 et seq. (Law. Co-op. 2003).

[20] See generally Sol L. Garfield, Some Comments on Empirically Supported Treatments, 66 J. CONSULTING & CLINICAL PSYCHOL. 121 n.1 (1998); Sol L. Garfield, Some Problems Associated With "Validated" Forms of Psychotherapy, 3 CLINICAL PSYCHOL.: SCI. & PRAC. 218 n.3 (1996); Dianne L. Chambliss, Empirically Validated Treatments, in PSYCHOLOGIST'S DESK REFERENCE (Gerald P. Koocher, John C. Norcross & Sam S. Hill, eds. 1998); Philip C. Kendall & Dianne L. Chambliss, Eds., Special Section: Empirically Supported Psychological Therapies, 66 J. CONSULTING & CLINICAL PSYCHOL. 3 (1998). Obviously, clinicians would be open to an ethical complaint and malpractice claim if it were shown that one procedure is empirically validated and the procedure chosen by the clinician has been empirically proven not to be valid for treating the problem presented by the patient.

[21] See generally GARY B. MELTON ET AL., PSYCHOLOGICAL EVALUATIONS FOR THE COURTS: A HANDBOOK FOR MENTAL HEALTH PROFESSIONALS AND LAWYERS (2nd ed. 1997).

[22] Daniel A. Krauss & Bruce D. Sales. Forensic Psychology's Inter-dependence with Law and Policy, in FORENSIC PSYCHOLOGY (Alan M. Goldstein, ed. 2003).

the legal rules for admissibility of expert testimony. We believe that it is impossible to evaluate how well the rules of evidence work without comparing their performance against the goals of the rules. It is ironic that although other authors have noted the importance of the goals of the rules in evaluating their performance, [23] we have discovered neither authors nor courts who have attempted to sort out the meaning of the goals and apply them to expert admissibility decisions.

Our analysis starts by asking in chapter 2, What are the articulated goals for having rules of evidence? In the case of the rules of evidence relating to the admission of expert testimony, we compare how well the operation of the rules achieves the goals for those rules.[24] We find the goals for the admissibility of expert testimony in the goals underlying the creation of all of the rules of evidence. In this book, we use the Federal Rules of Evidence to represent the rules that courts apply at trial, although they only apply in the federal courts. Nonetheless, most states have adopted similar versions of these rules, but, more important, the federal rules reflect leading evidence scholarship and legal analysis. As chapter 2 demonstrates, the goals articulated in the Federal Rules of Evidence are both simple and intricately complex. Some of the complexity derives from the fact that the underlying goals and the possible interpretations of the rules of evidence may lead courts facing the same facts to reach different decisions. These conflicting goals need to be recognized and respected to understand and evaluate how experts interact with courts and how they are likely to interact with them in the future.

Once the goals for the rules of evidence have been articulated, chapter 3 addresses the subset of the rules of evidence that focus on the admissibility of expert testimony and how these rules have evolved. This chapter travels from the early common law of evidence[25] to the modern Federal Rules of Evidence and their interpretation by the United States Supreme Court in *Daubert v. Merrell Dow Pharamceuticals, Inc.*,[26] *General Electric Co. v. Joiner*,[27]

---

[23] *See, e.g.*, Glen Weissenberger, *Evidence Myopia: The Failure to See the Federal Rules of Evidence as a Codification of the Common Law*, 40 WM. & MARY L. REV. 1539, 1551 (1999): "The importance of Rule 102 in the interpretation of the Rules is central because it supplies the interpretive directive by which all other Rules are to be construed."

[24] This approach is premised on the fact that there is a way to establish criteria for judging valid knowledge in a any field (i.e., its epistemology). *See generally* ALVIN I. GOLDMAN, EPISTEMOLOGY AND COGNITION (1986); ALVIN I. GOLDMAN, KNOWLEDGE IN A SOCIAL WORLD (1999); Brian Leiter, *The Epistemology of Admissibility: Why Even Good Philosophy of Science Would Not Make for Good Philosophy of Evidence*, 1997 BYU L. REV. 803, 817 (1997) ("No such [admissibility] standard can be formulated in indifference to the epistemic limits of the courts.").

[25] By common law rules of evidence, we to refer to the process of judge made law in cases decided prior to the codification of the rules of evidence. *See* OLIVER WENDELL HOLMES, JR, THE COMMON LAW (1881).

[26] 509 U.S. 579 (1993).

[27] 522 U.S. 136 (1997).

and *Kumho Tire Company v. Carmichael*.[28] This chapter is essential because it sets out the subset of evidence law that we evaluate in the book.

Having discussed the rules for the admissibility of expert testimony and the goals for those rules, we discuss in chapter 4 whether the goals of the rules have been well served by the Supreme Court's opinions and the opinions of the lower federal courts that have attempted to apply them to the admissibility of expert testimony. We find that the goals of the rules have not been fulfilled in the judicial decisions that have sought to implement *Daubert* and its interpretation of the Federal Rules of Evidence.

Chapter 5 focuses on how the law should evolve to use experts more effectively. Our discussion in this chapter is based on the results of our analyses in chapter 4 (i.e., how well the goals of the Federal Rules of Evidence are being applied to the subset of rules applicable to the admissibility of expert testimony). We urge a series of solutions that cut across the education and training of lawyers and judges as well as the criteria they use to determine the admissibility of experts.

Another way to evaluate the use of experts in court is to focus on the experts' behaviors rather than focusing solely on the language and implementation of the rules of evidence by the courts. Chapter 6 does this by asking how the behavior of experts can serve the goals of the rule of evidence. It identifies the way in which the behavior of experts may serve or frustrate the goals of the rules of evidence and offers specific recommendations for experts.

Our conclusions and recommendations in this book appear in chapters 5 and 6. Chapter 7 provides a brief epilogue by addressing questions raised by our proposed solutions to the problems we identify. It describes a research agenda that will create a better understanding of the attitudes and practices of trial courts regarding Federal Rule of Evidence 102's goals, the problems generated by *Daubert* and its progeny, and our proposed solutions to the *Daubert*-precipitated problems.

The main thrust of our argument throughout this book is novel. No other author has considered the application of Rule 102 to understanding the application of Federal Rule of Evidence 702 and its interpretation by *Daubert* and its progeny. For this reason, we have been meticulous in laying out our assertions and their justifications. There is a minor downside to this drafting approach. At some points in the text, readers may recognize that they are seeing information that was presented earlier. We only do this when the information is required to make our case under the different Rule 102 goals. We hope that readers will agree that the redundancy is justified to prove the validity of our analysis—one that has been completely overlooked to date.

---

[28] 526 U.S. 137 (1999).

2

GOALS FOR THE RULES OF EVIDENCE

The rules of evidence provide the framework for assessing challenges to the admissibility of all offers of evidence, including expert evidence. These rules limit and guide discretion when judges are required to make admissibility decisions. Although it is commonly assumed that the judge must rule on the admissibility of an expert's testimony before the expert is permitted to testify, that is not required by the rules of evidence. Judges rule on objections presented by lawyers, and in the absence of a timely and specific objection, the right to object to the introduction of evidence is waived.[1] Thus, only when a party objects to the admissibility of an opposing expert's testimony will the trial judge be asked to rule on the issue of admissibility.

As one noted evidence scholar, James Bradley Thayer, has observed, the rules of evidence are a product of the jury system.[2] Without a jury there is arguably no need for most of the rules of evidence.[3] As this relates to the presentation of expert testimony, the assumption is that although judges

---

[1] FED. R. EVID. 103 (a)(1).

[2] JAMES BRADLEY THAYER, A PRELIMINARY TREATISE ON EVIDENCE AT THE COMMON LAW 2 (1898).

[3] Two rules that are needed regardless of whether there is a jury are those addressing relevance (i.e., evidence that helps to prove or disprove an material issue in the case) and privilege (i.e., a rule protecting against the disclosure of certain confidential professional communications). The rule of relevance is needed to ensure that courts do not waste their time with the presentation of irrelevant information, whereas the rules relating to privilege ensure that certain protected confidences are not disclosed.

are sophisticated decision makers who are unlikely to need protection from *bad* information presented by unreliable experts at trial,[4] juries are naive about the dilemmas posed by some expert testimony, which when combined with the frailties of human decision making, is likely to cause jurors to over-weight the influence of the expert's opinion.[5] Thus, juries in our adversarial system of justice are assumed to require protection from irrelevant or unreliable evidence.[6]

The structure of the rules of evidence implicitly address the concerns about jury capabilities and behavior. The rules were developed over time, however, and encompass a broader set of goals. In the Federal Rules of Evidence, a set of codified rules governing the admissibility of evidence in the federal courts, these goals are contained in Rule 102:

> These rules shall be construed to secure fairness in the administration, elimination of unjustifiable expense and delay, and promotion of growth and development of the law of evidence to the end that the truth may be ascertained and proceedings justly determined.

INTERPRETING FEDERAL RULE OF EVIDENCE 102

Although only one sentence long, Federal Rule of Evidence (hereinafter *Fed. R. Evid.*) 102 combines five different concepts (fairness, efficiency, growth and development of the law, truth, and justice), strung together in

---

[4]Judges may suffer from similar limitations. *See* Chris Guthrie, Jeffrey J. Rachlinski & Andrew J. Wistrich, *Inside the Judicial Mind: Heuristics and Biases*, 86 Cornell L. Rev. 777, 821 (2001), who after studying a sample of 167 federal magistrate judges concluded that "[j]udges, it seems, are human. Like the rest of us, they use heuristics that can produce systematic errors in judgment."
[5]Some social scientists are not as pessimistic about the abilities of the jurors: Although jurors have greater difficulty with probabilistic and statistical evidence, there is little evidence that they are simply impressed by jargon and awed by experts' credentials to the point that they are overwhelmed by and uncritical of the testimony. Nor is there evidence that they simply ignore complex expert testimony. Although jurors struggle and are occasionally misled, they generally make reasonable use of complex material, utilizing the expert testimony when it is presented in a form that they can use. Their struggles suggest that there is room for improvement in the way that complex material is presented, and that advocates and experts who fail to address this need may, as a result, fail to persuade jurors that the testimony they are offering should be accepted. Neil Vidmar & Shari Seidman Diamond, *Juries and Expert Evidence*, 66 Brooklyn L. Rev. 1121, 1166–1167 (2001). For a more skeptical view of the ability of juries in complex cases, *see* Joseph Sanders, *Expert Admissibility Symposium: Reliability Standards—Too High, Too Low, or Just Right?: The Merits of the Paternalistic Justification for Restrictions on the Admissibility of Expert Evidence*, 33 Seton Hall L. Rev. 881, 901–907 (2003). For a general overview of the impact of expert testimony on jury decision making, *see*, Dennis J. Devine et al., *Jury Decision Making: 45 Years of Empirical Research on Deliberating Groups*, 7 Psychol. Pub. Pol'y & L. 622, 688 (2001).
[6]The rules of evidence, other than the rules on relevance and privilege, therefore, do not apply to administrative hearings or judicial proceedings not involving juries (e.g., federal criminal court sentencing; *see* Fed. R. Evid. 1101). Although the rules apply in bench trials, they are not as rigorously applied in those trials as in jury trials, nor are appellate courts as likely to reverse judicial admissibility decisions in bench trials as they are in jury trials. Indeed, few bench trials are reversed on evidentiary grounds.

a manner that can lead to several different interpretations of the goals of the rule.[7] It might be argued that the end phrase: "to the end that the truth may be ascertained and proceedings justly determined" is meant to modify the first three criteria (fairness, efficiency, growth and development of the law). Under this interpretation, Fed. R. Evid. 102 has three goals for the rules of evidence:

- Goal 1: "to secure fairness in the administration [of the law of evidence] . . . to the end that the truth may be ascertained and proceedings justly determined,"
- Goal 2: "to [eliminate] unjustifiable expense and delay [in the operation of the law of evidence] . . . to the end that the truth may be ascertained and proceedings justly determined," and
- Goal 3: "to [promote] growth and development of the law of evidence to the end that the truth may be ascertained and proceedings [be] justly determined."

We reject this first interpretation for two reasons. It is important to note that achieving truth and justice will not always advance all three goals. In regard to fairness (Goal 1), we know that fair procedures do not always achieve truth and that unfair procedures might yield truth. Consider torture as the method of finding truth. Even if torture were likely to elicit truthful responses, our society regards torture as an unfair method of gathering evidence. And what of the relationship of fairness to justice? Can justice emerge only when the procedures are fair? We think not. Justice can emerge when procedures are unfair. For example, one of the justifications for jury nullification is to allow juries to render justice when strict adherence to the rules of law might lead to an unjust result.[8] And injustice can occur when procedures are fair. For example, persons who have committed criminal offenses have been acquitted in fair trials, and persons who have been convicted in fair trials have later been proven innocent.[9]

Linking efficiency (Goal 2) to truth and justice is also illogical. Efficiency can defeat both. For example, the drive for efficiency may force litigants to go to trial prior to the opportunity to identify the author of the most relevant and reliable research that addresses a contested issue in the case. Litigants may instead use the most quickly available expert, with the

---

[7] See Andrew E. Taslitz, *Daubert's Guide to the Federal Rules of Evidence: A Not-so-Plain-Meaning Jurisprudence*, 32 HARV. J. ON LEGIS. 3 (1995) for a critique of the Supreme Court's plain meaning approach to interpreting the Federal Rules of Evidence.

[8] The process by which juries can ignore the law in its decision making. See Todd E. Pettys, *Evidentiary Relevance, Morally Responsible Verdicts, and Jury Nullification*, 86 IOWA L. REV. 467 (2001).

[9] Edward Connors et al., CONVICTED BY JURIES, EXONERATED BY SCIENCE: CASE STUDIES IN THE USE OF DNA EVIDENCE TO ESTABLISH INNOCENCE AFTER TRIAL (1996); Innocence Project, at http://www.innocenceproject.org/ (last visited March 4, 2003).

result that both truth and justice are compromised. Inefficiency may also lead to injustice, such as forcing litigants to wait years for their day in court. If the overarching goal is to achieve truth and justice, efficiency can be counterproductive. Therefore, an interpretation of Fed. R. Evid. 102 that invariably links efficiency to truth and justice appears inappropriate.

Finally, is it logical to link the promotion of the growth and development of the law of evidence (Goal 3) only to truth and justice? To judge the appropriateness of legal change against whether it will promote the finding of the truth and the achievement of justice is reasonable. But should not the growth and development of the law also seek to enhance the efficient administration of the courts and fairness in their administration? For example, Fed. R. Evid. 103(a) limits a party's predicating an appeal on an erroneous trial court evidentiary ruling "unless a substantial right of the party is affected." Unless the fairness of the proceeding is affected by the erroneous ruling, efficiency demands that the case not be reversed on that ground. Limiting the growth and development of the law only to the concerns of truth and justice then is both narrow and out of step with the evolution of judicial administration in America. Moreover, as we describe in the next subsection (Defining the Four Goals), this first interpretation of Fed. R. Evid. 102 should be rejected because it minimizes the independent importance of the separate goals of fairness, efficiency, truth, and justice.

Another possible interpretation of Fed. R. Evid. 102 would have the phrase "promotion of growth and development of the law of evidence" modify all of the goals articulated in the rule. The rule, as interpreted, would now read as follows:

> In order to promote the growth and development of the law of evidence, these rules shall be construed to secure fairness in the administration, eliminate unjustifiable expense and delay, to the end that the truth may be ascertained and proceedings justly determined.

We reject this interpretation because it forces an illogical grammatical construction of this rule. If the overarching goal for Fed. R. Evid. 102 is to promote the growth and development of the law of evidence, why would the drafters of the Federal Rules have embedded the phrase "promoting the growth and development" into the third phrase of the sentence (as set off by the commas within the sentence) instead of starting the rule with it? In addition, when the rule is rewritten to make this interpretation work, it is apparent that the end phrase referring to truth and justice also becomes an overarching goal that would require that the conjunction "and" precede the second phrase referring to efficiency.

The interpretation of Fed. R. Evid. 102, which we conclude is the correct one and which guides the analysis in this book, is to take the rule at its grammatical face value. "These rules shall be construed to secure Goal 1 . . . , Goal 2 . . . , Goal 3 . . . , and Goal 4," when:

- Goal 1: "to secure fairness in the administration [of the law of evidence],"
- Goal 2 "to [eliminate] unjustifiable expense and delay [in the operation of the law of evidence],"
- Goal 3: "to [promote] growth and development of the law of evidence to the end that the truth may be ascertained," and
- Goal 4: "to [promote] growth and development of the law of evidence to the end that the proceedings [be] justly determined."

Thus, we assume that the rule should be construed to achieve each of these goals independently. We refer to these four goals as fairness, efficiency, truth, and justice—although, as we discuss in the next subsection, the specific words suggest far more than these shorthand abbreviations capture.

Fairness

Fairness is usually understood in the law to embody procedural concerns, such as the time and manner of giving an opposing party notice of claims or defenses. By fair procedures, we refer to a set of rules that seek to provide litigants an unbiased approach to resolving disputes.[10] Fair procedures place litigants on a level playing field. The same rules apply to all litigants, with the process not favoring either side. In addition, fair procedures promise litigants that they will have a reasonable opportunity to tell their story to the decision maker.

Although some scholars speak of procedural fairness and procedural justice interchangeably,[11] it makes sense to distinguish the terms in this setting because the drafters of Fed. R. Evid. 102 list fairness and justice in different locations within the rule. Indeed, this interpretation is supported

---

[10] "The notion of fair procedure has evolved from the common law principle that a private association which controls a fundamental right, such as the right to pursue a livelihood, cannot engage in arbitrary exclusion practices. . . . Like its constitutional counterpart due process, fair procedure does not lend itself to rigid definition, but must be assessed on a case-by-case basis. The essence of both sets of rights is fairness; central to both are adequate notice of the charges and a reasonable opportunity to respond. . . . 'The common law requirement of a fair procedure does not compel formal proceedings with all the embellishments of a court trial . . . nor adherence to a single mode of process. It may be satisfied by any one of a variety of procedures which afford a fair opportunity for an applicant to present his position. As such, this court should not attempt to fix a rigid procedure that must invariably be observed. Instead, the associations themselves should retain the initial and primary responsibility for devising a method which provides an applicant adequate notice of the 'charges' against him and a reasonable opportunity to respond.'" Sywak v. O'Connor Hosp., 244 Cal. Rptr. 753, 758 (Cal. App. 6th Dist., 1988).
[11] Tom R. Tyler, *Citizen Discontent with Legal Procedures: A Social Science Perspective on Civil Procedure Reform*, 45 Am. J. Comp. L. 871 (1997).

by our earlier observation that procedures can be unfair yet result in a just outcome, and fair procedures can produce an unjust outcome. Finally, this interpretation is reinforced by the observation that the terms *fairness* and *justice* are used to refer to different goals: administration (fairness in the administration) and outcome (proceedings justly determined).

Efficiency

Fed. R. Evid. 102 does not demand the attainment of truth, fairness, or justice at all costs. The decision of the drafters to use considerations of efficiency, in addition to truth, fairness, and justice, contemplates that there will be limits on the time or money that can be allocated to achieve a just, fair, or truthful result. Legal disputes present questions that must be resolved in a relatively short period of time. We cannot permit criminal charges to remain pending for years, nor can we leave injured parties waiting indefinitely for compensation. Yet, the factual questions that underlie legal disputes may not be capable of resolution within a short time frame. For example, definitive scientific research may not be available, and it may take years to design, conduct, and analyze the research. In addition, the cost of conducting the scientific research or investigation necessary to resolve disputes accurately may exceed the financial interests at stake in the litigation. In these situations the rules of evidence contemplate that truth in decision making (by waiting for such research to be conducted) may be considered along with efficiency.[12] The dilemma of this approach is that Fed. R. Evid. 102 does not provide any particular clues as to what constitutes justifiable or unjustifiable expense or delay.

The concept of efficiency includes several micro- and macro-level concerns. Micro-level notions of efficiency refer to individual cases, and include concerns with the time lawyers spend preparing the case. These factors include the need for experts; how many experts are involved; how much time experts spend on case preparation; and how much time lawyers spend deciding when, whether, and how to challenge opposing experts (e.g., offering contrary expert testimony, preparing effective cross-examinations, making motions to dismiss the case on grounds that are unrelated to expert testimony), and the attendant costs. Macro-level efficiency refers to system-wide concerns with costs and time spent across cases as a function of the decision to admit or exclude certain testimony. This includes the total time spent by lawyers learning about science and other professional knowledge in preparing for cases involving expert witnesses; total time spent in the

---

[12] "In sum, the law cannot wait for future scientific investigation and research. We must resolve cases in our courts on the basis of scientific knowledge that is currently available." Moore v. Ashland Chemical Inc. 151 F.3d 269, 276 (5th Cir. 1998).

admissibility hearings for these experts;[13] total time spent for postlitigation challenges in cases involving expert witnesses; and total time spent by judges learning about science and other professional knowledge in preparing for cases involving expert witnesses. Although we have focused our discussion in terms of time spent, it is not the only concern of the legal system. The associated increase in costs is also an important consideration, both because of its implication for the notion of *justice for all* and its implication for the operation of the courts.

Truth

The goal of truth is most associated with the purpose for having a system of evidence rules. Fed. R. Evid. 102 recognizes this goal: "These rules shall be construed to [promote the] growth and development of the law to the end that the truth may be ascertained," but neither the rules nor the Advisory Committee Note[14] define truth for these purposes. The most obvious definition of truth is accuracy in decision making, which refers to an outcome that correctly reflects some external state of affairs. Although this definition reflects what scientists, as well as the lay public, would likely consider included in the concept of truth, the manner in which truth is described in Fed. R. Evid. 102 suggests the need for a more nuanced analysis of its meaning. It is necessary to consider why the drafters tied truth to the growth and development of the law, rather than stating it as a goal without any modifier. Once again, we have no clues in the language of the rules or the Advisory Committee Note,[15] but logic suggests that for the law to grow and develop it must acknowledge realistic limitations in achieving its goals in fact finding. Determining the truth is a Herculean task in many cases, for many reasons.

---

[13] For example, "[t]he controversy over the use of DNA evidence caused obvious problems for the courts. Successive pre-trial hearings, during which the reliability of scientific evidence is debated, impose costs on the legal system." Mike Redmayne, *Expert Evidence and Scientific Disagreement*, 30 U.C. Davis L. Rev. 1027, 1057 (1997).

[14] The Advisory Committee on Rules of Evidence, comprised of judges, lawyers, and law professors, was appointed by Chief Justice of the United States Supreme Court, under the authority of 28 U.S.C. §331 to study and make recommendations for procedural rules. The committee's report and its notes served as the foundation for the Federal Rules of Evidence, as modified by the Congress under its inherent authority. Committee on Rules of Practice and Procedure of the Judicial Conference of the United States, *Preliminary Draft of Proposed Rules of Evidence for the United States District Courts and Magistrates*, 46 F.R.D. 161 (1969).

[15] Flexibility and growth are the watchwords of the Federal Rules, and in the words of well-known commentators, "It is not an exaggeration to say that the keystone to the effective functioning of the federal rules is the discretion of the trial court. . . . The rules will remain a workable system only as long as trial court judges exercise their discretion intelligently on a case by case basis; application of arbitrary rules of law to particular situations only will have a debilitating effect on the overall system." David A. Sonenshein, *Circuit Roulette: The Use of Prior Convictions to Impeach Credibility in Civil Cases Under the Federal Rules of Evidence*, 57 Geo. Wash. L. Rev. 279, 299–300 (1988).

As evidence scholars remind us, we can never be 100% confident in the accuracy of the result, because truth is not necessarily discoverable in the context of a particular trial.[16] Trials are conducted within a limited time frame and ultimately must go forward whether all pertinent information is or will ever be available. In addition, some information relevant to the outcome of litigation will never be captured in a witness's perception, a videotape, or an audio recording. Lay witnesses can give, to the best of their knowledge, truthful testimony that is inaccurate because of the vagaries of attention, perception, memory, recall, and other cognitive and emotive factors.[17]

In addition, decisions about what is truth will depend on the point in time with which the trier of fact is concerned—past, present, or future events. Whereas we might hope to achieve a greater degree of accuracy in the determination of present events or conditions (e.g., competence to stand trial), our ability to determine past events (e.g., the defendant's mental state at the time of the offense) or future events (e.g., capital sentencing that turns on the risk of future violence) is limited by the ability to capture past evidence and accurately assess mental status retrospectively,[18] and to predict future behavior.[19] Even attempts to determine present events quickly devolve into the assessment of events past, as testimony in court about the present instantly becomes subject to the fallibility of memory and recall.[20]

As noted earlier, truth is not an absolute or penultimate value in litigation. For example, the Federal Rules of Evidence and case law recognize that relevant evidence may be excluded for reasons that frustrate truth (e.g., because a privilege prohibits its introduction[21]). Concerns with fairness and efficiency may also be a limitation on truth-seeking where it is not efficient to make the investment necessary to obtain truth. For example, in some litigation, truth will only be discoverable with scientific verification of the

---

[16] James Bradley Thayer, A Preliminary Treatise on Evidence at the Common Law (1898).
[17] Psychologists have long studied the factors affecting the inaccuracy of eyewitness identification, including stress and postevent assimilation of information. See, e.g., Michael R. Leippe, The Case for Expert Testimony About Eyewitness Memory, 1 Psychol. Pub. Pol'y & L. 909 (1995). Many courts recognize the value of such information in helping juries more accurately evaluate the accuracy of identification claims. See, e.g., Arizona v. Chapple, 660 P.2d 1208 (Ariz. 1983). And concerns with the inaccuracy of eyewitness identification testimony have been validated in cases in which persons convicted on the basis of eyewitness testimony have been exculpated by DNA evidence. Edward Connors et al., Convicted by Juries, Exonerated by Science: Case Studies in the Use of DNA Evidence to Establish Innocence After Trial (1996).
[18] Retrospective Assessment of Mental States in Litigation: Predicting the Past (Robert I. Simon & Daniel W. Shuman, eds. 2002).
[19] E.g., Vernon L. Quinsey et al., Violent Offenders: Appraising and Managing Risk (1998).
[20] Richard Rogers, Validating Retrospective Assessments: An Overview of Research Findings, in Retrospective Assessment of Mental States in Litigation: Predicting the Past (Robert I. Simon & Daniel W. Shuman, eds., 2002).
[21] See, e.g., Jaffee v. Redmond, 518 U.S. 1 (1996), recognizing a privilege protecting against court-ordered disclosure of psychotherapist–patient communications.

facts—something that efficiency may not allow or that cannot be done given the current development of scientific methodology.

In some instances, truth may not be measured by testimonial accuracy. For example, assume that in a child custody case the expert determines that the father is more demanding and the mother is more empathetic and therefore recommends that the mother be awarded custody. The finding with regard to parental traits may be accurate, but the expert's opinion, and its use by the fact finder to determine custody, requires the application of value judgments about what is in the best interests of the child.[22] The application of these value judgments is not a matter of truth as accuracy in any scientific sense of the concept.

This concern applies to all expert opinion. Unless scientific research provides results that can be presented to the court without interpretation by the expert, the expert's testimony will contain some value judgments about what is the truth of the situation, which leads to the proverbial battle of the experts. Finally, some scholars argue that science can never be value free because there are discretionary judgments that go into the design, conduct, and analysis of the research. According to this view, even when the researcher attempts to be unbiased in designing and conducting the research, the exercise of discretion will reflect the underlying values and biases of the researcher.[23]

Truth cannot be understood without reference to the adversarial context in which it arises. The adversarial approach to conflict resolution does not assume that each side's presentation of its case represents truth, because truth does not reside in any given witness' testimony or lawyer's argument. Rather it assumes that truth will result from the adversarial process, wherein the trier of fact reaches a determination based on hearing and weighing each component of both sides' adversarial representations. It is unfortunate that fact finders are subject to all of the frailties of human judgment when trying to discern which of each side's presented facts are accurate.[24]

The law may be designed to reflect a concern with legal decision making that transcends truthful results in individual cases. According to this interpretation of truth, the law is concerned with rules that inspire

---

[22] Daniel A. Krauss & Bruce D. Sales, *The Problem of "Helpfulness" in Applying Daubert to Expert Testimony: Child Custody Determinations in Family Law as an Exemplar*, 5 PSYCHOL. PUB. POL'Y & L. 78 (1999); Daniel A. Krauss & Bruce D. Sales, *Legal Standards, Expertise, and Experts in Child Custody Decision-Making*, 6 PSYCHOL. PUB. POL'Y & L., 843 (2000); Daniel W. Shuman, *What Should We Permit Mental Health Professionals to Say About "The Best Interests of the Child"?: An Essay on Commonsense, Daubert, and the Rules of Evidence*, 3 FAM. L. Q. 551 (1997).
[23] PAUL RICOEUR, LECTURES ON IDEOLOGY AND UTOPIA 162–172 (1986); Stephen J. Ceci et al., *Human Subjects Review, Personal Values, and the Regulation of Social Science Research*, 40 AM. PSYCHOL. 994, 1001 (1985).
[24] Michael J. Saks & Robert F. Kidd, *Human Information Processing and Adjudication: Trial by Heuristics*, 15 LAW & SOC'Y REV. 123 (1980).

confidence in the accuracy of legal decision making.[25] It is important not only that the law facilitate the attainment of truth, but also that the public believe that the law promotes accuracy in factfinding. If this does not occur, people will be less likely to respect and to adhere to legal decisions.

Finally, truth in some situations is best understood as justice and not accuracy in the trier of fact's judgment. Consider, for example, a personal injury case in which the jury is asked to commodify an intangible injury (e.g., pain and suffering) suffered by a plaintiff.[26] There is no measure of the accuracy of the plaintiff's suffering or the amount of money that should be awarded to compensate for it. A jury's verdict on intangible loss is best understood not as a truth, but as justice that results from combining and weighing social, moral, and legal values with the factual information presented.

These seven interpretations of truth find common ground in the fact that the courts are unlikely to find an absolute truth for understanding and resolving the dispute before the court that is immutable and accurate. Perhaps that is why truth is listed as the third goal. Although having trials reach truthful results is an important goal for our system of justice, failure to achieve it in any particular case does not negate the value of truth as a goal for the rules of evidence. These challenges to truthful decision making provide a cogent reason for the drafters to have couched truth in the phrase "promotion of growth and development of the law of evidence to the end that the truth may be ascertained," rather than simply as accuracy in factfinding.

Justice

Finally, Fed. R. Evid. 102 lists justice independently of truth or fairness as the fourth goal of the rules of evidence. ("These rules shall be construed to secure . . . [the] growth and development of the law of evidence to the end that . . . proceedings [be] justly determined."). This goal implies that justice is intended to convey something different from truth, fairness, or efficiency, but what does it mean for proceedings to be justly determined? In addition, why did the drafters believe it necessary to modify the goal of justice in the same way that it modified the goal of truth?

In regard to the former issue, it appears that the drafters intended justice to refer to outcome (i.e., was the outcome of the trial just?), which is a different criterion from that represented by fairness, efficiency, or truth.

---

[25] In re Winship, 397 U.S. 358 (1970).
[26] Randall R. Bovbjerg et al., *Valuing Life and Limb in Tort: Scheduling "Pain and Suffering,"* 83 Nw. U. L. Rev. 908 (1989).

But to better define and understand justice, we need to consider these four criteria juxtaposed to each other.

Understanding the differences between the concepts of justice and fairness requires going beyond the common usage of these terms, which often treats them as identical. This is necessary because the words of Fed. R. Evid. 102 make it clear that the drafters intended the concepts to refer to very different judgments. *Fairness* refers to a quality of the procedures used—are the rules of evidence applied fairly? *Justice* refers to a quality of the outcome of the proceeding—is the outcome justly determined? This distinction is reasonable because fair procedures can lead to an unjust outcome, and unfair procedures can result in a just one. As an example of fair procedures leading to unjust outcomes, consider pre-DNA cases that relied on eyewitness identification testimony for conviction of defendants charged with sexual assault. When new DNA technology was applied to the evidence years later, it was proved that in many of these cases, the defendant was innocent.[27] For an example of unfair procedures leading to just outcomes, we point to instances of jurors' responding to unfair procedures nullifying the instructions that have been given them to arrive at a just result.[28]

Distinguishing justice from efficiency is relatively straightforward. Because *efficiency* refers to a value judgment about the allocation of public and private resources, there may be a tension between justice and efficiency. Justice can be compromised by efficiency, as when the need to proceed speedily or with less cost compromises the ability to gather all of the facts relevant to the case. Justice can also be compromised by inefficiency, as when undue delay causes the loss of certain evidence, leading to an unjust outcome.[29] Efficiency is a value judgment about the resources used in the conduct of a proceeding (e.g., the application of the rules of evidence); justice is a value judgment about the appropriateness of the outcome of that proceeding.

Finally, whereas *truth* refers to the trier of fact being able to determine something about the facts in the case (i.e., the accuracy of conflicting pieces of evidence) and the accuracy of a result in light of the facts and the law, *justice* refers to a state of the outcome of the proceedings (i.e., is the outcome appropriate in light of the facts, the controlling law, and other social and moral standards). The use of both truth and justice in Fed. R. Evid. 102 suggests that the drafters recognized that determinations could ascertain

---

[27] Edward Connors et al., Convicted by Juries, Exonerated by Science: Case Studies in the Use of DNA Evidence to Establish Innocence After Trial (1996); Innocence Project, at http://www.innocenceproject.org/ (last visited March 4, 2003).

[28] Todd E. Pettys, *Evidentiary Relevance, Morally Responsible Verdicts, and Jury Nullification*, 86 Iowa L. Rev. 467 (2001).

[29] Daniel W. Shuman, *When Time Does Not Heal: Understanding the Importance of Avoiding Unnecessary Delay in the Resolution of Tort Cases*, 6 Psychol. Pub. Pol'y & L. 880 (2000).

truth without achieving a just outcome, could fail to ascertain truth but still achieve a just outcome, or could achieve both truth and justice. For example, as to the first category, a state might discover the truth about the role of former military leaders in torture and assassination, yet not achieve a result many of its victims find just when the defendants are found too infirm to stand trial.[30] As to the situation where the evidentiary approach is just but not truthful, consider jury nullification. With or without formal legal approval, from time to time jurors nullify the law and ignore certain facts to avoid reaching a verdict they find unjust. And in the best situation, the rules of evidence can facilitate a verdict that recognizes both the truth of the facts and the justness of a particular result.

Given the independence of the goal of justice from the other three goals in Fed. R. Evid. 102, why did the drafters find it necessary to modify that goal as they did with the goal of truth: "These rules shall be construed to secure . . . [the] growth and development of the law of evidence to the end that . . . proceedings [be] justly determined"? The drafters could have assumed that justice is an absolute state of affairs that flows from the correct application of the procedural and substantive rules of law. If they had made that assumption, it is reasonable to expect that the goal of justice would not have been modified in the rule. Neither the text of the rule nor the Advisory Committee Note inform us as to why the drafters chose to add the concern over growth and development of the law to the goal of justice, but logic suggests that we should use the same analysis that was appropriate for understanding the modification of the goal of truth. This analysis was predicated on the realization that the goal, in this case justice, is extraordinarily difficult to define as an absolute concept. There are numerous reasons for this.

The goal of reaching a just result is influenced by the adversarial context. The adversarial setting gives to the parties the strategic choice of what arguments to make, what evidence to present in support of those arguments, and what experts to present. As a consequence, the trier of fact is presented with choices limited by lawyers' strategic decisions. Change in the adversarial strategy of one or both of the parties can result in a different outcome.

---

[30] *See, e.g.*, In re Pinochet, [1999] 1 All E.R. 577. The potential disjunction of truth and justice also is poignant in toxic tort cases: "[I]t is certainly debatable whether the legal system—whose aim is to do justice—should use a scientific standard designed to defer resolution until an optimal amount of information is available. This is especially the case because plaintiffs are rarely in a position to initiate scientific research, have access to far less information than defendants have about its product, and often have fewer resources than defendants do. Nevertheless, many courts reject opinions based on epidemiological studies that fail to satisfy a .05 level of statistical significance as though these studies had no probative value." Margaret A. Berger, *Upsetting the Balance Between Adverse Interests: The Impact of the Supreme Court's Trilogy on Expert Testimony in Toxic Tort Litigation*, 64 Law & Contemp. Probs. 289, 301 (2001).

Lawsuits result when two or more parties assert a mutually exclusive claim on justice, and in cases resolved by a judge or a jury decision at least one party is likely to claim that the case was resolved unjustly. An individual's perception of justice is colored by whether the outcome conforms to that person's social or moral standards. This perception also may bias a person's belief about the facts and the law that should apply.

The bias in perception that affects litigants can also affect juries and judges. Neither is immune from the frailties of human decision making.[31] For example, each jury panel will adopt its own perception of justice. It is precisely for this reason that trial lawyers are so concerned about the jury selection process.[32]

Perceptions of justice can change over time, thus rendering justice a temporal concept. For example, consider the recent U.S. Supreme Court decision in *Atkins v. Virginia*.[33] In that case the Court concluded that a change in public consensus about executions of persons with mental retardation required a change in its interpretation of the cruel and unusual punishment clause of the Eighth Amendment to the U.S. Constitution to ban executions of persons with mental retardation.

Although it is well understood that different resources may produce different outcomes in similar cases, the rules of evidence make no effort to equalize these resource differences. For example, the rules of evidence do not try to equalize the disputing parties' access to relevant scientific information or other fundamental inequities in the quality of adversarial representation. The result is that the resources available to the differing parties can lead to outcomes that vary in the quality of justice that results.

Justice, like truth, is not an absolute or penultimate value in litigation. Fed. R. Evid. 102 does not list justice as the only goal of the rules of evidence, but notes other potentially conflicting goals. For example, in regard to justice versus fairness, as noted earlier, procedures may satisfy fundamental and legal notions of fairness while not enhancing just outcomes. For example, consider the decision to dismiss a child sexual abuse tort claim where the complainant has consistently remembered the abuse but has filed the action after the statute of limitations has run.[34] The statute of limitations exists out of a concern for fairness to the defendant and the defendant's ability to defend against stale claims. Although dismissal of the claim of child sexual abuse filed after the running of the statute of limitations might be

---

[31] Chris Guthrie, Jeffrey J. Rachlinski, & Andrew J. Wistrich, *Inside the Judicial Mind: Heuristics and Biases*, 86 CORNELL L. REV. 777 (2001).
[32] *See generally* David Suggs & Bruce D. Sales, *Juror Self-Disclosure in the Voir Dire: A Social Science Analysis*, 56 IND. L.J. 245 (1981).
[33] 536 U.S. 304 (2002).
[34] A statute of limitations describes the time period available to file a civil damage claim after a wrong has occurred.

fair to the defendant, it is arguably an unjust outcome, particularly when it is clear that the abuse has occurred.

Finally, we often hear and read the phrases *our system of justice, our justice system,* and *the criminal justice system.* What the phrasing implies is that justice as a goal is typically ascribed to the system level of analysis (the macro-level). Although we would like the system to dispense justice in every case (the micro-level of analysis), this may not occur in any given case.

Because of these limitations, justice cannot be perceived to be an absolute concept, nor is it an ultimate goal of the rules of evidence that is always recognizable and attainable in litigation. Thus understood, the decision of the drafters to couple justice with the "promotion of growth and development of the law of evidence"[35] becomes comprehensible. By so doing, the Federal Rules of Evidence acknowledge the long-term value of the goal of justice while recognizing its limitations as applied to any given case.

Importance of the Goals of the Federal Rules of Evidence for Our Analysis

As our analysis demonstrates, Fed. R. Evid. 102 specifies fairness, efficiency, truth, and justice as coequal goals for the Federal Rules of Evidence. Nothing in the text of Rule 102 suggests that one goal is to be considered more important than the others. Yet, in any given case, a conflict between these goals may require a court to choose between them, giving priority to one goal over another. It also is clear from our analysis that the four goals each have multiple definitions that can guide legal analysis. Thus, the values of the judges who interpret and apply them will affect both the priority given to the four goals and their meaning in specific cases.

In chapter 4, we ask how these goals have been implemented in the rules governing the admission of expert testimony. To answer this question, chapter 3 first provides the necessary background information about the historical development of the rules for the admissibility of expert testimony, Fed. R. Evid. 702 "Testimony by Experts," and the three United States Supreme Court decisions that have interpreted the application of this rule.

---

[35] Fed. R. Evid. 102.

3

ADMITTING EXPERT TESTIMONY: EVOLUTION AND INTERPRETATION

By the time common law courts evolved to their current approach based on trial by evidence rather than trial by ordeal,[1] they expected the jury to draw inferences from facts presented by witnesses to reach a decision in the case. Although lay witnesses were expected to provide factual information and not opinions, common law rules recognized exceptions permitting lay witnesses to give shorthand expressions of information amounting to opinions regarding matters such as speed, direction, and height.[2] But the common law rules recognized that, at times, lay testimony would not be sufficient to fully inform the fact finder. For example, although lay witnesses may describe their opinions about an automobile's speed, determining whether a specific speed limit (e.g., 35 mph) was violated may call for more exacting expert testimony about the application of radar to the case at hand.[3] Therefore, the common law permitted testimony from expert witnesses as well as lay witnesses.

Fearing that expert witnesses would dominate the trial process and result in jurors failing to engage in independent fact-finding, experts were

---

[1] Robert Bartlett, Trial by Fire and Water: the Medieval Judicial Ordeal (1986).
[2] 7 John Henry Wigmore, Evidence § 1977 (Chadbourn rev. 1978).
[3] City of Rochester v. Torpey, 128 N.Y.S.2d 864 (Cty. Ct. 1953).

only admitted to testify on matters beyond the common knowledge of lay witnesses.

> The rule is that the opinions of experts or skilled witnesses are admissible in evidence in those cases in which the matter of inquiry is such that inexperienced persons are unlikely to prove capable of forming a correct judgment upon it, for the reason that the subject-matter so far partakes of a science, art, or trade as to require a previous habit or experience or study in it, in order to acquire a knowledge of it. When the question involved does not lie within the range of common experience or common knowledge, but requires special experience or special knowledge, then the opinions of witnesses skilled in that particular science, art, or trade to which the question relates are admissible in evidence.[4]

When expert testimony was admissible to address an issue under the common law, the standard for admitting it was set rather low. Common law courts asked whether the proffered witness had the expert qualifications in the context of the particular case. To determine this, the courts evaluated whether the witness had the requisite education, training, skills, or experience necessary to permit him or her to assist the jury in resolving a question of fact in the case.[5] In cases where proffered experts had some credible claim to expertise, judges typically permitted the expert to testify, relegating disputes about the expert's qualifications to the fact finder when it assessed the weight to give the testimony.

In 1974, the Federal Rules of Evidence formalized the process for addressing whether proffered experts in the federal courts should be admitted to testify. Although not binding on the states, the majority of them have adopted these rules with some modification.[6] Rule 702, as originally codified in 1974 provided the following:

> If scientific, technical, or other specialized knowledge will assist the trier of fact to understand the evidence or to determine a fact in issue, a witness qualified as an expert by knowledge, skill, experience, training, or education, may testify thereto in the form of an opinion or otherwise.[7]

As enacted, the Federal Rules of Evidence did little to change the standards applied to assess whether an expert witness was qualified to testify on a particular topic. Like its common law predecessor, the federal rules leave the preliminary determination of qualification to the trial judge.[8] The

---

[4]Frye v. United States, 293 F. 1013, 1014 (D.C. Cir. 1923).
[5]Mason Ladd, *Expert Testimony*, 5 VAND. L. REV. 414 (1952).
[6]Faust F. Rossi, *The Federal Rules of Evidence—Past, Present, & Future: A Twenty-Year Perspective*, 28 LOY. L.A. L. REV. 1271 (1995).
[7]Federal Rules of Evidence for U.S. Courts and Magistrates, 56 F. R. D. 183, 282 (U.S. 1992).
[8]"[The] . . . court must determine admissibility under Rule 702 by following the directions provided in Rule 104(a)." Moore v. Ashland Chemical, Inc., 151 F.3d 269, 276 (5th Cir, 1998); "Preliminary questions concerning the qualification of a person to be a witness, the existence of a privilege, or the

rules create no rigid standard beyond directing the judge to consider what "knowledge, skill, experience, training, or education"[9] will be necessary to provide assistance to the fact finder.

For example, under the common law, the question of what mental health professional qualifications were required before a witness could serve as an expert occupied few reported decisions. Courts made categorical decisions about which of the mental health professional disciplines were qualified to testify on particular matters (e.g., psychiatrists versus psychologists on the insanity defense).[10] However, the question of which members of the profession possessed the education, training, and experience necessary to satisfy these categorical requirements was vested in the sound discretion of the trial court judge.[11] Over time, courts began to recognize psychologists as well as psychiatrists as experts on issues of mental status.[12] The Federal Rules of Evidence , which were adopted with the intent of liberalizing the admissibility of evidence in general[13] and expert evidence in particular,[14] did not result in a more restrictive application of the requirement that an expert be qualified by knowledge, skill, experience, education, or training.

Once a witness is qualified to testify as an expert, it is important to ask why anything more should be demanded before permitting the expert to testify. Why is being an expert not a sufficient guarantee of expertise? The manner in which courts have answered this question has shaped the evolution of evidence law.

At common law, when experts offered opinions on matters regarded as nonnovel science, the reliability of the expert's methods and procedures was not an issue that needed to be addressed separately in the admissibility of the expert's testimony. It was instead an issue of the believability of the expert's testimony for the fact finder to assess. For example, in the typical personal injury case in which a mental health professional testified that the accident caused the plaintiff's anxiety and that the injury could be expected to have a long-term impact on the plaintiff, it did not occur to lawyers or judges to demand research supporting the expert's ability to make this causal nexus or prediction. Only when the expert offered novel science (i.e., new

---

admissibility of evidence shall be determined by the court, subject to the provisions of subdivision (b). In making its determination it is not bound by the rules of evidence except those with respect to privileges." FED. R. EVID. 104(a).

[9] FED. R. EVID. 702.

[10] See, e.g., Jenkins v. United States, 307 F.2d 637 (D.C. Cir. 1962).

[11] See, e.g., Hagen v. Swenson, 236 N.W.2d 161 (Minn. 1975).

[12] See, e.g., State v. Robertson, 278 A.2d 842 (R.I. 1971).

[13] Beech Aircraft Corp. v. Rainey, 488 U.S. 153, 169 (1988) ("We see no reason to strain to reach an interpretation of Rule 803(8)(C) that is contrary to the liberal thrust of the Federal Rules.").

[14] Daubert v. Merrell Dow Pharmaceuticals, Inc., 509 U.S. 579, 588: ("Moreover, such a rigid standard would be at odds with the Rules' liberal thrust and their general approach of relaxing the traditional barriers to 'opinion' testimony.").

and not yet generally accepted science) did some courts look for more than qualifications in making their admissibility determination.

In addressing a proffer of novel science, the courts that looked for more than qualifications assessed the methods and procedures that the expert relied on to reach a judgment. The most well known approach to accomplishing this task is found in *Frye v. United States*,[15] a 1923 decision of the District of Columbia Court of Appeals. In that case the defendant offered testimony from an expert witness who conducted a test of deception on the defendant and concluded that he was not being deceptive in his denial of the crime charged. The test for deception was a measure of systolic blood pressure. The expert asserted that the defendant's emotions would influence blood pressure because they would trigger changes in the sympathetic nervous system resulting in a rise in systolic blood pressure. He claimed that scientific experiments

> have demonstrated that fear, rage, and pain always produce a rise of systolic blood pressure, and that conscious deception or falsehood, concealment of facts, or guilt of crime, accompanied by fear of detection when the person is under examination ... raises the systolic blood pressure in a curve, which corresponds exactly to the struggle going on in the subject's mind, between fear and attempted control of that fear, as the examination ... touches the vital points in respect of which he is attempting to deceive the examiner.[16]

To determine whether to admit this evidence, the court fashioned a test that envisioned science to be a linear evolutionary process:

> Just when a scientific principle or discovery crosses the line between the experimental and demonstrable stages is difficult to define. Somewhere in this twilight zone the evidential force of the principle must be recognized, and while courts will go a long way in admitting expert testimony deduced from a well-recognized scientific principle or discovery, the thing from which the deduction is made *must be sufficiently established to have gained general acceptance in the particular field in which it belongs.*[17] [Emphasis added]

Under the *Frye* test, when a challenge is made by an opponent to the admissibility of an expert's testimony, the judge is required to determine whether the proffered information is generally accepted in the particular field in which it belongs.[18] The judge is not required to evaluate its scientific

---

[15] 293 F. 1013 (D.C. Cir. 1923).

[16] *Id.* at 1013–1014.

[17] *Id.* at 1014.

[18] In the case of the deception test, the court considered that field to be both physiology and psychology: "We think the systolic blood pressure deception test has not yet gained such standing and scientific recognition among physiological and psychological authorities as would justify the

validity independently. Although *Frye* became one of the more important tests for the admissibility of expert testimony, that did not occur until long after it was decided.[19]

As *Frye* was applied with increasing frequency, it came under increased criticism.[20] Some critics addressed pragmatic aspects of the application of *Frye* (i.e., what had to be generally accepted, by whom, and with what level of support). Other commentators addressed the underlying assumption on which *Frye* was based, arguing that general acceptance addressed the popularity of a scientific proposition, not its validity. The ferocity of this debate intensified as proffers of scientific evidence increased, yet the Federal Rules of Evidence that were adopted in 1974 curiously made no mention of *Frye*.

The Federal Rules of Evidence, promulgated in 1974 to govern the trial of cases in the federal courts, sought to make the rules of evidence more accessible by codifying the multitude of common law cases.[21] The federal rules also sought to modernize evidence law by encouraging a preference for admitting relevant evidence, absent a convincing justification for its exclusion.[22] This approach contrasted with the common law approach that sought to protect uneducated and naive jurors by restricting the admissibility of expert testimony. The modernization effort contained in the Federal Rules of Evidence was carried forward in the vast majority of state courts that chose to codify their rules.[23]

The drafters of the Federal Rules of Evidence sought to incorporate their preference for admitting relevant expert testimony in the language of a number of rules that address the admissibility of expert testimony. Common law courts, protective of juries, admitted expert testimony only when it was "beyond the ken" of the jury. Rule 702 sought to increase the admissibility of expert testimony by requiring only that the expert testimony "assist the trier of fact."[24] The common law had often excluded expert testimony because the facts on which the expert based an opinion were not admissible in evidence.[25] Rule 703 permitted an expert to base an opinion on facts that were not admissible if they were the type of information "relied upon by

---

courts in admitting expert testimony deduced from the discovery, development, and experiments thus far made." *Id.* at 1014.

[19] Paul C. Giannelli, *The Admissibility of Novel Scientific Evidence: Frye v. United States, A Half Century Later*, 80 Colum. L. Rev. 1197 (1980).

[20] *Id.* at 1208–1228.

[21] Faust F. Rossi, *The Federal Rules of Evidence—Past, Present, & Future: A Twenty-Year Perspective*, 28 Loy. L.A. L. Rev. 1271 (1995).

[22] *See* Fed. R. Evid. 402: "All relevant evidence is admissible, except as otherwise provided by the Constitution of the United States, by Act of Congress, by these rules, or by other rules prescribed by the Supreme Court pursuant to statutory authority. Evidence which is not relevant is not admissible."

[23] Faust F. Rossi, *The Federal Rules of Evidence—Past, Present, & Future: A Twenty-Year Perspective*, 28 Loy. L.A. L. Rev. 1271 (1995).

[24] Fed. R. Evid. 702.

[25] *See generally* Fed. R. Evid. 703 Advisory Committee Note.

experts in the particular field in forming inferences or opinions on the subject."[26] Finally, the common law excluded expert opinions that touched on an ultimate issue in the case because it intruded on the function of the jury.[27] Rule 704, as originally enacted, did away with the ultimate opinion rule and permitted qualified opinions that were helpful to the jury without regard to whether they intruded on the ultimate issue before the fact finder.[28] These differences collectively represent the attempt of the drafters of the Federal Rules of Evidence to liberalize the admissibility of expert testimony.

The debate over the standard that should govern the admissibility of scientific evidence did not occur in a vacuum. Paralleling, and perhaps driving, this debate was a surge in proffers of increasingly complex scientific evidence. In the face of this surge, some argued that courts should respond by more carefully evaluating both the expert's qualifications and the expert's expertise.[29] Against this background and all of the changes in the rules for admissibility of expert testimony under the Federal Rules of Evidence noted above, the drafters still did not explicitly address the distinction between experts and expertise, or the test that should apply to evaluate the latter (i.e., the continued viability of *Frye*). As noted earlier, with the exception of the way some courts addressed the admissibility of novel science claims,[30] the common law rules did not distinguish experts from their expertise.[31] Once the expert's qualifications were found satisfactory, the expert's methods and procedures were rarely subject to rigorous scrutiny as a condition of admissibility. In a similar way, in the decade following the adoption of the Federal Rules of Evidence, most federal courts did not assess the reliability of an expert's information separately from the expert's qualifications.[32] Thus, the admission decisions were often likely to be similar to decisions under the prior common law.[33]

---

[26] The facts or data in the particular case upon which an expert bases an opinion or inference may be those perceived by or made known to the expert at or before the hearing. If of a type reasonably relied on by experts in the particular field in forming opinions or inferences on the subject, the facts or data need not be admissible in evidence for the opinion or inference to be admitted. Facts or data that are otherwise inadmissible shall not be disclosed to the jury by the proponent of the opinion or inference unless the court determines that their probative value in assisting the jury to evaluate the expert's opinion substantially outweighs their prejudicial effect. *See* FED. R. EVID. 703.

[27] *See, e.g.,* FED. R. EVID. 704 Advisory Committee Note. For example, expert testimony about the accuracy of the eyewitness in a criminal case is typically denied admission because the expert testimony would intrude on the province of the jury. It is the jury's role to judge the credibility of witnesses. *See, e.g.,* United States v. Brown, 511 F.2d 920 (2nd. Cir. 1975).

[28] FED. R. EVID. 704 as originally enacted.

[29] *See, e.g.,* Peter W. Huber, GALILEO'S REVENGE: JUNK SCIENCE IN THE COURTROOM 206-09 (1991).

[30] *See generally* United States v. Addison, 498 F.2d 741 (D.C. Cir. 1974).

[31] Daniel W. Shuman & Bruce D. Sales, *The Admissibility of Expert Testimony Based Upon Clinical Judgment and Scientific Research,* 4 PSYCHOL. PUB. POL'Y & L. 1226, 1235 (1998).

[32] *See generally* United States v. Downing, 753 F.2d 1224 (3d Cir. 1985).

[33] *See, e.g.,* A Special Theme Issue: Daubert's Meaning for the Admissibility of Behavioral and Social Science Evidence, 5 PSYCHOL. PUB. POL'Y & L. 3 (1999) (Daniel W. Shuman & Bruce D. Sales, Guest Editors).

Daubert v. Merrell Dow Pharmaceuticals, Inc.

When federal courts have addressed offers of novel scientific evidence and separately considered the expert from the expertise in deciding whether to admit the testimony, they have disagreed over whether the test to be applied in assessing admissibility of expert testimony was *Frye* or a test not predicated on general acceptance of the relevant scientific community.[34] The U.S. Supreme Court chose to address this issue in 1993 in *Daubert v. Merrell Dow Pharmaceuticals, Inc.*[35] *Daubert* was originally filed in a California state court seeking redress for injuries to children born with limb reduction birth defects. It was subsequently removed to the federal district court on the basis of the parties' diversity of state citizenship, as permitted by the U.S. Constitution[36] and federal statutes.[37]

The plaintiffs' tort claim alleged that the birth defects were caused by the mother's ingestion of Bendectin, a prescription antinausea drug, during the first trimester of pregnancy. The defendant moved for summary judgment on the basis of the affidavits of a physician and epidemiologist who reviewed the published studies on Bendectin and reported that none found it to be capable of causing malformations in human fetuses. In response, the plaintiffs offered the opinions of eight well-qualified experts who concluded that the drug caused the birth defects.

> Their conclusions were based upon "in vitro" (test tube) and "in vivo" (live) animal studies that found a link between Bendectin and malformations; pharmacological studies of the chemical structure of Bendectin that purported to show similarities between the structure of the drug and that of other substances known to cause birth defects; and the "reanalysis" of previously published epidemiological (human statistical) studies.[38]

The federal district court granted the defendant's motion for summary judgment and dismissed the lawsuit.[39] It concluded that the plaintiffs' experts could not demonstrate that the defendant's drug caused the plaintiffs' injury because epidemiological studies were the only generally accepted method (the *Frye* standard) of proving this link, and the epidemiological studies failed to demonstrate such a causal relationship. The U.S. Court of Appeals affirmed this decision,[40] and the Supreme Court granted review.

---

[34] Paul C. Giannelli, *The Admissibility of Novel Scientific Evidence: Frye v. United States, A Half Century Later*, 80 COLUM. L. REV. 1197, 1228–1231 (1980).
[35] 509 U.S. 579 (1993).
[36] U.S. CONST. art. III, § 2 cl. 1.
[37] 28 U.S.C. § 1332 (1996).
[38] *Daubert*, 509 U.S. 579 at 583.
[39] 727 F. Supp. 570 (S.D. Cal. 1989).
[40] 951 F.2d 1128 (9th Cir. 1991).

The Supreme Court began its opinion by recognizing that "[i]n the 70 years since its formulation in the *Frye* case, the 'general acceptance' test has been the dominant standard for determining the admissibility of *novel scientific evidence* at trial."[41] The plaintiffs argued that the *Frye* standard applied by the district court had been superseded by the Federal Rules of Evidence. To evaluate the merits of this claim, the Court looked to the text of Rule 702 of the Federal Rules of Evidence[42] and concluded that "[n]othing in the text of this Rule [or its drafting history] establishes 'general acceptance' as an absolute prerequisite to admissibility. Nor [is there] . . . any clear indication that Rule 702 or the Rules as a whole were intended to incorporate a 'general acceptance' standard."[43] The Court also reasoned that the Federal Rules of Evidence were intended to relax traditional barriers to opinion testimony by experts and that continued reliance on the *Frye* general acceptance standard would thwart this goal.[44] It then concluded that the Federal Rules of Evidence had displaced the *Frye* standard.

The Court next considered the trial court's obligation to screen proffers of expert testimony and the standard that would govern this scrutiny. Reasoning that the Federal Rules of Evidence required trial judges to admit only relevant and reliable expert testimony, the Court next considered what reliability means in the context of scientific expert testimony. The Court began its analysis by noting the following:

> The adjective "scientific" implies a grounding in the methods and procedures of science. Similarly, the word "knowledge" connotes more than subjective belief or unsupported speculation. The term "applies to any body of known facts or to any body of ideas inferred from such facts or accepted as truths on good grounds." . . . Of course, it would be unreasonable to conclude that the subject of scientific testimony must be "known" to a certainty; arguably, there are no certainties in science. . . . But, in order to qualify as "scientific knowledge," an inference or assertion must be derived by the scientific method.[45]

The Court concluded that the "[p]roposed testimony must be supported by appropriate validation—*i.e.*, 'good grounds,' based on what is known. In short, the requirement that an expert's testimony pertain to 'scientific

---

[41] 509 U.S. at 585 (emphasis added).

[42] "If scientific, technical, or other specialized knowledge will assist the trier of fact to understand the evidence or to determine a fact in issue, a witness qualified as an expert by knowledge, skill, experience, training, or education, may testify thereto in the form of an opinion or otherwise." [as originally enacted]

[43] 509 U.S. at 585.

[44] *Id.* ("The drafting history makes no mention of *Frye,* and a rigid 'general acceptance' requirement would be at odds with the 'liberal thrust' of the Federal Rules and their 'general approach of relaxing the traditional barriers to "opinion" testimony.' Beech Aircraft Corp. v. Rainey, 488 U.S., at 169, 109 S.Ct., at 450 (citing Rules 701 to 705).").

[45] *Id.* at 590.

knowledge' establishes a standard of evidentiary reliability."[46] It distinguished scientific validity (proof of what something is intended to prove) from scientific reliability (consistency in application of the science) and concluded that in cases involving scientific evidence, *evidentiary reliability* will be based on *scientific validity.*[47]

The Court removed any suggestion that the scrutiny be limited to "novel" scientific evidence.

> Although the *Frye* decision itself focused exclusively on "novel" scientific techniques, we do not read the requirements of Rule 702 to apply specially or exclusively to unconventional evidence. Of course, well-established propositions are less likely to be challenged than those that are novel, and they are more handily defended.[48]

Although Rule 702 applies to technical or other specialized knowledge, the Court noted that its opinion was limited to the case before it, which involved scientific evidence. The Court addressed offers of expert testimony grounded in technical or other specialized knowledge in a subsequent opinion, *Kumho Tire Co.v. Carmichael,*[49] which we discuss later in this chapter.

Once the applicability of *Frye* had been addressed, the Court went on to consider the meaning and importance of the phrase "assist the trier of fact to understand the evidence or to determine a fact in issue" in Rule 702.[50] The Court determined that the phrase applied to the issue of relevance.

> "Expert testimony which does not relate to any issue in the case is not relevant and, ergo, non-helpful." . . . ("An additional consideration under Rule 702—and another aspect of relevancy—is whether expert testimony proffered in the case is sufficiently tied to the facts of the case that it will aid the jury in resolving a factual dispute"). The consideration has been aptly described . . . as one of "fit." "Fit" is not always obvious, and scientific validity for one purpose is not necessarily scientific validity for other, unrelated purposes. . . . Rule 702's "helpfulness" standard requires a valid scientific connection to the pertinent inquiry as a precondition to admissibility.[51]

Once it considered both the requirements of the reliability and the relevance of the testimony, the Court laid out its approach to judging the admissibility of proffers of scientific testimony. Trial judges must first determine whether the expert is offering scientific testimony or evidence. If so, the judge must then determine whether that testimony or evidence

---

[46] *Id.*
[47] *Id.*
[48] *Id.* at 593.
[49] 526 U.S. 137 (1999).
[50] 509 U.S. at 591.
[51] *Id.* at 591–592.

will assist the trier of fact to understand or determine a fact that is in issue in the trial. To accomplish these two determinations, the judge must evaluate "whether the reasoning or methodology underlying the testimony is scientifically valid and of whether that reasoning or methodology properly can be applied to the facts in issue."[52]

Although the framework of the decision to this point relied on the explicit text of the Federal Rules of Evidence, the Court then left the text of the rules and delved into the philosophy of science to formulate the factors that courts should consider when assessing whether the reasoning or methodology underlying the testimony is scientifically valid:

> Ordinarily, a key question to be answered in determining whether a theory or technique is scientific knowledge that will assist the trier of fact will be whether it can be (and has been) tested. "Scientific methodology today is based on generating hypotheses and testing them to see if they can be falsified; indeed, this methodology is what distinguishes science from other fields of human inquiry." Green 645. See also C. Hempel, Philosophy of Natural Science 49 (1966) ("[T]he statements constituting a scientific explanation must be capable of empirical test"); K. Popper, Conjectures and Refutations: The Growth of Scientific Knowledge 37 (5th ed. 1989) ("[T]he criterion of the scientific status of a theory is its falsifiability, or refutability, or testability").[53] [Emphasis deleted]

Although the Court opined that trial judges were capable of successfully carrying out these scientific assessments, it did not specify how they should do so.[54] Rather, it provided what it referred to as "general observations,"[55] noting that many factors including the general observations will bear on the admissibility decision, and that it did not want to limit the trial courts discretion in evaluating proffered testimony.[56]

Following up on its discussion of the philosophy of science and acceptance of Popper's notions, the first observation the Court offered was that for a theory or technique to be scientific knowledge, it must be testable and ideally should have been tested. Second, it observed that it is pertinent whether the knowledge has been subjected to peer review and publication.

---

[52] *Id.* at 592–593.
[53] *Id.* at 593. Not all agree that the Court was wise in adopting Popper's philosophy of science. *See* e.g., Jan Beyea & Daniel Berger, *Complex Litigation at the Millennium: Scientific Misconceptions Among Daubert Gatekeepers: The Need for Reform of Expert Review Procedures*, 64 LAW & CONTEMP. PROB. 327 (2001); Joseph Sanders, *Complex Litigation at the Millennium: Kumho and How We Know*, 64 LAW & CONTEMP. PROB. 373 (2001).
[54] "We are confident that federal judges possess the capacity to undertake this review." 509 U.S. at 593.
[55] *Id.*
[56] "Many factors will bear on the inquiry, and we do not presume to set out a definitive checklist or test." *Id.* at 592.

The Court noted that publication does not guarantee evidentiary reliability (i.e., scientific validity), but it is a relevant consideration because it demonstrates that the knowledge has been subjected to the scrutiny of other experts in the field, which in turn increases the probability that problems in the proffered knowledge would have been detected. Third, the Court recommended that trial courts consider the known or potential error rate for the knowledge, and standards regulating how the technique is to be applied. It did not elaborate on this observation to indicate why error rate is important, what might be an unacceptable error rate, or what is the importance of considering the standards controlling the measurements. Fourth, and finally, having rejected *Frye*'s general acceptance test, the Court opined that widespread acceptance was a relevant consideration in admissibility decisions because it reflects support for the knowledge in the relevant scientific community.[57]

The Court provided little guidance as to how these general observations should be applied (i.e., whether they were conjunctive requirements, whether some mattered more than others). Instead, the Court noted, simply, that these observations were to be applied flexibly. "The inquiry envisioned by Rule 702 is, we emphasize, a flexible one. Its overarching subject is the scientific validity."[58]

What are we to make of these new criteria? Were they intended to raise or lower the bar for the admissibility of expert testimony? Was the Court's rejection of *Frye* and substitution of a set of pragmatic considerations a liberalization of expert admissibility requirements or an attempt to respond to *Frye*'s scientific failings? Some of these concerns were raised by the parties and addressed by the Court in the final section of its opinion.[59] The defendant, who prevailed under the *Frye* test at trial and in the court of appeals, argued that abandoning *Frye* would result in a "free-for-all" in which unreliable evidence would be admitted because of the lack of the need to prove general acceptance of the scientific information by the relevant scientific community. And once admitted, this information would overwhelm the abilities of juries. The Court responded that this concern was unduly critical of the abilities of juries and did not recognize the ability of the adversary system to use cross-examination and opposing experts to compensate for less reliable testimony.[60] The Court also noted the trial judge's ability to keep cases from the jury that were not supported by sufficient evidence.

---

[57] Even if the proffered testimony is admissible under the *Daubert* considerations, FED. R. EVID. 403 admonishes that if evidence, although relevant, is substantially outweighed by the risk that it may confuse rather than enlighten the jury, it may be excluded.

[58] 509 U.S. at 594.

[59] *Id.* at 59–97.

[60] *Id.* at 596. ("In this regard respondent seems to us to be overly pessimistic about the capabilities of the jury and of the adversary system generally. Vigorous cross-examination, presentation of contrary

The plaintiffs in *Daubert*, who lost at trial and in the court of appeals under *Frye*, argued that a rigid threshold would stifle the search for truth by only admitting testimony that conformed to the scientific orthodoxy. The Court responded by acknowledging that whereas science's search for truth was subject to perpetual revision, the law demanded timely and final resolution of disputes. It recognized that asking the trial judge to play the role of gatekeeper would "inevitably on occasion . . . prevent the jury from learning of authentic insights and innovations. That, nevertheless, is the balance that is struck by Rules of Evidence designed not for the exhaustive search for cosmic understanding but for the particularized resolution of legal disputes."[61]

After the decision in *Daubert* was announced, many, including mental health professionals, wondered whether the decision, which arose in the context of scientific expert evidence, governed the admissibility of non-scientific expert evidence.[62] Rule 702 recognized that expertise might be grounded not only in science, but also in technical, or other specialized knowledge. Would these latter types of expert testimony have to satisfy *Daubert's* requirements, which were born of a discussion of the demands for the scientific enterprise?

Kumho Tire Co. v. Carmichael

The answer came in the Court's 1999 decision in *Kumho Tire Co. v. Carmichael*.[63] The plaintiff in that case brought a product liability claim against the manufacturer and retailer of a tire that allegedly failed and caused an accident in which several persons were seriously injured and one person died. The plaintiff's liability claim rested on the testimony of an expert in tire failure analysis. On the basis of observational and technical information about tire design and wear, the expert concluded that the blowout was caused by a defect in the tire's design or manufacture. He also refuted the proposition that the blowout could have been caused by tire misuse, which he referred to as overdeflection (i.e., underinflation of the tire or the imposition of an excessive load on it).

The trial court concluded that the expert's methodology did not satisfy *Daubert's* reliability factors and did not admit it.[64] The plaintiffs asked for

---

evidence, and careful instruction on the burden of proof are the traditional and appropriate means of attacking shaky but admissible evidence.").

[61] *Id.* at 596–597.

[62] *See, e.g.,* C. Robert Showalter, *Distinguishing Science From Pseudo-Science in Psychiatry: Expert Testimony in the Post-Daubert Era,* 2 VA. J. SOC. POL'Y & L. 211 (1995).

[63] 526 U.S. 137 (1999).

[64] 526 U.S. at 145 ("The court . . . examined Carlson's methodology in light of the reliability-related factors that *Daubert* mentioned, such as a theory's testability, whether it 'has been a subject of peer review or publication,' the 'known or potential rate of error,' and the 'degree of acceptance . . . within the relevant scientific community.' 923 F.Supp., at 1520 (citing Daubert, 509 U.S., at

reconsideration of the decision, arguing that the court was too inflexible in applying *Daubert* to technical testimony. The court agreed to reconsider the issue, and concluded that *Daubert* "should be applied flexibly, [and] that its four factors were simply illustrative, and that other factors could argue in favor of admissibility."[65] But after reviewing the methods used by the expert, it affirmed its decision to exclude the testimony because it lacked the necessary indicia of reliability. The court of appeals reversed the trial court's decision, concluding that *Daubert* only applied to scientific testimony. It then remanded the case to the trial court to reevaluate its admissibility decision, using non-*Daubert* criteria under Fed. R. Evid. 702.[66]

The U.S. Supreme Court agreed to review the court of appeals decision and noted that under Fed. R. Evid. 702 trial judges have an obligation to determine that the proffered expert testimony is both relevant and reliable, whether it be offered as scientific, technical, or other specialized knowledge. This gatekeeping responsibility is important because, as discussed earlier, experts are granted wide latitude to present their opinions. However, the Court was clear in asserting that this discretion cannot allow the admission of testimony "where the discipline itself lacks reliability, as, for example . . . theories grounded in any so-called generally accepted principles of astrology or necromancy."[67]

In determining evidentiary reliability, the Court opined that *Daubert*'s factors may, but need not, be applied in admissibility decisions.

> We also conclude that a trial court may consider one or more of the more specific factors that Daubert mentioned when doing so will help determine that testimony's reliability. But, as the Court stated in Daubert, the test of reliability is "flexible," and Daubert's list of specific factors neither necessarily nor exclusively applies to all experts or in every case. Rather, the law grants a district court the same broad latitude when it decides how to determine reliability as it enjoys in respect to its ultimate reliability determination. See General Electric Co. v. Joiner, 522 U.S. 136, 143, 118 S.Ct. 512, 139 L.Ed.2d 508 (1997) (courts of appeals are to apply "abuse of discretion" standard when reviewing district court's reliability determination).[68]

Daubert's factors, a theory's testability, peer review and publication, its known or potential error rate, and its acceptance in the relevant scientific community, make sense in evaluating the reliability of a scientific expert's methods. However, because some technical or other specialized testimony

---

589–595, 113 S.Ct. 2786). The District Court found that all those factors argued against the reliability of Carlson's methods, and it granted the motion to exclude the testimony. . . .").
[65] *Id.* at 145–146.
[66] Carmichael v. Samyang Tire Inc., 131 F3d 1433 (11th Cir. 1997).
[67] 526 U.S. at 151.
[68] *Id.* at 141–142.

is not premised on science, "no one denies that an expert might draw a conclusion from a set of observations based on extensive and specialized experience."[69] The Court noted that the *Daubert* criteria cannot be logically applied to this latter category of proffered testimony.[70] To judge the reliability of this latter testimony, the Court concluded that a trial court could use any other factors it deemed appropriate. In explaining its reasoning, the Court noted that "Engineering testimony rests upon scientific foundations, the reliability of which will be at issue in some cases. . . . In other cases, the relevant reliability concerns may focus upon personal knowledge or experience."[71] The Court observed that "[t]he factors identified in *Daubert* may or may not be pertinent in assessing reliability, depending on the nature of the issue, the expert's particular expertise, and the subject of his testimony."[72]

In an effort to capture the wisdom of *Daubert* and *Kumho*, the drafters of the Federal Rules of Evidence amended Rule 702 from its original version, which read

> If scientific, technical, or other specialized knowledge will assist the trier of fact to understand the evidence or to determine a fact in issue, a witness qualified as an expert by knowledge, skill, experience, training, or education, may testify thereto in the form of an opinion or otherwise.

to read, as amended,

> If scientific, technical, or other specialized knowledge will assist the trier of fact to understand the evidence or to determine a fact in issue, a witness qualified as an expert by knowledge, skill, experience, training, or education, may testify thereto in the form of an opinion or otherwise, if (1) the testimony is based upon sufficient facts or data, (2) the testimony is the product of reliable principles and methods, and (3) the witness has applied the principles and methods reliably to the facts of the case.

As noted by the drafters of the 2000 Amendment to the rule, it "requires that the testimony must be the product of reliable principles and methods that are reliably applied to the facts of the case."[73]

---

[69] *Id.* at 156.
[70] *Id.* at 150.
[71] 526 U.S. at 150. ("*Daubert* makes clear that the factors it mentions do *not* constitute a 'definitive checklist or test.' Daubert, 509 U.S. at 593. And *Daubert* adds that the gatekeeping inquiry must be 'tied to the facts' of a particular 'case.' *Id.* at 591.").
[72] 526 U.S. at 150.
[73] FED. R. EVID. 702, 2000 Amendment Advisory Committee Note.

General Electric Co. v. Joiner

One other U.S. Supreme Court case, *General Electric Co. v. Joiner*,[74] deserves mention. *Joiner* addressed the standard that appellate courts should apply when reviewing trial court expert admissibility determinations. Robert Joiner, an electrician at the Water & Light Department of the city of Thomasville, Georgia, worked with electrical transformers that used a liquid coolant that was shown to be contaminated with polychlorinated biphenyls (PCBs). "Joiner often had to stick his hands and arms into the fluid to make repairs. The fluid would sometimes splash onto him, occasionally getting into his eyes and mouth."[75] Joiner and his wife sued General Electric Company, Westinghouse Electric Corporation, and Monsanto Company, manufacturers of the electrical transformers, the coolant, and the PCBs, claiming that he had small-cell lung cancer injuries resulting from his on-the-job exposure to PCBs. The district court

> granted summary judgment for [the defendants] because (1) there was no genuine issue as to whether Joiner had been exposed to furans and dioxins, and (2) the testimony of Joiner's experts had failed to show that there was a link between exposure to PCBs and small cell lung cancer. The court believed that the testimony of respondent's experts to the contrary did not rise above "subjective belief or unsupported speculation." . . . . Their testimony was therefore inadmissible.[76]

The court of appeals reversed, holding that "[b]ecause the Federal Rules of Evidence governing expert testimony display a preference for admissibility, we apply a particularly stringent standard of review to the trial judge's exclusion of expert testimony."[77] The U.S. Supreme Court reversed, holding that a standard more deferential to the trial court—abuse of discretion—applies to reviews of all evidentiary determinations, and that *Daubert* did not change this standard.

Thus, because the Federal Rules of Evidence require judges to act as gatekeepers for the reliability of the proffered expert testimony and allow them leeway in judging that reliability, a court of appeals cannot overturn the trial court's decision unless it is determined that the trial court abused its discretion.[78] Although seemingly a technical legal point, this standard has been cited as another pragmatic consideration to add to *Daubert*'s general observations,[79] and has a potentially profound impact on how *Daubert* is implemented. Because each trial court's admissibility determinations are

---

[74] 522 U.S. 136 (1997).
[75] *Id.* at 139.
[76] *Id.* at 140.
[77] Joiner v. General Elec. Co., 78 F.3d 524, 529 (11th Cir. 1996).
[78] 522 U.S. at 142.
[79] Fed. R. Evid. 702, 2000 Amendment Advisory Committee Note.

reviewable only for an abuse of discretion, it is possible that, absent a determinative U.S. Supreme Court decision on a particular category of evidence (e.g., recovered memories), there may be different rules for the admissibility of the same evidence in different trial courts.

Conclusion

Daubert answered the question about *Frye*'s continued viability, substituting a set of pragmatic criteria for trial courts to consider when addressing the admissibility of scientific expert testimony. *Kumho* and *Joiner* made these criteria applicable to all expert testimony, but reviewable only for an abuse of discretion. Although seemingly complete as a judicial response to a related series of questions, this trilogy raises more questions than it answers. If *Daubert*'s pragmatic criteria need not be applied in each and every case and a trial court's application of these criteria are granted deference by appellate courts, what should guide the trial court's exercise of its discretion? For the answer, the next chapter addresses how courts are making admissibility decisions post-*Daubert* and how Fed. R. Evid. 102 helps us understand and assess the quality of these decisions.

4

PROBLEMS IN IMPLEMENTING THE
GOALS FOR THE RULES OF EVIDENCE

Daubert, *Kumho*, and *Joiner* are not independent efforts by the United States Supreme Court to create rules for the admissibility of expert testimony. Rather, they are judicially crafted efforts to implement the rules of evidence. Thus, to assess their wisdom, it is necessary to evaluate them against the background of the goals articulated in the Federal Rules of Evidence (i.e., fairness, efficiency, truth, and justice). As we argue in this chapter, the gatekeeping process envisioned by Fed. R. Evid. 702, and the Supreme Court decisions that interpret it, present trial and appellate courts with difficult choices in the implementation of these goals, lead to some of the goals being compromised in individual cases, and may result in judicial inconsistency in admissibility decisions across cases. To make our case, this chapter uses the post-*Daubert* case law. Because our concern is with Fed. R. Evid. 702, and *Daubert*, *Joiner*, and *Kumho*'s implementation of the epistemology of the rules, we do not here address state court decisions that have rejected the federal rules.[1]

---

[1] Alice B. Lustre, *Post-*Daubert *Standards for Admissibility of Scientific and Other Expert Evidence in State Courts*, 90 A.L.R. 5th 453 (2001).

FAIRNESS

The decision of the drafters of the Federal Rules of Evidence to list fairness as the first goal of the rules of evidence is a powerful statement about the importance of process to the courts. Fair procedures are intended to guarantee a level playing field to all parties. We recognize that this concern is likely to seem strange to our scientist readers. A scientist would not seek to evaluate a colleague's research by using the construct of fairness. Science is concerned with process only so far as it promotes a valid outcome. In the law, however, fairness is critical, independent of any possible relationship to the efficiency, truth, or justice of the process, because it will promote the perceived legitimacy of, and satisfaction with, the legal system.[2]

Let us consider how the goal of fairness plays out in the Fed. R. Evid. 702 decision making. When a challenge is made to the admissibility of expert evidence, the Supreme Court has instructed federal judges to act as gatekeepers and make a threshold determination of whether the proffered expert information is reliable for evidentiary purposes. As the Supreme Court noted in *Daubert*: "[U]nder the Rules the trial judge must ensure that any and all scientific testimony or evidence admitted is not only relevant, but reliable."[3] For offers of scientific information, evidentiary reliability means scientific validity.[4] For nonscientific expert opinion, *Kumho* instructs that "Rule 702 grants the district judge the discretionary authority . . . to determine reliability in light of the particular facts and circumstances of the particular case."[5] This means that a judge may reach a decision on the basis of some criterion other than the validity of the methods on which the expert relied.

Keeping in mind the distinction between scientific and nonscientific expert testimony, what criteria should guide trial courts when reaching an admissibility decision if the determination is to be fair? The short answer is that courts should apply consistent, unbiased criteria for Fed. R. Evid. 702 admissibility decisions because they are more likely to lead to uniform decision making that does not favor any particular litigant or type of litigant.[6] Although consistency may advance the goal of fairness, its impact on truth

---

[2] *See e.g.,* Tom R. Tyler, Why People Obey the Law (1990); Daniel W. Shuman et al., *Jury Service—It May Change Your Mind: Perceptions of Fairness of Jurors and Nonjurors,* 46 SMU L. Rev. 449 (1992).

[3] 509 U.S. 579, 589 (1993).

[4] *Id.* at 590 ("In a case involving scientific evidence, *evidentiary reliability* will be based upon *scientific validity.*" [emphasis in original]).

[5] Kumho Tire Co. v. Carmichael, 526 U.S. 137, 158 (1999).

[6] *See supra* text accompanying chapter 2, notes 10–11.

and justice is another matter. Whether criteria that will advance fairness will also advance the pursuit of these other two goals is discussed under their respective subsections below.

Is the goal of fairness likely to be achieved under Fed. R. Evid. 702 as interpreted by *Daubert*, *Joiner*, and *Kumho*? The answer is that there are a number of reasons why the courts are likely to experience substantial problems advancing the goal of fairness under the judicial analysis of scientific, technical, and specialized information required by these decisions.

First, courts do not always rely on the same type of information in similar cases when reaching an admissibility decision. This promotes inconsistency in judicial decision making, which undercuts the goal of fairness. Although inconsistency in decision making is an inherent problem of the adversary system, *Daubert* and its progeny exacerbate this problem by demanding the lawyers and judges engage in an independent assessment of the reliability of expert testimony.

To elaborate, when determining whether to admit an expert's testimony, *Daubert* admonishes courts to determine whether the proffered information is reliable (in addition to relevant). To make this decision, courts rely on several sources of information—*primary*, *secondary*, and *tertiary* authority. These sources can be categorized along a continuum that varies in its determination of their adequacy for proving the scientific validity of the principles and methods underlying the proffered expert's testimony, or for proving the evidentiary reliability of the nonscientific expert's principles and methods for reaching his or her conclusions. Some of these sources will be easy for a judge to understand and evaluate, while others will require judges to have scientific, technical, or specialized training. And, unfortunately, it is the sources that are less reliable that are typically easiest for judges to understand and apply.

In the case of science, courts can look to the *primary* scientific literature. This literature is composed of the original scientific articles published in peer-reviewed journals or technical reports, which directly addresses the scientific validity of the principles or methods at issue in the admissibility decision. Courts can also consider *secondary* reviews of this literature by other scientists or experts. In this type of literature, scientists or other experts review the primary literature, providing their opinion as to its adequacy and value for addressing certain issues. *Tertiary* analyses are analytical law review articles authored by law students, law professors, lawyers, or judges, or judicial opinions in other cases addressing the merits of admitting similar types of expert information. Relying on one source of information to the exclusion of the other two, or using them in different combinations, can lead to different conclusions on the same issue and inconsistencies in decision making.

Neither Fed. R. Evid. 702 nor the Supreme Court's decisions in *Daubert*, *Joiner*, and *Kumho* provide guidance to trial court judges about the sources of information to rely on in their gatekeeping responsibilities. Indeed, *Joiner's* *abuse of discretion* standard for appellate review of trial court evidentiary decisions appears to insulate the trial judge's decision about which sources to use and in what order of importance.[7] Thus, in a case where all three sources are available, one trial judge might use primary sources while another trial judge might use secondary or tertiary sources, or a trial judge might use tertiary sources in one case and in a similar case use primary sources. These choices will be under the "radar-screen of likely Supreme Court review"[8] because these differences in trial courts' decisions are not cognizable as reversible error under *Joiner's* abuse of discretion standard for appellate review.

Second, as a product of our adversarial system and practice within it, judges are not expected to play the primary role in raising challenges to proffered expert testimony, nor in identifying the information that will be presented in a challenge to the admissibility of the expert evidence. It is the lawyer's responsibility to object to the opposing expert's testimony. The failure to make a timely and specific objection to expert testimony waives an objection to its admission under Fed. R. Evid. 103.[9] The logic of this practice is consistent with the adversarial system's approach to place control over the presentation of the case, along with the legal arguments and objections, with the parties. Yet, this facet of the adversary system also opens the door to similar trials having different outcomes because of the differing abilities or tactics of the lawyers. These differences may lead to inconsistencies in the implementation of Fed. R. Evid. 702 as interpreted by *Daubert*, *Joiner*, and *Kumho*.

Third, of the pragmatic considerations *Daubert* articulated to assess evidentiary reliability, which ones should the judge apply to which specific facts?[10] In what order should they be applied? What weight should the different pragmatic considerations be given in reaching an ultimate judgment? As noted in both *Daubert* and *Kumho*, which of these guidelines or considerations courts should apply in any given case, or to a particular category of expertise, rests within the sound discretion of the trial court.[11]

---

[7] *See* Michael H. Gottesman, *From* Barefoot *to* Daubert *to* Joiner: *Triple Play or Double Error?* 40 ARIZ. L. REV. 753, 775 (1998) ("Joiner is a paean to 'anything goes.'").

[8] *Id.* at 778.

[9] FED. R. EVID. 103(a)(1): "Error may not be predicated upon a ruling which admits or excludes evidence unless a substantial right of the party is affected, and . . . [i]n case the ruling is one admitting evidence, a timely objection or motion to strike appears of record, stating the specific ground of objection. . . . "

[10] *See supra* text accompanying chapter 3, notes 53–54.

[11] A trial judge determining the admissibility of an engineering expert's testimony *may* consider one or more of the specific *Daubert* factors. The emphasis on the word "may" reflects *Daubert's*

There is "little consensus [among trial judges] regarding how to weight or combine the *Daubert* criteria."[12] *Kumho* teaches that judges can ignore all of these pragmatic considerations and use other considerations if they so choose, as long as they are "reasonable measures of the reliability."[13] The result is that judicial decisions will vary on the basis of the judges' decision making processes, and these variations are not likely to be adjusted by the appellate courts. As explained in *Joiner*, review of the trial court's decision will be by way of an *abuse of discretion* standard that defers to the decision of the trial court judge in all but the most egregious of errors. Disparate application of criteria and their weighting is a major challenge to achieving fairness under Fed. R. Evid. 702 as interpreted by *Daubert*, *Joiner*, and *Kumho*.

This dilemma is equally important for nonscientifically derived clinical opinion testimony after *Kumho*. Although *Kumho* opines that the *Daubert* criteria can apply to nonscientific expert testimony,[14] a category in which clinical opinion testimony fits, an attempt to do so with any of the pragmatic considerations except general acceptance is problematic. Clinicians have not recognized or applied commonly agreed on criteria to test the validity of clinically derived opinions.[15] Thus, courts have no clear professional metric to which to resort, as did the *Daubert* Court in its application of the methods of epidemiology. The resulting uncertainty will affect the consistency in the application of the criteria across similar cases, which presents a challenge to the goal of fairness.

For example, consider the Ninth Circuit Court of Appeals decision in *United States v. Hankey*,[16] which was decided in light of *Kuhmo*. Hankey and a codefendant were prosecuted for distribution of PCP, but the co-defendant testified that Hankey was not involved in illegal activities. To impeach the codefendant, the government presented the testimony of a police officer as an expert witness, who testified that Hankey and the co-

---

description of the Rule 702 inquiry as "a flexible one." 509 U.S., at 594, 113 S.Ct. 2786. The *Daubert* factors do *not* constitute a definitive checklist or test, *id.*, at 593, 113 S.Ct. 2786, and the gatekeeping inquiry must be tied to the particular facts, *id.*, at 591, 113 S.Ct. 2786. Those factors may or may not be pertinent in assessing reliability, depending on the nature of the issue, the expert's particular expertise, and the subject of his testimony. Some of those factors may be helpful in evaluating the reliability even of experience-based expert testimony, and the Court of Appeals erred insofar as it ruled those factors out in such cases. In determining whether particular expert testimony is reliable, the trial court should consider the specific *Daubert* factors where they are reasonable measures of reliability.

Kumho Tire Co. v. Carmichael 526 U.S. 137, 138 (1999).

[12] Sophia I. Gatowski et al., *Asking the Gatekeepers: A National Survey of Judges on Judging Expert Evidence in a Post-Daubert World*, 25 LAW & HUM. BEHAV. 433, 448 (2001).

[13] *Kumho Tire*, 526 U.S. at 152.

[14] *Kumho Tire*, 526 U.S. at 138. ("Some of those factors may be helpful in evaluating the reliability even of experience-based expert testimony, . . .")

[15] Indeed, they could not without applying scientific methods of validation, which they do not use. *See infra* text accompanying chapter 4, notes 119–120.

[16] 203 F.3d 1160 (9th Cir. 2000).

defendant were gang members and that testifying against the fellow gang member was traditionally punished by death or serious injury. According to the government's expert, this would explain why the co-defendant would perjure himself by denying Hankey's complicity in the crime. The trial court admitted the expert's testimony over Hankey's objection, and Hankey appealed the decision to the Ninth Circuit Court of Appeals. In upholding the trial court's decision, the court of appeals noted that "[t]he *Daubert* factors (peer review, publication, potential error rate, etc.) simply are not applicable to this kind of testimony, whose reliability depends heavily on the knowledge and experience of the expert, rather than the methodology or theory behind it."[17] Expanding on the *Kumho* decision, which opined that expert testimony can be based on a set of observations grounded in extensive and specialized experience, the *Hankey* court noted that the admissibility decision could also focus on the expert's knowledge, skill, experience, training, or education. The use of these criteria presents the risk of inconsistent admissibility decisions from court to court over the same facts. Lacking some validated criteria to evaluate the sufficiency of experience, the judge's values shaped by his or her own experiences with police officers as witnesses may result in a disparate pattern of decisions from judge to judge.

Fed. R. Evid. 702 as interpreted and applied post-*Daubert* seems unlikely to result in fairness if fairness is gauged by consistency of decisions in like cases. The differing sources of information on which courts can rely, the differing abilities of trial court judges to understand theses sources, and the wide margin appellate courts have been instructed to give trial courts in their application of the *Daubert* criteria, lead to the conclusion that whatever other goals *Daubert* might advance, fairness is not one of them.

EFFICIENCY

Fed. R. Evid. 102's concern with efficiency would dictate that we evaluate *Daubert* and its progeny's impact on cost-efficiency and time-efficiency for lawyers and the courts. For example, does the cost-efficiency and time-efficiency for lawyers' performance differ before and after the adoption of Fed. R. Evid. 702? Is it less time consuming and costly to assess the admissibility of expert testimony admitted post-702 than pre-702 when holding the reliability of that testimony constant? The answer to such questions addresses the efficiency of Fed. R. Evid. 702 and its implementation post-*Daubert*.

---

[17]*Id*. at 1169.

To explore these questions and find the answers, we need to remember that the Federal Rules were intended to adopt a more liberal thrust in favor of the admissibility of evidence. If the Federal Rules of Evidence are more liberal, they should admit more proffered expert testimony to inform the fact-finder.[18] This would affect efficiency in two ways: the first concerns the admissibility decision itself, and the second concerns the consequences of that decision for the resolution of the case.

If the Federal Rules of Evidence increase efficiency, the same testimony offered after their enactment should require less time and expense on the part of lawyers to prepare for and less time for judges to reach an admissibility decision on when compared to pre-Federal Rules of Evidence cases. Under this hypothesis, lawyers working under pre-Federal Rules of Evidence should have spent significantly more time and expense developing expert evidence than would be generally accepted by the relevant scientific community, and judges should have spent more time in assessing an expert's satisfaction of the general acceptance standard. This might have required a longer and more intense search for experts who could substantiate that the proffered expert testimony was generally accepted and a longer and more complex admissibility determination. Conversely, under this same hypothesis, the liberal thrust of the Federal Rules of Evidence should have made lawyers' work more efficient by requiring less time and money to secure experts to convey admissible information and should have made judge's work less time consuming to determine admissibility.

The problem with this hypothesis is that there is no evidence to support it and much to argue against it. Under the common law's broad relevancy approach to admissibility, if the proffered expert was qualified and the testimony was relevant, it would get to the jury. This was highly efficient in terms of lowered lawyer trial preparation and costs for judging the admissibility of expert testimony.

Under *Frye*, the lawyer's work may have been somewhat increased, but that was not consistent across jurisdictions.[19] Whereas some courts accepted the testimony of a single expert or the decision of another court to satisfy *Frye*, others required the concurrence of more than one expert or the introduction of scientific literature supporting general acceptance. This absence of consensus about what *Frye* required contributed to criticism of

---

[18] *See* FED. R. EVID. 702, 2000 Amendment Advisory Committee Note. ("A review of the case law after Daubert shows that the rejection of expert testimony is the exception rather than the rule."); *See also* Heller v. Shaw Industries, 167 F.3d 146, 155 (3rd Cir. 1999) ("Given the liberal thrust of the Federal Rules of Evidence, the flexible nature of the Daubert inquiry, and the proper roles of the judge and the jury in evaluating the ultimate credibility of an expert's opinion, we do not believe that a medical expert must always cite published studies on general causation in order to reliably conclude that a particular object caused a particular illness.").

[19] Paul C. Giannelli, *The Admissibility of Novel Scientific Evidence:* Frye v. United States, *a Half-Century Later*, 80 COLUM. L. REV. 1197, 1215–1219 (1980).

it as a standard for admissibility of expert testimony and called into question its efficiency across cases. In addition, because *Frye's* application was limited to novel science, evidence that had been regularly admitted did not come under its scrutiny.[20] This limited application of *Frye* meant it did not change the efficiency of admissibility determinations in most cases.

The Federal Rules of Evidence did not likely create greater efficiency. The consequence of the *Daubert* decision, when combined with the Court's subsequent decision in *Kumho,* is clear. *Daubert* does not grant regularly used, nonnovel, expert testimony immunity from its scrutiny. Thus, it presents more instances of its application, which will increase costs when compared to *Frye.*

In addition, the available evidence after the *Daubert* decision indicates that substituting *Daubert's* pragmatic criteria for judging evidentiary reliability for *Frye's* general acceptance test decreases efficiency insofar as it increases the costs of admissibility decision making. *Daubert's* inefficiency in the costs of decision making about admissibility, relative to *Frye,* is due to its requirement that the lawyer prove the validity of the scientific testimony rather than simply its general acceptance. Proving validity under *Daubert* requires lawyers and judges to address whether the relevant hypotheses can be and have been tested, the error rate for research and methods for controlling it, whether the research has been subjected to peer review through publication or others methods, and whether it is generally accepted. Application of additional criteria (i.e., more criteria than required under *Frye*) should increase the time it takes a lawyer to prepare an expert for trial or to challenge an expert's admissibility. It should also take more time for judges to complete their admissibility analysis and reach an admissibility decision. The result will be increased delay and cost in lawyer and court time spent. Thus, *Daubert's* interpretation of 702 does not well serve the epistemological goal of avoiding increased expense or delay.[21] Rather than increasing the efficiency of the judicial decision making process for admissi-

---

[20] *See* Randolph N. Jonakait, *The Standard of Appellate Review for Scientific Evidence: Beyond* Joiner *and* Scheffer, 32 U.C. Davis L. Rev. 289 (1999).

[21] Daubert did not function well at all. The Supreme Court sought to encourage liberal admissibility. It believed it was abolishing a strict Frye test in favor of a more liberal factor balancing analysis. But instead of liberal admissibility, the direct opposite occurred. First, all "scientific" evidence was now subject to Daubert's five factor analysis, including scientific evidence in civil cases never previously exposed to significant gatekeeping. When a gatekeeping test is applied where one was not before, less expert witness testimony is admissible, which is hardly a liberalization. In situations where Frye previously had been applied, while probably not resulting in many expert opinions being excluded where previously admitted, Daubert hardly significantly liberalized admissibility. Very little, if anything, is admitted in the federal courts using Daubert that is excluded in state courts still following Frye.

Michael H. Graham, *The Expert Witness Predicament: Determining "Reliable" Under the Gatekeeping Test of* Daubert, Kumho, *and Proposed Amended Rule 702 of the Federal Rules of Evidence,* 54 U. Miami L. Rev. 317, 324 (2000).

bility, at least when all or most of its criteria are applied,[22] *Daubert* demands more time and expense to satisfy this threshold.[23] This conclusion is supported by recent empirical findings. In a review of pre- and post-*Daubert* federal district court judges' survey responses, judges reported a substantial increase in the number of pretrial hearings on the admissibility of expert testimony.[24]

The efficiency of *Daubert* may also be affected by lawyers' and judges' scientific knowledge. Although the scientific proficiency of judges and lawyers will have a bearing on the efficiency of the admissibility of experts under any test, *Daubert* exacerbates this relationship between scientific proficiency and efficiency because it requires the court to make an independent assessment of evidentiary reliability based on arguments presented by the lawyers. This may affect efficiency in two ways. One is that more scientifically proficient judges and lawyers may resolve admissibility issues more expeditiously than less scientifically proficient judges because they have the capacity to cut to the heart of the issues quickly. Conversely, there is the possibility that greater scientific proficiency may result in more time being spent on subtle issues that those less knowledgeable in science would miss. We can point to no studies or cases that directly address these hypotheses.

The best evidence we have available points to the fact that judges have struggled with application of the *Daubert* criteria because of a lack of knowledge about concepts that are fundamental to science: falsifiability and error rate.[25] We assume that if lawyers were surveyed, they would respond

---

[22] Lawyers and courts could ignore the *Daubert* mandate and continue to use old practices and logic. A *Special Theme Issue:* Daubert's *Meaning for the Admissibility of Behavioral and Social Science Evidence,* 5 PSYCHOL. PUB. POL'Y & L. 3 (1999) (Daniel W. Shuman & Bruce D. Sales, Guest Editors) found this to be the case in their review of the way courts scrutinized the admissibility of behavioral and social science evidence in child custody, guardianship, and testamentary capacity litigation.

[23] My biggest problem comes from the push initially by the Supreme Court, then by courts of appeal, and then by lawyers, to have a Daubert hearing in virtually every case involving expert testimony. This is not simply a matter of "You're in trial, you've gotten to that point, and then there's some Daubert issue to be decided by the judge as to whether perhaps the final bottomline opinion comes in or not." Rather, it involves a request by one side or the other, and let's be frank about it, most of these come up in the context of a defendant seeking to have me reject a plaintiff's expert's testimony with at least the goal in mind of attempting to get summary judgment or at least eliminate certain aspects of the case. So it tends to be one-sided in terms of how it comes up. But my experience is that, almost invariably, where there's going to be a need for expert testimony by the plaintiff in order to establish either reliability or some aspect of damages, the defendant will ask for a hearing in advance of trial, before me, to make the Daubert presentation which may involve hearing a number of witnesses, and that is very time-consuming.
Sam C. Pointer, Jr., *Response to Edward J. Imwinkelried, The Taxonomy of Testimony Post-*Kumho: *Refocusing on the Bottomlines of Reliability and Necessity,* 30 CUMB. L. REV. 235, 236 (2000).

[24] See Carol Krafka et al., *Judge and Attorney Experiences, Practices, and Concerns Regarding Expert Testimony in Federal Civil Trials,* 8 PSYCHOL. PUB. POL'Y & L. 309, 321 (2002).

[25] Shirley A. Dobbin et al., *Applying* Daubert: *How Well Do Judges Understand Science and Scientific Method?* 85 JUDICATURE 244 (2002).

similarly to the judges. But this does not resolve the rival hypotheses about the impact of this lack of scientific knowledge. These judges lacking scientific proficiency may resolve admissibility issues more slowly (i.e., less efficiently) because they lack an understanding of the scientific meaning of the *Daubert* criteria and therefore struggle with its application. Alternatively, these judges may be more efficient because they will spend less time on subtle scientific issues that they fail to identify.

To see how each of our rival hypotheses would affect efficiency, we first need to remember that we concluded that the increase in criteria under *Daubert*, as compared to *Frye*, would lower efficiency. If judges then struggle with the application of the *Daubert* criteria because they do not understand the science, this will further decrease efficiency. This seems likely to occur in the many cases in which judges with poor scientific knowledge carefully attempt to apply *Daubert*'s more scientifically arduous criteria (i.e., falsifiability and error rate). If, however, judges spend less time on the science that they do not understand, this will increase efficiency and offset the potential efficiency decrease caused by the increase in the number of criteria. The logic here is that some judges may be influenced by their lack of scientific knowledge to opt for the easiest solution to the admissibility decision or to miss the issues all together. They might look to the tertiary literature, including what other court opinions have held, or rely on evidence of peer review or general acceptance in the relevant scientific community. If this occurred, it would offset the potential effect on efficiency of having to deal with more criteria. We conclude, therefore, that the combined effect of the *Daubert* criteria and the lack of scientific knowledge has probably resulted in a nuanced effect on efficiency rather than a monolithic response.

Moreover, efficiency cannot be measured using a single dimension. If there is decreased efficiency in the admission of expert testimony post-*Daubert*, it may be offset by greater overall efficiency in the trial process. Despite taking more time to deal with admissibility, case outcome may be determined more efficiently if cases in which expert testimony is not admitted are disposed of more readily because the expert testimony was, as a matter of law or tactics, necessary to make out a claim or defense. In addition, extra time spent for admissibility decision making may well dissuade potential litigants from instituting nonmeritorious claims.

Would the result of our efficiency analysis be different if we were considering a proffer of expert testimony not grounded in scientific research pre-Fed. R. Evid. 702 and post-*Kumho*? The answer depends on the type of testimony that the expert offers. Where the testimony is based on pure clinical opinion without reliance on scientific literature or techniques, the post-*Kumho* efficiency has mirrored that which occurred pre-702 in many cases. For example, consider the decision in *United States v. Hankey*,[26] discussed above, in which the court admitted a police officer's testimony relating to gang behavior by focusing on the expert's knowledge, skill, experience, training, or education. The court's approach to admissibility is identical to what most courts would have done prior to Fed. R. Evid. 702.

Not all courts approach this issue in the same manner, however. In the case of clinical medicine, for example, some courts have taken an approach that does not result in equivalent efficiency.[27] Consider the case of *Moore v. Ashland Chemical Inc.*[28] In this case, an *en banc* decision of the Fifth Circuit Court of Appeals rejected the use of clinical medicine to demonstrate a causal link between the defendant's chemicals and the plaintiff's injuries, demanding scientific proof instead. This court's approach differs from what most courts would have done pre-Fed. R. Evid. 702, and would result in the lawyers and the courts expending significantly more resources in preparing and judging the admissibility of the expert testimony.

The difference between the efficiencies in these two cases was the result of the courts requiring different thresholds for ascertaining truth as accuracy from the two disciplines: medicine and law enforcement. According to the logic of the *Moore* decision, medical experts, even if presenting clinical information, should derive their results using scientifically based premises to increase its testimonial accuracy. This would result in a difference in the ways lawyers would prepare for cases and courts would judge admissibility pre-Fed. R. Evid. 702 and post-*Kumho*. The *Hankey* court did not demand similar scientific rigor for police observations of gang behavior.

Yet many social scientists, particularly those in sociology and criminology, would respond to this purported distinction in two ways. They would expect police experts to ground their testimony in existing social science research on gangs. And if no research were available, they would question why unsystematic observations that have not been scientifically verified should be admitted as expert testimony.

If these criticisms of the attempts to distinguish the judicial scrutiny of medical and law enforcement observations are fair, lawyers would need to prepare for *Hankey* type cases, and judges would need to scrutinize the

---

[26] 203 F.3d 1160 (9th Cir. 2000).
[27] Courts have not been uniform in applying *Daubert* when assessing the methodology of clinical medicine to prove causation. *See* Hollander, 289 F.3d at 1209–1210 (comparing Westberry v. Gislaved Gummi AB, 178 F.3d 257, 262–266 (4th Cir. 1999) and Glastetter v. Novartis Pharm. Corp., 252 F.3d 986, 989 (8th Cir. 2001). *See also* Federal Judicial Center, Reference Manual on Scientific Evidence, 34–38 (2d ed. 2000) (comparing Moore v. Ashland Chemical Inc., 151 F.3d 269 (5th Cir. 1998), *cert. denied*, 526 U.S. 1064, 119 S.Ct. 1454, 143 L.Ed.2d 541 (1999), and Heller v. Shaw Industries, Inc., 167 F.3d 146 (3rd Cir. 1999)).
Christian v. Gray, 65 P.3d 591, 605 n.18 (Okla. 2003).
[28] 151 F.3d 269 (5th Cir. 1998).

proffers of expert testimony by police, using a similar approach to that found with clinical medical experts relying on the *Moore* approach. The result would be that the efficiencies related to the attempted use of both types of testimony would be similar, and that similarity would differ from that which occurred prior to the introduction of the Fed. R. Evid. 702. One implication of our analysis is that efficiency, one of the goals of the rules of evidence, is unlikely to play a role in these courts' decisions about the admissibility threshold.

Even when efficiency does play a role, the efficiencies of post-*Daubert* and *Kumho* cases are not likely to be uniform. First, under *Joiner*, appellate courts are instructed to give great deference to trial courts' Fed. R. Evid. 702 decisions, and overturn them only where the decision is clearly erroneous. The practical result is that Fed. R. Evid. 702 decisions made by trial judges will likely stand. Second, under *Kumho*, trial judges are permitted to exercise discretion concerning which of *Daubert*'s pragmatic criteria to apply. A trial judge who, on efficiency grounds, applies only the fourth of *Daubert*'s criteria—general acceptance—may well take much less time to reach a decision than a fellow judge in a similar case who applied all of the *Daubert* criteria.

In addition to failing to address the costs of deciding whether to admit the expert's testimony, these decisions also fail to address the efficiency implications of an admissibility decision for the entire case. When expert testimony is required to make out a *prima facie* case for a claim or defense, excluding expert testimony may result in avoiding a trial with a summary judgment or ending a trial with a directed verdict. For example, for the plaintiff to have prevailed in *Daubert*, expert testimony was required to prove that Bendectin caused the plaintiff's limb reduction birth defects. Thus, once the decision was made to exclude that expert testimony, the case was dismissed because no alternate method of proving this element of the plaintiff's case existed. Did this result in greater efficiency in the processing of this case or the series of cases seeking similar relief? Answering that question requires a comparison of the time and expense of the admissibility hearing with the time and expense of trial. For example, when the trial court declines to admit expert testimony, the costs of the hearing might be compared with the cost savings avoided by the trial, offset by the costs of appeal. When the trial court admits the testimony, the costs of the hearing might be compared with the costs of trial, offset by the resulting potential for settlement. None of these decisions, nor any others we were able to identify, explicitly addressed these issues.

Whether Fed. R. Evid. 702, as interpreted by *Daubert* and its progeny, necessarily and justifiably involve greater expense and delay than *Frye* to achieve greater accuracy in decision making (i.e., a goal of truth seeking) is a question that we consider in the subsection on truth. Additionally, none of these decisions consider the implications of increased or decreased efficiency on the pursuit of the other goals of fairness and justice in the Federal Rules of Evidence. For example, one might evaluate whether expense or delay are justifiable in relationship to the financial or societal interests at stake in the litigation. Thus, litigation concerning only private interests or seeking minor damages would seem to justify less expense or tolerance of delay than litigation concerning important public interests[29] or significant damages. Fed. R. Evid. 702 and the *Daubert*, *Kumho*, and *Joiner* trilogy make no explicit reference to such distinctions. That may be because these concerns were not at issue in any of those cases, and it would have been inappropriate for the Court to comment on an issue that was not raised and briefed by the parties. And of course, ironically, cases involving less significant interests are not likely to be the ones that parties would pursue to the United States Supreme Court.

Moreover, *Daubert* and its progeny appear to decrease efficiency for the admission of scientific evidence. We use the word "appear" because there have been no empirical studies to document our conceptual analysis to date. For the admissibility of nonscientific evidence, the picture is mixed. For those courts that have tried to increase the rigor of the evidentiary reliability analysis of the proffered evidence, efficiency appears to have once again suffered when compared to pre-Federal Rules of Evidence. But in a number of cases, the courts' evaluation of the nonscientific information appears no more rigorous than what occurred prior the Fed. R. Evid. 702, leaving efficiency unchanged.

TRUTH

As noted in chapter 2, there are a number of possible ways to understand the meaning of truth in the context of the Federal Rules of Evidence: (a) truth referring to accuracy of the testimony conveyed in court; (b) truth referring to the an outcome that culminates after the adversarial process occurs, rather than an absolute discernable state of knowledge;[30] and (c) truth referring to a systemwide goal for all trials without regard to whether that goal is achieved in any one case.[31]

---

[29] Determining what issue or issues are societally important is in and of itself a complex decision making task. For example, are all issues raising distributive justice concerns societally important? If not, what criteria define which subset of those issues that are above threshold? We do not try to analyze this issue because it is unnecessary for purposes of the goal of this book.

[30] *See* Shari Seidman Diamond, *Truth, the Jury, and the Adversarial System: Truth, Justice, and the Jury,* 26 HARV. J.L. & PUB. POL'Y 143 (2003).

[31] *See* Shari Seidman Diamond, *Truth, the Jury, and the Adversarial System: Truth, Justice, and the Jury,* 26 HARV. J.L. & PUB. POL'Y 143 (2003); Marianne Wesson, *Historical Truth, Narrative Truth, and Expert Testimony,* 60 WASH. L. REV. 331 (1985).

Truth as Accuracy

Perhaps the most appealing interpretation of truth as it is applied to 702 and its interpretation through *Daubert* is that it encourages the search for truth using an approach that scientists would respect. Built on Karl Popper's notion of falsifiability as the hallmark of the scientific enterprise,[32] *Daubert*'s pragmatic criteria seem to encourage admissibility decisions based on the scientific accuracy of the proffered information.[33] *Daubert*, unlike *Frye*, does not ask courts to defer to accepted, but not necessarily scientifically valid, science. It treats all claims of expertise, both new and old similarly, demanding that they all pass muster under the criteria laid down.[34]

There are 11 reasons to doubt that *Daubert*'s interpretation of 702 will always lead to accurate testimony, however, the first two of which could apply to any admissibility standard.

Scientific Agreement

Scientists do not always agree on what is scientifically proven.[35] When the scientific community cannot agree on what information is accurate, the judge will be less likely to consistently and accurately exclude unreliable

---

[32] KARL R. POPPER, CONJECTURES AND REFUTATIONS (1965).

[33] *See Daubert*, 509 U.S. at 593 "K. Popper, Conjectures and Refutations: The Growth of Scientific Knowledge 37 (5th ed. 1989) ('[T]he criterion of the scientific status of a theory is its falsifiability, or refutability, or testability') (emphasis deleted)."; *see also* "Jan Beyea & Daniel Berger, *Complex Litigation at the Millennium: Scientific Misconceptions Among Daubert Gatekeepers: The Need for Reform of Expert Review Procedures*, 64 LAW & CONTEMP. PROB. 327, 332 (2001). ("Popper's view has had a 'profound effect on the theories of scientific method.' . . . Scientific inference under this view is a mixture of intuition, which is subjective, and logical reasoning. Deductive logic can be applied only to the hypothesis when the hypothesis is assumed to be 100% true."); *see also*

> Not all agree that the Court in Daubert was consistent in its claim of reliance on Popper: The Supreme Court's opinions in Daubert v. Merrell Dow Pharmaceuticals, Inc. General Electric Company v. Joiner, and Kumho Tire v. Carmichael contain two inconsistent views of science. In some places, the Court views science as an imperfect "process" for refining theories, whereas in other places, the Court views science as universal knowledge derived through "formal logic." The latter view, long out of favor with philosophers and historians of science, comports with the current cultural vision of science and is likely to be adopted by district and appeals court judges, without vigorous "education," or until such time as higher courts recognize that the two views need to be synthesized into a consistent whole . . .

Id. at 328.

[34] *But see* United States v. Hines, 55 F. Supp. 2d 62, 66 (D. Mass., 1999) ("Traditional science, generally accepted by judges for decades, may not need the same kind of rigorous analysis as 'new' science which lacks the legitimacy of a chorus of sponsors. As to the latter, the Daubert analysis is critical, and the court should be an especially vigilant gatekeeper.").

[35] [I]n the Daubert decision, the Supreme Court demands that an expert testify to "scientific knowledge," when neither it nor anyone else can possibly recognize "scientific knowledge" due to its abstract and amorphous nature. The ipse dixit of the Supreme Court that "federal judges possess the capacity" to undertake a proper review is not an answer. No scientific instrument or meter can be held over expert testimony to identify scientific knowledge; no algorithm can tell us which testimony is valid and which is not. By failing to resolve the semantic problems that engulf the concept of scientific knowledge, the Supreme Court has encouraged lower courts to undertake hopeless searches for scientific Holy Grails. The resulting confusion will surely lead to judicial error, primarily because the courts have no institutional mechanisms for peer review by

---

expert information. For example, a report of the National Research Council, studying effects of PCBs, dioxin, and other substances, was unable to reach unanimity because

> Some of the differences [between the conclusions of committee members] reflect areas where additional research would help; others reflect differing judgments about the significance of the existing information. The differences are not confined to this committee but are reflected in the scientific community at large. Some differences appear to stem from different views of the value of different kinds of evidence obtained by experiments, observations, weight-of-evidence approaches, and extrapolation of results from one compound or organism to others, as well as allowable sources of information and criteria for arriving at meaningful conclusions and recommendations.[36]

Daubert's teachings can only be used to judge information offered by the experts. When the experts disagree, it becomes inherently more difficult for a nonscientist judge to accurately determine the scientific validity of the proffered information.

Completeness of Information

In a system that primarily relies on the adversarial presentation of retained experts, there will always be questions about the completeness of the information presented. Relevant information to which these experts do not have access (i.e., research does not yet exist; research is not generally available), or to which these experts do not refer in their testimony, is unlikely to be scrutinized by the court. Although the information could be gathered by the judge or the judge's clerk, that is an uncommon event. The result is that accuracy in fact-finding may be compromised.

Clarity of the General Observations

The criteria articulated in *Daubert/Kumho* (i.e., whether the underlying theory or technique can be and has been tested, whether it has been subjected to scrutiny by others in the field through peer review and publication, whether the error rate and standards for controlling it are acceptable, and the degree of acceptance within the scientific community) do not always provide clear guidance for judges. For an example, how should each criterion

scientists to minimize the amount of scientific error that will creep into legal decisions and precedents. The courts will end up enforcing a kind of quasi-scientific orthodoxy that, in the absence of reform, could well institutionalize unfairness and bring disrespect to the judiciary. Jan Beyea & Daniel Berger, *Complex Litigation at the Millennium: Scientific Misconceptions Among Daubert Gatekeepers: The Need for Reform of Expert Review Procedures*, 64 LAW & CONTEMP. PROB. 327, 338–339 (2001).

[36] NATIONAL RESEARCH COUNCIL, HORMONALLY ACTIVE AGENTS IN THE ENVIRONMENT 2 (1999).

be interpreted and implemented? In the case of the criterion of error rate, how much error should be acceptable?[37]

For a more detailed elaboration of the absence of clarity in an individual criterion, consider peer review, a criterion that would seem to be easy to interpret and implement. *Peer review* refers to the process of vetting one's work before other experts so that its flaws may be revealed and its content improved. But all peer-reviewed publications do not provide the same level or type of vetting. Peer-reviewed journals may not actually have peer review or not always apply it to all submitted manuscripts.[38] In some cases, the editor may decide to accept an article without sending it out for peer review. Where peer reviewers are used, there is substantial variation in the number of peer reviews a manuscript may receive. Some may receive one peer review, others two, and some may receive as many as nine. Peer review may be selectively applied, and peer reviewers may not be uniform in the quality of their reviews. Indeed, there are large differences in the quality of reviews. This problem is exacerbated by the fact that most journals do not require authors to supply copies of the original data or statistical analyses for the reviewers to consider. And because reviewing is a completely voluntary activity in an often already busy schedule, some potentially good reviewers provide inadequate reviews on occasion. Even if the journal editor accepted the manuscript for publication on scientific grounds because of peer reviewers' recommendations, "a large number of published studies actually turn out to be wrong. Indeed, the scientific literature is full of 'peer-reviewed', but inaccurate articles and theories."[39] Not surprisingly, one study concluded that the journal peer review process is far less accurate than traditionally assumed.[40]

Peer review can also refer to presenting one's work in conferences or other forums, such as workshops. Vetting one's work is the critical component of peer review, not publication in a peer-reviewed journal. Yet, this type of public vetting raises concerns that are similar to those posed by peer review in journals. Consider the case of *State v. Anderson*.[41] The New Mexico

---

[37] *See* Christopher Slobogin, *The Admissibility of Behavioral Science Information in Criminal Trials: From Primivitsm to* Daubert *to Voice*, 5 Psychol. Pub. Pol'y & L. 100 (1999); Daniel A. Krauss & Bruce D. Sales, *The Problem of "Helpfulness" in Applying* Daubert *to Expert Testimony: Child Custody Determinations in Family Law as an Exemplar*, 5 Psychol. Pub. Pol'y. & L. 78 (1999); and Daniel A. Krauss & Bruce D. Sales, *Legal Standards, Expertise, and Experts in Child Custody Decision-Making*, 6 Psychol. Pub. Pol'y. & L., 843 (2000).

[38] Lois A. Colaianni, *Peer Review in Journals Indexed in Index Medicus*, 272 J. Am. Med. Ass'n 156 (1994).

[39] William L. Anderson, Barry M. Parsons, & Drummond Rennie, Daubert's *Backwash: Litigation-Generated Science*, 34 U. Mich. J.L. Reform 619, 628–629 (2001). "Neither courts nor scientists should blithely assume that publication in a purportedly 'peer-reviewed' journal is a seal of approval for a particular methodology or theory." *Id.* at 636–637.

[40] Michael L. Callaham et al., *Reliability of Editors' Subjective Quality Ratings of Peer Reviews of Manuscripts*, 280 J. Am. Med. Ass'n 229 (1998).

[41] 881 P.2d 29 (N.M. 1994).

courts were faced with the admissibility of FBI DNA identification evidence that relied on research that was not published in a peer-reviewed journal. Anderson was convicted of kidnapping, second-degree criminal sexual penetration, aggravated battery, extortion, and two counts of first-degree criminal sexual penetration, in part on the basis of FBI DNA evidence linking him to the crimes. Anderson unsuccessfully objected to the admission of this testimony. The New Mexico Court of Appeals reversed the admissibility decision and remanded the case for retrial. The New Mexico Supreme Court affirmed the trial court's admission of the contested evidence and upheld the admissibility of the DNA evidence, including evidence obtained through methods used by the FBI. In reaching its decision, the court noted that publication in a peer-reviewed journal provides helpful information to the court about the testimony's evidentiary reliability but "is not a *sine qua non* of admissibility."[42] Because the FBI's DNA technique had not been subject to vetting through peer-reviewed publication, the court independently reviewed the FBI's evidence in support of admitting the testimony. The court reasoned that the FBI technique had been subjected to peer review because the technique had been discussed "at scientific conferences, workshops and other forums for the exchange of ideas and through the dissemination of unpublished and non-peer-reviewed writings."[43]

What the court did not consider was that conferences are often open door invitations to scientists and professionals to speak as long as they pay the registration fee. Often their ideas and the methodology used to derive them are not scrutinized. In addition, conferences allow the speaker to present only summaries of their ideas and ignore the audience's comments, whereas the journal peer review process gives the editor gatekeeping control over whether to publish an article, forcing the authors to attend to the *audience's comments*. Workshops are also problematic. They are typically opportunities to disseminate practice strategies and not to provide a critical forum for peer review. The court did not consider these issues, nor did it identify what constituted the other forums for exchanging ideas. The defendant's four experts, scientists from the University of Washington; the University of California, Irvine; the University of Minnesota; and the

---

[42] *Id.* at 44.
[43] Among them are F. Samuel Baechtel, *A Primer on the Methods Used in the Typing of DNA*, 15 Crime Lab. Dig. 3 (Supp. No. 1 1988); Bruce Budowle et al., *An Introduction to the Methods of DNA Analysis Under Investigation in the FBI Laboratory*, 15 Crime Lab. Dig. 8 (1988); F. Samuel Baechtel, *Recovery of DNA from Human Biological Specimens*, 15 Crime Lab. Dig. 95 (1988); Bruce Budowle, *The RFLP Technique*, 15 Crime Lab. Dig. 97 (1988); Catherine Theisen Comey, *The Use of DNA Amplification in the Analysis of Forensic Evidence*, 15 Crime Lab. Dig. 99 (1988); Dwight E. Adams, *Validation of the FBI Procedure for DNA Analysis: A Summary*, 15 Crime Lab. Dig. 106 (1988); William G. Eubanks, *FBI Laboratory DNA Evidence Examination Policy*, 15 Crime Lab. Dig. 114 (1988). *Id.* at 45.

University of California, Los Angeles, found serious flaws in the FBI technique. Not surprisingly, rather than addressing the merits of these scientific criticisms, the court reasoned that peer review had occurred and then noted that the FBI published numerous articles, although it appears that these articles were in a non-peer-reviewed journal, *Crime Lab Digest*.[44] Because of the lack of clarity provided by *Daubert* and *Kumho* about the assessment of the peer review process, the New Mexico Supreme Court's reasoning is understandable.

This lack of clarity regarding the *Daubert* criteria can jeopardize the attainment of truth-as-accuracy in trials. For example, a journal may have accepted and published an article because it would stimulate important discussion and debate in the field, even though on purely scientific grounds it should not have been accepted. If the judge admitted expert testimony on the basis of this article because it was published in a peer-reviewed journal, the goal of truth as accuracy would be compromised. It is unlikely that the judge would be aware that peer review for the article meant something very different than a full and appropriate vetting. Journal editors do not typically tell readers why they accept manuscripts for publication.

Order and Weighting of General Observations

Because the criteria are guidelines only, courts can heavily emphasize one pragmatic criteria over others in their decision making, with no recommended fixed order or priority to their use,[45] and "no single factor ... necessarily dispositive of the reliability of a particular expert's testimony."[46] If judges can use different criteria to reach admissibility decisions about scientific validity, then they may reach inconsistent conclusions about the evidentiary reliability of identical proffered testimony, some of which must be wrong.

Judicial Competence

No matter how clear the criteria or the rules for ordering them, the scientific competence of judges limits the application of the admissibility

---

[44] *Id.*

[45] *See supra* text accompanying chapter 3, notes 53–58. For example, the 2000 Amendment Advisory Committee Note discusses five other criteria that courts have used as pragmatic considerations in interpreting and applying *Daubert*. FED. R. EVID. 702, 2000 Amendment Advisory Committee Note: (1) whether the testimony logically flows from the research conducted independent of the litigation, (2) the analytical gap between the data and the expert's conclusions, (3) consideration of alternative causes for the event, (4) whether the testimony employs the same degree of rigor that characterizes the expert's work outside of litigation, and (5) the reliability of the field that the expert represents and the reliability of the field for the type of the opinions that the expert offers.

[46] FED. R. EVID. 702, 2000 Amendment Advisory Committee Note.

rules.[47] Judges are not chosen because of their scientific training or acumen. Lack of understanding of the methods that experts use, and the conclusions they draw from their methods, will lead to inappropriately inconsistent admissibility decisions and frustrate Fed. R. Evid. 102's goal of truth as accuracy. This is not an idle concern. A recent study of state trial judges found that although half of the judges surveyed had confidence in their ability to evaluate adequately proffers of scientific testimony, almost all acknowledged that they never had training in scientific methods and principles.[48] This finding supports Chief Justice Rehnquist's doubts about whether federal trial judges would understand notions of falsifiability and implicitly the criteria that the court developed relying on falsifiability.[49] Even if judges attempt greater rigor in gatekeeping through an application of *Daubert*'s pragmatic criteria, standing alone, there is little assurance it will lead to the appropriate exclusion of unreliable expert testimony.[50] Supporting Justice Rehnquist's doubts, a recent study of trial judges found that

> [w]hile judges found falsifiability to be useful when determining the merits of proffered scientific evidence, they did not fully understand its scientific meaning. As a result, judges were unsure how to properly apply the criterion of falsifiability as an admissibility guideline. Indeed, when asked how they would apply the guideline of falsifiability when making a determination about the admissibility of proffered scientific evidence, the majority of judges expressed some hesitancy or uncertainty. Only 6 percent of the responses demonstrated a clear understanding of the scientific meaning of falsifiability.[51]

These concerns are amplified by the fact that "many obscure theories/studies that are published in second- or third-tier journals . . . never receive any

---

[47] See Joseph T. Walsh, *Keeping the Gate*, 83 JUDICATURE 140, 143 (1999). In discussing why *Daubert* granted the gatekeeping responsibility for admissibility decisions, Judge Walsh notes that the
  rationale is built on two underlying assumptions: (1) that the trial judge is more knowledgeable in assessing complex scientific testimony than is the average lay juror and (2) that each judge brings to the specific task of gatekeeping a general attitude or philosophy concerning the level of scrutiny appropriate for scientific gatekeepers. Experience, however, has demonstrated that judges are not fungible. Intelligence aside, judges vary considerably in how they view their role in the courtroom; active or passive, dominating or deferential to counsel, prone to independent inquiry or content to let the lawyers try the case.
[48] Sophia I. Gatowski et al., *Asking the Gatekeepers: A National Survey of Judges on Judging Expert Evidence in a Post-Daubert World*, 25 LAW & HUM. BEHAV. 433 (2001).
[49] Daubert v. Merrell Dow Pharmaceuticals, Inc., 509 U.S. 579, 598 (1993). "[T]he researchers could only infer a true understanding of the scientific meaning of falsifiability in 6% (n=23 of 400) of the judge's responses." Gatowski, *supra* note 48 at 444.
[50] Lloyd Dixon & Brian Gill, *Changes in the Standards for Admitting Expert Evidence in Federal Civil Cases Since the Daubert Decision*, 8 PSYCHOL. PUB. POL'Y & L. 251 (2002).
[51] Shirley A. Dobbin et al., *Applying Daubert: How Well Do Judges Understand Science and Scientific Method?*, 85 JUDICATURE 244, 246–247 (2002).

significant attention or criticism,"[52] and by studies demonstrating the problems that judges have in assessing scientific information.[53]

The problem of achieving the goal of truth as accuracy will likely be compounded when the proffered testimony is based on complex science. Some more basic scientific techniques (e.g., basic experiments that manipulate only one variable) are likely to be understood by intelligent laypersons. But more complex scientific research techniques require more specialized knowledge of research methodology and statistics that individuals without scientific training are not likely to grasp. Thus, as the complexity of the science at issue increases, there will be an increase in the disagreement in judicial rulings on the same question, resulting in some of the decisions being inaccurate,[54] as well as an increase in judges' avoiding actually evaluating the validity of the science. For example, let us return to the court's opinion in *State v. Anderson.*[55] In discussing the error rate for the FBI's DNA technique, the court correctly noted that there are two measurements of concern: how well DNA examiners could perform their tasks and how accurate are the DNA measurements using the technique. In regard to the first criterion, human error in measurements taken, the defendant mounted a powerful set of arguments refuting the conclusion that the FBI's technique yielded a low error rate. Citing a report of the prestigious National Research Council, one of the defendant's experts noted that the FBI had never done what is known as blind proficiency testing of their examiners, which is essential to proving a low error rate for examiners. In addition, the FBI tested only nine

---

[52] William L. Anderson, Barry M. Parsons, & Drummond Rennie, Daubert's *Backwash: Litigation-Generated Science*, 34 U. Mich. J.L. Reform 619, 630 (2001).

[53] *See* Sophia I. Gatowski et al., *Asking the Gatekeepers: A National Survey of Judges of Judging Expert Evidence in the Post-*Daubert *World*, 25 Law & Hum. Behav. 433 (2001); Margaret Bull Kovera & Bradley D. McAuliff, *The Effects of Peer Review and Evidence Quality on Judge Evaluations of Psychological Science: Are Judges Effective Gatekeepers?*, 85 J. of Applied Psychol. 574 (2000); Margaret Bull Kovera, Melissa B. Russano, & Bradley D. McAuliff, *Assessment of the Commonsense Psychology Underlying* Daubert: *Legal Decision Makers' Abilities to Evaluate Expert Evidence in Hostile Work Environment Cases*, 8 Psychol. Pub. Pol'y & L. 180 (2002). As one legal scholar has noted, *Daubert* assumes that the expert is testifying honestly. Where that is the case, it is unlikely that judges will be better equipped than the expert to address the reliability of the expert's opinion. Michael H. Gottesman, *From Barefoot to* Daubert *to Joiner: Triple Play or Double Error?*, 40 Ariz. L. Rev. 753, 758–759 (1998).

[54] Some have serious doubts about the judges' ability in this regard: "Most federal judges are bright individuals but we sorely underestimate the complexity of many scientific controversies, particularly those involving complex quantitative analyses, when we presume that nonscientist judges can master the technical issues to the point that they should feel comfortable deciding what is or is not good science in a particular case." Paul S. Milich, *Controversial Science in the Courtroom: Daubert and the Law's Hubris*, 43 Emory L. J. 913, 919 (1994). For a specific example of the complexity science raises for the judiciary even in the most common of legal cases—child custody, see Daniel A. Krauss & Bruce D. Sales, *The Problem of "Helpfulness" in Applying* Daubert *to Expert Testimony: Child Custody Determinations in Family Law as an Exemplar*, 5 Psychol. Pub. Pol'y & L. 78 (1999); and Daniel A. Krauss & Bruce D. Sales, *Legal Standards, Expertise, and Experts in the Resolution of Contested Child Custody Cases*, 6 Psychol. Pub. Pol'y & L. 843 (2000).

[55] 881 P.2d 29 (N.M. 1994).

simulated cases and the examiners knew that they were tests. Despite these and other criticisms that were raised by the defense expert, the FBI did not offer any evidence to refute the criticisms. Although a scientist would conclude that the problem with establishing the technique's error rate presented a serious and perhaps dispositive challenge to its scientific validity, the court concluded that the evidence should be admitted, with its credibility left up to the jury. The only justification for its conclusion was that courts in New York and Colorado reached a similar conclusion.[56] An equally plausible explanation is that the judge did not understand the real meaning of error rate. The results of a recent survey of state trial judges supports this interpretation.

> [J]udges surveyed did not fully understand the scientific meaning of "error rate," and often were unsure how to use the concept to assess the admissibility of proffered evidence. For most of the judges surveyed (86 percent), understanding of the scientific concept of error rate was questionable at best, with a clear understanding evident in only 4 percent of responses.[57]

The court ruled similarly in regard to the accuracy of the FBI testing procedure. Anderson claimed that the FBI's procedure was inappropriate because it relied on a sample that was not proven to represent the population being studied. His argument was supported by the National Research Council, which recommended that an alternative procedure be used by organizations like the FBI. Once again, however, the court avoided directly evaluating the scientific issues, concluding that the arguments for both sides could be presented to the jury. Thus, the court admitted the FBI DNA testimony, leaving it to the jury to weigh its credibility. The court engaged in no independent analysis of the issue nor did they opine how the jury would be able to assess the reliability of the FBI's technique in reaching its conclusions. The court ignored the peer review advice of the National Research

---

[56] There is good reason to doubt that this decision will lead to substantially greater accuracy in decision making. For example:

> It may be a greater mistake to be overly optimistic than overly pessimistic about the capabilities of juries when it comes to complex scientific issues, . . . particularly those involving sophisticated quantitative analysis. The Bendectin trials, for example, asked jurors to evaluate competing epidemiological and statistical theories and analyses. As Professor Sander's excellent study of the trials shows, even though the basic scientific issue remained the same, of twenty Bendectin trials that went all the way to jury verdict, plaintiffs won eight and defendants won twelve . . . . An optimist might point to the fact that the jury got it right 60% of the time . . . A pessimist would say this is not much better than flipping a coin.

Paul S. Milich, *Controversial Science in the Courtroom: Daubert and the Law's Hubris*, 43 EMORY L.J. 913, 922 (1994).

[57] Shirley A. Dobbin et al., *Applying Daubert: How Well Do Judges Understand Science and Scientific Method?* 85 JUDICATURE 244, 247 (2002). *See also* Sophia I. Gatowski et al., *Asking the Gatekeepers: A National Survey of Judges on Judging Expert Evidence in a Post-Daubert World*. 25 LAW & HUM. BEHAV. 433 (2001).

Council and avoided dealing with the scientific merits of the proffered testimony, rejecting its *Daubert* gatekeeper role in favor of the pre-*Daubert* approach of minimal judicial scrutiny of the reliability of the expert's methods and procedures.

Sources of Information

Techniques that judges use to overcome their lack of expert knowledge can present their own unique problems. Judges attempt to make up for their own lack of expert knowledge by relying on the opinions of experts or other sources of expert information. Unfortunately, because some judges lack the education necessary to become sophisticated consumers of scientific knowledge, their reliance on these sources can easily lead to inaccurate information being admitted into trials or accurate information being denied admission.

Judges have available to them three types of information: *primary*, *secondary*, and *tertiary*. Scientists would want courts to review the *primary* scientific information (i.e., review the original scientific research as published in peer-reviewed scientific journals, and the actual methods and analyses that underlay the expert testimony) because it contains the needed information to determine if the proffered information is valid for the purpose it is being offered. Some judges do this quite well.[58] Consider the decision in *Valentine v. Pioneer Chlor Alkali Co.*[59] Plaintiffs sued alleging neurotoxic effects of breathing in chlorine. As part of its decision the court was faced with the plaintiff's expert's assertion that relied on one article that the defendants argued was not published in a scientifically credible journal. Rather than relying on the article's assertions about the science, the court proceeded to engage in a well-constructed scientific critique of the author's methodology that formed the basis for the article and reached the following conclusion:

> In summary, Dr. Kilburn's study suffers from very serious flaws. He took no steps to eliminate selection bias in the study group, he failed to identify the background rate for the observed disorders in the Henderson community, he failed to control for potential recall bias, he simply ignored the lack of reliable dosage data, he chose a tiny sample size, and he did not attempt to eliminate so-called confounding factors which might have been responsible for the incidence of neurological disorders

---

[58] Sophia I. Gatowski et al., *Asking the Gatekeepers: A National Survey of Judges on Judging Expert Evidence in a Post-*Daubert *World*, 25 Law & Hum. Behav. 433 (2001) (concluding that most judges understand the concept of peer review. However, their research only addressed judicial knowledge that peer review entails an evaluation of submitted manuscripts by other experts prior to a decision to publish a manuscript. It did not consider the variations, vagaries, and biases that can occur in the peer review process.). We elaborate on these concerns below.
[59] 921 F. Supp. 666 (D. Nev. 1996).

in the subject group. As a result, his conclusions that the plaintiffs' exposure to atmospheric chlorine caused their neurological disorders cannot be said to be derived from acceptable scientific methodology.[60]

But not all judges engage in this type of analysis. Some simply accept the expert's testimony concerning the methodological rigor of the research underlying the testimony:

> The Court finds that Dr. Benoit's testimony regarding the Able Assessment satisfies the first part of the *Daubert* analysis. Not only did Dr. Abel participate in a research study which tested the Abel Assessment which was published in *Sexual Abuse: A Journal of Research and Treatment*, Vol. 10, No. 2, pp. 81–95, but four independent research studies have been performed on the Abel Assessment. Each study found the Abel Assessment to be valid. Moreover, the results of the studies were presented at the Association for the Treatment of Sexual Abusers national convention on September 20, 1999 and were thus subjected to peer review.[61]

The validity studies referred to were not evaluated by the judge or a journal for that matter. They were simply presented at a national conference of clinicians engaged in the treatment of sexual offenders. Although, as noted earlier, it is appropriate under the reasoning in *Daubert* to look for peer review outside of formal publication, in this case the judge did not engage in an evaluation of the rigor of the peer review process for being accepted to present one's ideas at this annual meeting, and there was no evaluation of the rigor of the peer review process at the meeting. Some professional conferences accept almost all submitted papers as long as the submitter holds a professional degree or equivalent credential and pays the conference registration fee. Indeed, it is reasonable to assume that the conference would have accepted invalid studies for presentation if they contained ideas that were worthy of discussion and debate among clinicians on the front line of assessment and treatment. A similar concern applies to the published article to which the judge refers. Although it was published in a highly respected clinical journal, it is a journal for disseminating ideas to and sharing ideas with those who work with sex offenders. As such, the journal would publish manuscripts that would be valuable for clinicians to read and think about even if the results reported were not proven scientifically valid.

This is particularly troubling because uncritical acceptance by judges of claims that information has been scientifically derived risks judges' missing

---

[60]*Id.* at 678.
[61]United States v. Robinson, 94 F. Supp. 2d 751, 753 (W.D. La. 2000).

the fact that the research may have been compromised not only by intentionally biased science but also by more subtle threats to scientific validity.[62] These threats include the researchers' scientific values and biases and the sources of funding that affect their selection of the scientific questions being asked, the methods used to answer those questions, the statistics selected to analyze the data, and the interpretations applied to the results.[63] For example, consider an expert testifying on the inability of juries to comprehend a significant portion of the instructions presented by the judge to the jury.[64] Such research will be significantly affected by the choice of dependent measures used to test juror comprehension of the instructions. Should the researcher choose a true–false response paradigm, multiple choice, short answer, or other possible measurement strategy? Choice of a particular measure will likely change the results of the studies. Yet, ironically, this has not been the focus of systematic research in this area.[65]

Scientists also read and value *secondary* sources for the insights they bring to understanding the primary sources and, not surprisingly, the courts have done the same.[66] *Secondary* sources are writings by scholars who review the *primary* scientific literature. *Secondary* reviews can be accurate in judging the validity of the primary work. This is most likely to occur where the secondary source is the consensus of a distinguished panel of scientists working on behalf of a federal agency[67] or a learned society. Consider the court's decision in *Sterling v. Velsicol Chemical Corp*,[68] in which residents adjoining the defendant's landfill brought suit seeking damages for exposure to chemicals known to cause cancer and affect the central nervous system. The only expert testimony the adjoining residents presented linking their health problems to the defendant's landfill relied on clinical ecology. The court of appeals rejected this evidence, noting that the "leading professional societies in the specialty of allergy and immunology, the American Academy of Allergy and Immunology (AAAI) and the California Medical Association (CMA) . . . [had] rejected clinical ecology as an unproven methodology lacking any scientific basis in either fact or theory . . . ."[69] Consequently, it

---

[62] William L. Anderson, Barry M. Parsons, & Drummond Rennie, Daubert's *Backwash: Litigation-Generated Science*, 34 U. MICH. J. L. REFORM 619 (2001).

[63] Mark R. Patterson, *Conflicts of Interest in Scientific Expert Testimony*, 40 WM. & MARY L. REV. 1313 (1999).

[64] *See* Gacy v. Welborn, 994 F. 2d. 305 (7th Cir. 1993) (admitting expert testimony on juror comprehension and rejecting the defendant's argument that this research rose to the level of presenting constitutional flaws in the fairness of the trial process).

[65] Joel D. Lieberman & Bruce D. Sales, *What Social Science Teaches Us About Jury Instructions*, 3 PSYCHOL. PUB. POL'Y & L. 589 (1997).

[66] *See, e.g.*, United States v. Cordoba, 991 F. Supp. 1199 (C.D. Cal. 1998).

[67] *E.g.*, National Institutes of Health Consensus Development Program, available at http://consensus.nih.gov/default.html, last visited October 20, 2003.

[68] 855 F.2d 1188 (6th Cir. 1988).

[69] *Id.* at 1208.

reversed the trial court's admission of the expert testimony and the resulting decision of the jury in favor of the plaintiffs.

But even when consensus has been reached, the problem for trial judges trying to rely on consensus agreements is that not all of them will necessarily result in scientific truths that stand the test of time. For example,

> in 1990, a Committee of the United States National Research Council [NRC1] . . . was appointed to examine the use of DNA technology in forensic science. The Committee's most important recommendations addressed the controversial question of how match probabilities should be calculated . . . .One might have thought that a report by a prestigious committee would have ended the controversy over the use of DNA evidence in the courts. NRC1 was able to examine the issues in a nonadversarial context, away from the heated atmosphere of the court-room . . . . However, if NRC1 is judged in terms of its success in ending the controversy and in easing the reception of DNA evidence by the courts, it was a dismal failure . . . . The report was criticized in strong terms by some scientists, . . . [J]ust as the report was released, a number of studies were published that appeared to tip the balance in the scientific debate . . . Owing to the failure of NRC1 to resolve the DNA contro-versy, in 1993 a second committee was convened under the auspices of the National Research Council. To date, the second report (NRC2) appears to have had a positive reception, at least so far as its recommen-dations on match probability calculation are concerned.[70]

Secondary sources are not always accurate. And, because they are reviews, they are prone to introduce another level of values and bias into the interpretation of the scientific findings. This is a real concern when the author of the *secondary* review is paid by an organization that has an interest in the outcome of the review (e.g., a review written by a scientist paid by the tobacco industry to review research and publish the findings on the impact of smoking on health). In addition, years of secondary writings also have led scholars in all disciplines to recognize that they should not uncritically accept the methods and conclusions of the secondary author without checking the conclusions against the *primary* literature. Reviewers make numerous discretionary decisions about what literature to review, what variables to critically consider, what method to use in the reviews, and how to interpret results that are in the mid-range rather than presenting clear-cut findings. The result is that subtle theoretical and methodological values and biases may distort the conclusions drawn by the secondary reviewer.

---

[70] Mike Redmayne, *Expert Evidence and Scientific Disagreement*, 30 U.C. Davis L. Rev. 1027, 1057–1060 (1997). "The existence of regulatory bodies would not ensure that novel scientific evidence is problem free. The intense scrutiny engendered by adversarial litigation will often reveal difficulties that never came to light outside the courtroom." *Id.* at 1075.

Yet, when courts rely on *secondary* authorities for making admissibility determinations, they rely on expert opinions that are as much in need of critical assessment as the proffered expert's testimony. Unfortunately, some courts uncritically rely on secondary sources, including the opinions of experts to reach conclusions about the validity of proffered information and its admissibility.[71]

Finally, some courts rely on *tertiary* sources of information when reaching admissibility decisions. This approach involves relying on the conclusions of nonexperts, such as law students or lawyers who author law review articles or the opinions of judges in other cases, for making judgments about the admissibility of expert information. Errors made by these third parties in their reviews of the literature are perpetuated by the courts who rely on it.

This is what occurred in the South Dakota case of *State v. Edelman*, in which the defendant challenged the trial court's admission of the prosecution's expert's testimony regarding Child Sexual Abuse Accommodation Syndrome (CSAAS).[72] The South Dakota Supreme Court affirmed the trial court's admission of the CSAAS testimony on the basis of the expert's testimonial support of it and decisions of courts in other jurisdictions to admit it. Neither the trial court nor the state supreme court did an independent evaluation of the validity of the underlying writings on CSAAS or the reliability of the proffered expert's methodology in arriving at his opinions.

Scientists would not accept such *tertiary* sources when trying to judge the validity of expert information because there is no reason to assume, without more supporting information, that law students, lawyers, or judges would have the requisite specialized expertise in evaluating knowledge in another discipline or profession.[73] The problem is compounded by the fact that these law student and lawyer authors are often trying to advance a particular perspective and use expert information selectively to bolster that perspective, not to engage in a neutral examination of the basis for the science. Indeed, even if these authors seek to engage in a neutral examination of the science, do they possess the training or expertise to identify, evaluate, and apply the information appropriately?

Relying on the ruling of a judge in another case assumes that the other judge understood the expert information and was able to evaluate it accurately. This is an assumption that we have already questioned. Yet, because of the use of precedent in the law, judges are prone to both look for and weigh heavily the opinions of other judges. Although it may be

---

[71] United States v. Crumby, 895 F. Supp. 1354 (D. Ariz. 1995).

[72] 593 N.W.2d 419 (S.D. 1999).

[73] *See* Perry v. United States, 755 F.2d 888, 892 (11th Cir. 1985), ("[T]he examination of a scientific study by a cadre of lawyers is not the same as its examination by others trained in the field of science or medicine.").

appropriate to rely on other judges' opinions about questions of law, extending that approach to other judges opinions about questions of science in the law may lead to consistency across judges, but it is gives no assurance of accuracy in making admissibility judgments.[74]

In conclusion, although scientists know and understand the importance of relying on *primary* sources when evaluating a body of research, the U.S. Supreme Court's guidance to trial judges, who are not selected because of any nonlegal expertise, fails to require judges to prioritize the types of information on which they rely. And because courts are prone to listen to other courts (*tertiary*) or experts' (*secondary*) opinions about the science, rather than looking at the *primary* literature, accuracy in judicial decision making may be compromised. Indeed, judges should be as leery as scientists when looking at all *tertiary* sources. If they turn to *secondary* authorities for making admissibility determinations because these authorities make it easier for the judges to believe they understand the quality of the proffered information, judges risk relying on inaccurate summaries and conclusions about the proffered expert information, which decreases the certainty of accuracy in decision making. Because *Daubert* requires judges with little or no training in the methods of science to make rigorous decisions about the reliability of proffered expert information, judges should turn to the *primary* sources. But when they do so, they are unlikely to have the skills to assess critically the information contained in these sources.

Policy Choices

The above concerns about judicial inconsistency and judges' ability to exclude unreliable expert testimony may occur even when trial courts understand science sufficiently well to apply the *Daubert* criteria. Judges, no less than scientists, inevitably make and advance their own policies that may have an impact on the admissibility of the proffered evidence. For example, law professor Margaret Berger argues that in toxic tort cases,

> Some [judges] endorse science's strict standard because they doubt that such litigation serves a useful social purpose. Others point to the need to deter future risks and to compensate those exposed to excessive risk through no fault of their own . . . .The point is that whatever standard of proof is chosen—whether by the scientific or legal community— reflects and furthers the policy objectives that the particular discipline

---

[74]Two law professors have recommended that judicial acceptance of scientific expert information be given precedential value. Laurens Walker & John Monahan, *Scientific Authority: The Breast Implant Litigation and Beyond*, 86 Va. L. Rev. 801 (2000); John Monahan & Laurens Walker, *Social Authority: Obtaining, Evaluating, and Establishing Social Science in Law*, 134 U. Pa. L. Rev. 477 (1986).

is seeking to achieve. When judges exclude scientific evidence in some of the particular circumstances discussed below, their decisions reflect a policy choice; they are not making value-free determinations that are the inevitable consequence of a system of rational proof.[75]

Additional Evaluative Criteria

Trial courts are allowed to ignore the criteria articulated in *Daubert* and adopt any other metric they think appropriate as long as the ultimate standard is the application of Fed. R. Evid. 702. When judges apply one of these additional criteria, additional problems in achieving truth as accuracy may occur. For example, the Advisory Committee for the 2000 Amendment to the Federal Rules of Evidence lists "Whether the expert has adequately accounted for obvious alternative explanations"[76] as one additional criterion. But will this criterion add or detract from achieving the goal of truth as accuracy?

Scientists would be supportive of it. For example, if one's research design or logic leaves the causal relationship between the data and the hypothesis suspect, scientists would demand that the alternative, explanatory hypotheses for the data be considered. Some courts also agree. Consider the case of *Claar v. Burlington Northern Railroad Company*.[77] Plaintiffs worked for Burlington Northern's Livingston, Montana, shop, where they were exposed to chemicals that they claimed resulted in their suffering a number of injuries. Plaintiffs retained two physician experts who provided affidavits supporting the plaintiffs' claim. The trial court then ordered the experts to file a second set of affidavits explaining the scientific basis for their opinions. After reviewing these affidavits, the trial court granted the defendant's motion for summary judgment, noting "that the affidavits still failed to explain [the expert's] reasoning and methods,"[78] and concluding that "without the affidavits, plaintiffs could not demonstrate a causal relationship between chemical exposure and their injuries."[79] The plaintiffs appealed. The court of appeals affirmed the trial court's exclusion of the plaintiffs' experts' testimony partially because the experts failed to explore alternative causes of the plaintiffs' injury other than workplace chemical exposure. The trial court "found that neither [of the experts] made any effort to rule out other possible causes for the injuries plaintiffs complain of, even though

---

[75] Margaret A. Berger, *Upsetting the Balance Between Adverse Interests: The Impact of the Supreme Court's Trilogy on Expert Testimony in Toxic Tort Litigation*, 64 Law & Contemp. Probs. 289, 301–302 (2001).
[76] Fed. R. Evid. 702, 2000 Amendment Advisory Committee Note.
[77] 29 F.3d 499 (9th Cir. 1994).
[78] *Id.* at 500.
[79] *Id.*

they admitted that this step would be standard procedure before arriving at a diagnosis."[80]

Although the criterion makes excellent sense from a scientific and clinical point of view, it raises a new dilemma for the trial judge. How would the judge know whether there are rival hypotheses that might explain the resulting data? Although the expert need not rule out every possible alternative explanation, she or he should rule out the obvious ones.[81] The only possible way for the judge to know whether this occurred is through the cross-examination of the expert by the opposing lawyer or the presentation of additional data by the opposing side's expert. Thus the goal of achieving truth as accuracy is limited to the success of the adversarial system. Where one side is less effective than the other in its expert preparation, courts are likely to be uninformed about potential rival hypotheses.

Lack of Appellate Scrutiny

Compounding all of the above problems with the admissibility decisions is the fact that judicial decisions on this matter are unlikely to be scrutinized by an appellate court. As noted in the prior chapter, the United States Supreme Court in *General Electric Co. v. Joiner*[82] held that appellate review of a trial court's application of *Daubert's* pragmatic considerations was to be judged under an abuse of discretion standard. The result is that the vast majority of trial court admissibility decisions are unlikely to be overturned if appealed. Thus, litigants who received an adverse ruling on an admissibility decision would be less likely to expend the money to seek appellate review. This conclusion holds true even where the trial court chose not to use any of the *Daubert* or additional criteria. The result is that errors in admissibility decisions are unlikely to be appealed and corrected.

For example, consider the decision of the Second Circuit Court of Appeals[83] to affirm without analysis the federal district court's opinion in *Mancuso v. Consolidated Edison Co.*[84] *Mancuso* concerned the admissibility of expert testimony purporting to link the plaintiff's learning disabilities to exposure to PCBs. The trial court admitted the testimony of a clinical psychologist, a person the court considered well qualified in the area of her testimony, to address whether the plaintiff had a learning disability. The district court noted that there are multiple pathways to acquiring and demonstrating expertise (i.e., training, experience, and self-education), that the expert relied on her clinical judgment rather than on scientifically valid

---

[80] *Id.* at 502.
[81] Daniel J. Capra, *The* Daubert *Puzzle*, 32 GA. L. REV. 699 (1998).
[82] 522 U.S. 136 (1997).
[83] Mancuso v. Consolidated Edison, Co., 216 F.3d 1072 (2d. Cir. 2000).
[84] 967 F. Supp. 1437 (S.D.N.Y. 1997).

methods, and admitted the testimony because "in an area of science as grey as learning disabilities . . . counter-evidence properly goes to the weight, not to the admissibility of [the expert's] testimony."[85]

Use of qualifications, although understandable when there are no scientifically valid methods for making the clinical determination in question,[86] avoids the issue of the evidentiary reliability of the testimony. Because *Joiner* instructs appellate courts to overturn only the most blatant cases of erroneous decision making, a trial court decision that relies on qualifications as a circumstantial indicator of evidentiary reliability may well be considered a discretionary decision that is not clearly erroneous. In regard to this case, the court of appeals uncritically accepted that there were good grounds for the clinical judgment and no relevant, valid scientific research to rely on. Use of credentials as the primary indicator of evidentiary reliability is ironic, however, because it draws the trial court full circle to the pre-*Frye* and pre-*Daubert* common law approach to admissibility of expert testimony.

> The earliest test articulated for admissibility of expert testimony that was developed by the common law courts turned exclusively on the qualifications of the expert . . . .There is an historically compelling logic for this approach. There are ample records of the use of expert "scientific" testimony dating from the Seventeenth Century, yet little scientific research existed during that period and for a substantial time later. Thus, for most legally relevant issues, the best that the scientific community had to offer could be found in the clinical opinions of those who were most qualified on the subject by virtue of their education, training, and experience in the field, and not because of their scientific research findings . . . . Ultimately, as the fields of science and available empirical research findings developed in the Twentieth Century, an exclusive

---

[85] *Id.* at 1456.

[86] There are numerous other cases we could cite on this point, which rely on nonscientific criteria to judge the admissibility of proffered clinical information. For example, in Berry v. City of Detroit, 25 F.3d 1342 (6th Cir. 1993), the court was faced with proffered expert testimony by a sociologist who worked as a Sheriff and was serving as a consultant in the case and wanted to offer opinion testimony on the effect of police policy and failure to discipline an officer on the cause of a shooting death. The court noted that his proffered testimony was nonscientific expert testimony and ruled that for this kind of testimony to be admissible, a foundation would have to be laid based on the witness's firsthand familiarity with disciplining police officers and the effect of lax discipline on the entire force. This requirement of firsthand experience has little to do with evaluating good science, and speaks most directly to the person's experience with the topic—something the courts have looked at historically in regard to admitting opinion testimony. In addition, the court invoked a slight variant of the *Frye* rule, asking whether the expert's theory of the problem had been subjected to peer review publication and peer review by colleagues. Because there are numerous professional journals, the mere fact of publication means little in regard to an article's scientific validity. Finally, the court opined that the admissibility determination should not focus on the qualifications of a witness in the abstract, but on whether those qualifications provide a foundation for a witness to answer a specific question. Although all of the above concerns may provide greater confidence in the expert's experience with and knowledge about an issue, none speak directly to the scientific validity of the proffered testimony.

focus on the witness's qualifications could no longer be justified. This shift in approach is perhaps most clearly seen in the 1923 decision of the Court of Appeals for the District of Columbia in *Frye v. United States* . . . .What is perhaps most significant about *Frye's* role in shaping judicial scrutiny of scientific expert evidence is that it moves the analysis beyond consideration of just the reputation and the qualifications of the expert witness as the test for admissibility. Acknowledging the qualifications of the expert who offered the test results, the court imposed an additional level of analysis on the admissibility decision. In this second level, the court focused its appraisal on the quality of the underlying science offered by the expert, assuming that the relevant scientific community's general acceptance of that science attests to its quality. Witness qualifications were a necessary, but not sufficient, condition of admissibility.[87]

Confounding the expert's qualifications with the evidentiary reliability of the testimony risks the possibility that the court will admit expert testimony "just because somebody with a diploma says it is so."[88]

This is not to argue that an expert's qualifications are irrelevant to a judge's gatekeeping responsibility. Fed. R. Evid. 702 instructs judges to consider the witness' qualifications as a prerequisite to evaluating the merits of proffered testimony: "[A] witness qualified as an expert . . . may testify thereto in the form of an opinion or otherwise, if . . . (2) the testimony is the product of reliable principles and methods, and (3) the witness has applied the principles and methods reliably to the facts of the case." Yet, qualifications should not be seen as a substitute for directly assessing the evidentiary reliability of the testimony.

Dilemma of Evaluating Nonscientific Testimony

This discussion raises another significant dilemma for achieving accuracy in admissibility decisions: attempting to apply *Daubert* as elaborated through *Kumho*. *Kumho* applied *Daubert* to technical and specialized information, which is not necessarily dependent on a scientific foundation. Even though the science has not specified the exact steps a nonscientific expert should use in reaching an opinion, the expert's testimony could be indirectly based on science. Science may provide partial guidance in approaches to use or in ways of analyzing problems. But there is no requirement that these nonscientific experts offer opinions that are tied to a reliable scientific base.[89]

---

[87] Daniel W. Shuman & Bruce D. Sales, *The Admissibility of Expert Testimony Based Upon Clinical Judgment and Scientific Research*, 4 PSYCHOL. PUB. POL'Y & L. 1226, 1235–1236 (1998).
[88] United States v. Ingham, 42 M.J. 218, 226 (1995).
[89] For example, when mental health practitioners engage in therapy, they can seek to rely on the available scientific research about treatment. But if the translation of the science into practice standards occurs without scientific research to prove that the translation was accurate, we are left with speculation about whether the practice methods are scientifically valid. *See, e.g.,* Peter J.

Expert opinions are not reports of the results of scientific research. Rather, they are personal observations and conclusions that have not been proven by prior scientific research.

In addition, although *Kumho* did not address it, scientists can also opine on the witness stand. For example, after reciting the results of research findings, the expert witness scientist can be asked by the lawyer whether, in her opinion, something had occurred or is likely to occur. When the expert witness scientist steps away from the actual data and moves to offer an opinion that was not directly studied in the scientific research, the expert testimony is opinion testimony similar to that of the expert conveying technical or other specialized knowledge.[90]

The accuracy dilemma for judges is that, as contrasted with research findings, there are no external criteria against which to evaluate the validity of the expert opinion testimony. To compound the problem, neither the Supreme Court in *Kumho* nor the Fed. R. Evid. 702 Advisory Committee Note defines evidentiary reliability for purposes of nonscientific testimony.[91] The Court did note that

> a trial court *may* consider one or more of the more specific factors that *Daubert* mentioned when doing so will help determine that testimony's reliability. But, as the Court stated in *Daubert*, the test of reliability is "flexible," and *Daubert*'s list of specific factors neither necessarily nor exclusively applies to all experts or in every case. Rather, the law grants a district court the same broad latitude when it decides *how* to determine reliability as it enjoys in respect to its ultimate reliability determination.[92]

Daubert's definition of reliability for proffers of scientific testimony does not resolve the dilemma, however. Because the Court in *Daubert* was faced with the admissibility of scientific evidence, it limited its language to defining reliability in that specific domain:

> Proposed testimony must be supported by appropriate validation—i.e., "good grounds," based on what is known. In short, the requirement that an expert's testimony pertain to "scientific knowledge" establishes a standard of evidentiary reliability. n9

Bieling & Willem Kuyken, *Is Cognitive Case Formulation Science or Science Fiction?*, 10 CLIN. PSYCHOL.: SCI. & PRAC. 52 (2003). A similar problem can occur with diagnoses using the American Psychiatric Association's *Diagnostic and Statistical Manual of Mental Disorders*. See, e.g., Laura E. Boeschen, Bruce D. Sales, & Mary P. Koss, *Rape Trauma Experts in the Courtroom*, 4 PSYCHOL. PUB. POL'Y & L. 414 (1998) (discussing problems with the use of the diagnostic category of posttraumatic stress disorder to prove that a rape victim was subjected to a traumatic experience).
[90] Daniel W. Shuman & Bruce D. Sales, *The Admissibility of Expert Testimony Based Upon Clinical Judgment and Scientific Research*, 4 PSYCHOL. PUB. POL'Y & L. 1226 (1998).
[91] Robert J. Goodwin, *Roadblocks to Achieving "Reliability" for Non-Scientific Expert Testimony: A Response to Professor Edward J. Imwinkelrie*, 30 CUMB. L. REV. 215 (1999-2000).
[92] Kumho Tire Co. v. Carmichael, 526 U.S. 137, 141–142 (1999).

n9 . . . our reference here is to evidentiary reliability—that is, trust-worthiness. . . . In a case involving scientific evidence, evidentiary reliability will be based upon scientific validity.[93]

For nonscientific expert testimony, scientific validity is an oxymoron. So how might the court attempt to judge the trustworthiness of the testimony? One way is to assess the experience and knowledge of the expert with the issue that he or she will be testifying about. *United States v. Hankey*,[94] addressing the admissibility of a police gang expert who would testify that gang members who testify against each other are customarily killed or severely beaten, exemplifies this approach. But prior experience, standing alone, does not provide any assurance that what will be said on the witness stand will be accurate. Absent some method of testing the validity of the experience, there is no way to know whether the expert's opinion is the product of a mistake that has been made repeatedly.

Another approach courts use for determining the evidentiary reliability of nonscientific expert testimony under *Kumho* is to ask whether other similar experts would apply the same method to address the question. This approach to assessing evidentiary reliability under *Kumho* was reflected in a federal district court's application of *Daubert* to the admissibility of mental health professional expert testimony regarding the restoration of a defendant's competence to stand trial.[95] No scientific information was offered in that case to address the process relied on by the expert, and the court solely sought to ascertain whether other mental health professionals relied on the same methodology. Quoting *Kumho*, the trial court stated, "The court must ensure that an expert witness 'employs in the courtroom the same level of intellectual rigor that characterizes the practice of an expert in the relevant field.' . . . Trial judges have 'considerable leeway' in making this determination."[96] Lacking any basis for consideration of *Daubert*'s two critical scientific pragmatic criteria (testability and error rate), the trial court looked to whether other mental health professionals performing a competency evaluation would have used the same or similar process for reaching a decision. Ironically, this approach to assessing admissibility, relying on peer judgment without independent judicial assessment of its scientific validity, reflects a return to the general acceptance standard that deferred to what other experts considered acceptable practice, rather than asking the judge to act as an independent gatekeeper in judging the evidentiary reliability of the proffered testimony.

---

[93] 509 U.S. 579, 590 (1993).
[94] 203 F. 3rd 1160 (9th Cir. 2000).
[95] United States v. Duhon, 104 F. Supp. 2d 663 (W.D. La. 2000).
[96] *Id.* at 677.

The dilemma for achieving Fed. R. Evid. 102's goal of truth as accuracy is that ascertaining whether a task was performed in a manner consistent with what other professionals would have done does not directly address whether that approach will result in accurate decisions by these professionals. It also does not ensure that the judge's admissibility decision will promote only accurate information being conveyed by experts in the courtroom.

Assuming that consistency in the behavior of professionals is a measure of accuracy risks permitting scientific reliability to replace scientific validity as the criterion for evidentiary reliability. One interesting example of the problem created by this approach is presented in *Walker v. Soo Line Railroad Co.*,[97] in which a psychologist's opinion was offered to address the plaintiff's IQ and intellectual functioning prior to an accident on the job. The psychologist based his opinion partly on information about the claimant's educational history, which he gathered from the patient's self-report and the claimant's sister. The psychologist did not attempt to verify the accuracy of the information, which the trial judge found to be erroneous. Nonetheless, the appellate court held that the trial judge erred in excluding this testimony. The appellate court based its decision on the belief that the jury was the appropriate body to determine whether this testimony should be considered accurate, based on cross-examination of the expert and any other conflicting testimony.

For the appellate court, "[t]he critical point is that Dr. Pliskin employed a proper methodology to determine Mr. Walker's pre-incident IQ. It was appropriate for Dr. Pliskin to rely on . . . the sources of information which he employed."[98] The sources to which the court refers included the patient's history,[99] which in this case would include the plaintiff's educational history, as reported by the patient and his sister. The appellate court's confidence in its decision was grounded in its conclusion that other professionals would also rely on the use of a patient history and that a jury could decide whether to rely on the expert's conclusions.[100]

Although this court heeded *Daubert*'s language that the trial judge's focus should be on the methods and not the conclusions,[101] the way this appellate court interpreted and applied this language creates multiple dilemmas. The court did not assess whether a self-reported patient history, medical history, and professional history (including educational history) is a scien-

---

[97] 208 F.3d 581 (7th Cir. 2000).

[98] *Id.* at 587.

[99] *Id.* at 586 ("Medical professionals reasonably may be expected to rely on self-reported patient histories.").

[100] *Id.* at 587 ("'[T]he accuracy and truthfulness of the underlying [educational] history is subject to meaningful exploration on cross-examination and ultimately to jury evaluation.' *Cooper*, 211 F.3d at 1008.").

[101] 509 U.S. at 580 ("The inquiry is a flexible one, and its focus must be solely on principles and methodology, not on the conclusions that they generate.").

tifically valid approach to reaching a professional opinion about the patient. The court simply noted that it is commonly relied on, even though self-reports are often inaccurate. In addition, the court did not ask if the particular method used by the expert for gathering this history relied on the same methods that other professionals rely on (i.e., would other professionals have relied on the sister to corroborate the self-reported educational history?). By simply asking if the titular method used (i.e., gathering a self-reported patient history) is the same as what other professionals would use, the court ignored asking whether the professional's methods were scientifically valid (i.e., would they produce accurate information?). Ironically, while attempting to rely on whether similar professionals would use the same methods, the court ignored scientific concerns with scientific reliability by admitting this testimony. If it does not matter whom the expert asks for corroborative information about the patient's educational history, then the expert could have asked a mother or a brother for this information. Yet, memories of different family members could dramatically differ about the same factual event, yielding unreliable data.

If the court was truly concerned with truth as accuracy, why did it let such testimony get to the jury? The obvious answers are that it believed it was applying *Daubert* correctly, and that it perceived the jury to be capable of discerning the accuracy and the relevance of this information.[102] This may be because the court assumed that psychological assessments are either transparent to juries or given so little weight that the risk of the jury being overwhelmed by its problems was not great. Although this conclusion might advance other Fed. R. Evid. 102 goals, such as justice or fairness, it poses significant problems for 102's goal of truth as accuracy.

We draw another important lesson from *Soo Line*—it is inherently problematic to judge pure clinical opinion by applying *Daubert*. *Daubert* was responding to the admissibility of scientific information purportedly derived according to the accepted methods of science. The validity of such information can be tested using the scientific method. Clinical opinion is very different because it is typically not predicated on prior tests of its validity. An expert's clinical opinion is one person's view or judgment about a particular matter, influenced by his or her professional experiences that have not been scientifically studied. Although these judgments might be subjected to scientific testing one day, until then they are opinion and not scientific

---

[102] "Based on such evidence, a jury reasonably might have chosen not to credit Dr. Pliskin's testimony. Evidence demonstrating that other events in Mr. Walker's life affected his functioning might have led a jury to conclude that, even if Mr. Walker's IQ had dropped after the incident, that decrease was not due to any electrical trauma. On the other hand, the jury might have been convinced that, evaluating Dr. Pliskin's testimony in its entirety, his conclusions remained sound despite the defects in the patient history." Soo Line, 208 F.3d at 587.

findings.[103] In addition, if the expert clinical opinion (e.g., this patient has cancer) can be validated by a scientific test (e.g., a biopsy of a tumor to prove the existence of cancer), why require that a test prove the accuracy of the opinion? The science would make the opinion unnecessary.

Kumho and lower courts side step this problem of subjectivity of expert clinical opinion testimony by looking for indicia of evidentiary reliability typically outside the realm of scientific validity. In seeking the admission of clinical opinion testimony, "the trial court as gatekeeper should determine whether the doctor's proposed testimony as a clinical physician is soundly grounded in the principles and methodology of his field of clinical medicine."[104] Clinical medicine by definition involves subjective gathering and interpretation of information, much of which is not scientifically verifiable. One doctor may order scientifically valid tests but then, of necessity in a clinical practice, have to combine that information with other nonscientifically verifiable information to reach a conclusion. Another doctor may order different tests, while a third doctor may order no tests in reaching a decision about how to respond to the patient. Consequentially, those courts that have attempted to apply the Kumho and Daubert decisions to determine which clinical opinion to admit have demanded that "the expert's opinion will have a reliable basis in the knowledge and experience of his discipline."[105] And the reliable basis that they are supposed to be assessing is very different from scientific validity. As noted earlier, the focus in clinical practice is on doing the same thing in similar situations. Although scientific reliability is a necessary ingredient of good science, it does not guarantee that the consistent methods are related to valid methods or outcomes. Thus, a unitary focus on scientific reliability diminishes the likelihood of achieving the Fed. R. Evid. 102 goal of truth as accuracy.

Perhaps truth as accuracy could be achieved if clinical experts were required to have science at least partially supporting the logic of their reasoning. For example, consider the case of Kennedy v. Collagen Corp,[106] in which the plaintiff claimed to have a debilitating and incurable autoimmune disease, atypical systemic lupus erythematosus, following injections with the defendant's product, Zyderm®. The plaintiff sought injections of Zyderm® into her facial wrinkles to provide a smoother, younger appearance. Plaintiff's expert was excluded by the federal district court, which then granted summary judgment. On appeal, the Ninth Circuit Court of Appeals applied Daubert to assess whether the lower court erred in denying admissibility of this expert.

---

[103] See, e.g., ROBYN M. DAWES, HOUSE OF CARDS: PSYCHOLOGY AND PSYCHOTHERAPY BUILT ON MYTHS (1994).
[104] Moore v. Ashland Chemical, Inc., 126 F.3d 679, 689–690 (5th Cir. 1997).
[105] Kumho Tire Co. v. Carmichael, 526 U.S. 137, 138 (1999).
[106] 161 F.3d 1226 (9th Cir. 1998).

The court of appeals noted that the plaintiff's expert relied on a number of different sources of information in reaching his medical opinion. Part of the information was purely clinical: his examination of the plaintiff, the plaintiff's medical history, and the plaintiff's medical reports. But to this he added the plaintiff's medical laboratory tests and a survey of peer-reviewed articles relevant to whether the active ingredient in Zyderm® could cause autoimmune reactions, clinical trials and product studies conducted by the defendant, and the Texas Department of Health's investigation of the product. The appellate court opined that all *Daubert* requires is that the expert's "analogical reasoning [be] based on objective, verifiable evidence and scientific methodology of the kind traditionally used by [like experts]"[107] and that "the 'analytical gap' between the data and the expert's conclusion [not be] too great."[108] Given that scientific studies had proven that the active ingredient in the defendant's product could cause autoimmune reactions, and given that the clinical observations of the plaintiff suggested that the plaintiff experienced such a reaction following the administration of the third injection of defendant's product, the appellate court ruled that it was error for the district court to deny the admission of this expert's testimony. To the court, the expert's sources of information were objective and verifiable, and therefore met *Daubert*'s demands.

Even though the court focused on the chain of reasoning leading to the expert's opinion, with some of that reasoning based on science, achieving the goal of truth as accuracy is still problematic. What the expert could say about general causation relying on science is that the active ingredient in the defendant's product can cause an autoimmune reaction. Science did not provide a basis for specific causation that this plaintiff's autoimmune reaction was caused by the defendant's product.[109] Is the causal connection possible? Yes. Did this causal connection occur as argued by the plaintiff's expert? We do not know from the evidence. Thus, as with pure clinical opinion, the interpretation of *Daubert* to permit the use of clinical opinion to draw inferences from the science to the facts of a particular case leaves us with limited confidence that this approach advances the goal of truth as accuracy.

The problem does not necessarily evaporate when a court critically applies numerous specific evaluative criteria to judging clinical opinion. For example, in *Antoine-Tubbs v. Local 513 Air Transp. Div.*[110] the federal district

---

[107] *Id.* at 1230.
[108] *Id.* at 1228.
[109] *Id.* at 1229–1230 ("Here, based on his knowledge of the connection between collagen and various autoimmune disorders, combined with his observation of Mrs. Kennedy's injuries and her medical history and laboratory tests, Dr. Spindler concluded that Zyderm, a collagen product, had caused Mrs. Kennedy's particular auto-immune disorder, atypical SLE.").
[110] 50 F. Supp. 2d 601 (N.D. Tex. 1998).

court tried to use formal criteria to aid in its evaluation of the admissibility of clinical testimony. In this case, the plaintiff offered testimony by a Doctor of Osteopathy to establish a causal linkage between the defendant's alleged sexual harassment and the plaintiff's preclampsia and miscarriage. Relying on a Fifth Circuit Court of Appeals decision,[111] the district court stated that a *Daubert* analysis of clinical testimony would use the following criteria: (a) personal examination of the plaintiff by the doctor; (b) personally taking a detailed medical history from the plaintiff; (c) using differential diagnosis and etiology; (d) reviewing tests, reports, and opinions of other doctors; (e) reviewing other facts or data reasonably relied on by medical experts in forming opinions or inferences as to medical causation; (f) reference to medical literature; and (g) using the doctor's training and experience.

These criteria are used daily by physicians in making life and death decisions; should they be used in deciding whether testimony is sufficiently reliable from an evidentiary perspective to be admitted? Courts often assume that what is good enough for clinical practice in which life and death decisions are made relying on this information ought to be good enough for legal purposes. Thus, for example, Fed. R. Evid. 703 permits the use of hearsay to support an expert opinion where that hearsay is the sort of information that is relied on regularly by experts in the field in forming opinions.

> [T]he rule is designed to broaden the basis for expert opinions beyond that current in many jurisdictions and to bring the judicial practice into line with the practice of the experts themselves when not in court. Thus a physician in his own practice bases his diagnosis on information from numerous sources and of considerable variety, including statements by patients and relatives, reports and opinions from nurses, technicians and other doctors, hospital records, and X rays. Most of them are admissible in evidence, but only with the expenditure of substantial time in producing and examining various authenticating witnesses. The physician makes life-and-death decisions in reliance upon them. His validation, expertly performed and subject to cross-examination, ought to suffice for judicial purposes.[112]

Do the seven criteria applied in *Antoine-Tubbs v. Local 513 Air Transp. Div.* assist in judging the validity of the expert's judgment? The first criterion, a personal examination of the plaintiff by the physician, is subject to the idiosyncrasies attendant to personal observation.[113] What the physician selectively asks about and attends to, what he or she considers particularly

---

[111] Moore v. Ashland Chemical, Inc., 126 F.3d 679 (5th Cir. 1997).

[112] FED. R. EVID. 703 Advisory Committee Note, Rules of Evidence for United States Courts and Magistrates, 56 F.R.D. 183, 283 (U.S. 1972).

[113] *See generally* HEURISTICS AND BIASES: THE PSYCHOLOGY OF INTUITIVE JUDGEMENT (Thomas Gilovich, Dale W. Griffin & Daniel Kahneman, eds. 2002).

important or at least more important than other information, and how he or she combines the pieces of important information together for diagnostic use are all based on the personal subjective approach of the individual provider. As such, this information may contribute to valid opinions, but we have no way of knowing so without the application of scientific tests.

The second criterion, personally taking a detailed medical history from the plaintiff, raises similar concerns. For example, the taking of medical history involves asking questions that are not rigidly specified and applied by all practitioners. Variations exist among physicians in the questions they ask. And once the information is noted, the subjective assignment of importance to it and how it is combined is based on the subjective experiences and decisions of the provider. Thus, it is unfortunately all too common that two physicians can identify different information from the same patient when taking a history and reach different conclusions from that information, leading to different treatment recommendations.[114]

The third criterion, differential diagnosis, describes the process used by physicians to determine all plausible causes of any injury and then to rule out the least likely causes until only the most likely cause remains. Although commonly used in clinical settings, the evidentiary reliability of differential diagnosis and etiology has been hotly debated in the courts,[115] and the validity of differential diagnosis should be suspect. Clinicians may have scientific research showing that a particular drug or chemical can cause a particular adverse reaction in people, but absent scientific evidence showing that the adverse reaction was caused by the drug or chemical in the particular patient, clinicians must infer this causal sequence in the individual case. What makes the causal inference likely to be accurate? We have already ruled out clinical experience as a good indicator of accuracy. Relying on similar cases also is problematic. If it were not, then scientists would not have to collect randomized data in controlled studies and analyze that data using appropriate statistical techniques. Instead, researchers could eyeball nonsystematic events and draw conclusions, as is done by clinicians in differential diagnosis. If this is a completely unacceptable approach for the scientific derivation of truth, what makes it accurate for clinical opinion? It does not. The same result occurs where courts allow experts to testify as to their differential diagnosis even where no science is available for any part of the causal chain. In such cases, the expert is solely relying on the nonsystematic *eyeballing* of past case reports, which is arguably even more

---

[114] David A. Nardone, *Differential Diagnosis and Heuristics*, 254 J. Am. Med. Ass'n 2890 (1985).

[115] *See, e.g.*, cases finding differential diagnosis sufficient to satisfy *Daubert*: Turner v. Iowa Fire Equip. Co., 229 F.3d 1202, 1209 (8th Cir. 2000); Westberry v. Gislaved Gummi AB, 178 F.3d 257, 262–266 (4th Cir. 1999); Glaser v. Thompson Med. Co., 32 F.3d 969, 975 (6th Cir. 1994); *but see* cases rejecting differential diagnosis as satisfying *Daubert*: Glastetter v. Novartis Pharms. Corp., 252 F.3d 986, 991 (8th Cir. 2001); Casey v. Ohio Med. Prods., 877 F. Supp. 1380, 1385 (N.D. Cal. 1995).

unreliable than when science is available for the first part of the causal chain. Ironically,

> [m]ost circuits have held that a reliable differential diagnosis satisfies Daubert and provides a valid foundation for admitting an expert opinion. The circuits reason that a differential diagnosis is a tested methodology, has been subjected to peer review/publication, does not frequently lead to incorrect results, and is generally accepted in the medical community.[116]

These courts fail to recognize that although differential diagnosis might help physicians as a clinical methodology, we lack scientific evidence that it provides an accurate conclusion on its first application in an individual case.

The fourth criterion, reviewing tests, reports, and opinions of other physicians, is only as valid as the weakest link in the information provided and how that information is used. When the written materials contain the results of scientifically valid tests, administered according to the test protocol and interpreted according to the test's normed and validated standards, then this step would increase the validity of the information used by the physician. But if the other physicians relied on their subjective experiences to identify that certain information was important, and reached opinions and conclusions based on this subjective information, then their opinions are clinical and not scientific, and therefore subject to all the uncertainties attendant to clinical judgments. Where then is the science or the consequent validity in such opinions and conclusions?

The fifth criterion, reviewing other facts or data reasonably relied on by medical experts in forming opinions or inferences as to medical causation, sounds like a sensible way to increase accuracy, but is it? What other physicians rely on is based on what they have done in the past, and this approach is not likely to change unless new information becomes available that proves there is a better way to proceed, the physician is familiar with this information, and the physician knows how to apply the information. Thus, what facts or data other physicians rely on may be based on "this is what I have always looked at" and not on what is the scientifically valid information to look at, in what order, and with what weight to assign to each piece of information, to reach an accurate conclusion.[117]

The sixth criterion, reference to medical literature, sounds like its use would lead to more accurate conclusions. When the literature is reporting on the results of science, that is likely to be the case. But even this criterion is suspect, because physicians and the court talk about medical literature

---

[116] Turner v. Iowa Fire Equip. Co., 229 F.3rd 1202, 1208 (8th Cir. 2000).
[117] See Cynthia D. Mulrow & Kathleen N. Lohr, *Proof and Policy from Medical Research Evidence*, 26 J. HEALTH POL. POL'Y & L. 249 (2001).

that includes nonscientific writings by physicians. When this occurs, truth as accuracy becomes a more elusive goal.

The final criterion, using the physician's training and experience as a measure of the evidentiary reliability of the testimony, even where that training and experience is current, is to rely on the experience and opinions of each physician. How is the court to know then whether the physician's opinions and conclusions are valid? It cannot without independent corroboration of a scientific test.

The dilemma with trying to use this approach to achieve truth as accuracy in the courts is that each source of information relied on by the expert in reaching his conclusion may provide subjective, nonscientific information, which when combined by the practitioner in unspecified ways to reach a decision leads to a conclusion that bears no resemblance to the way scientific conclusions are derived. Clinically derived conclusions and opinions may be valid, but we have no way of knowing that. The extent to which this risk is acceptable for clinical practice is because the opinions and conclusions of practitioners can often be revised in the next meeting between the physician and the patient. The dilemma for physicians and patients regarding the lack of foreknowledge about validity of these opinions and conclusions becomes acute when physicians apply irreversible procedures. An elegant example of this problem from the field of orthopedic surgery was recently published in the New England Journal of Medicine.[118] Each year surgeons perform more than 650,000 arthroscopic procedures on the knee for osteoarthritis, with patients often reporting improvement following the surgery although the physiological basis for the reduction in pain is unclear. In this study, 180 patients were randomly assigned into one of 2 groups. One group had the surgery, while the other group had placebo surgery in which they received an incision but without insertion of the arthroscope. The researchers found no difference in the outcomes of both groups either in terms of pain reduction or better knee function.

If the goal of the courts in the admission of evidence is truth as accuracy, then the methods used to produce the expert's opinions and conclusions should be likely to produce valid results. The study published in the New England Journal of Medicine demonstrates that clinicians' opinions and conclusions are often wrong even when using accepted clinical methods and procedures. Indeed, the only way to know if the clinician's opinions and conclusions are valid is to have scientific research available on the accuracy of the clinician's methods or scientific research on the validity of the clinician's conclusions. The lesson from this study is that

---

[118] J. Bruce Moseley et al., A Controlled Trial of Arthroscopic Surgery for Osteoarthritis of the Knee, 347 New. Eng. J. Med. 81 (2002).

expert testimony based on clinical criteria that are considered good for clinical practice do not necessarily yield testimony that meets the legal system's goal of truth as accuracy.[119]

Focusing on Expert Methods and Not on Conclusions

By focusing on the methods and procedures underlying the expert's opinions, rather than on the validity of the conclusions, *Daubert* opens the door to additional problems for judicial decisions about admissibility because methods and conclusions are not entirely distinct. The Supreme Court acknowledged this dilemma in *Joiner*: "conclusions and methodology are not entirely distinct from one another."[120] The importance of focusing on the validity of the conclusions and not just the expert's methods and procedures in reaching those conclusions was highlighted in *United States v. Hines*.[121] This case addressed the admissibility of the testimony of a handwriting expert who was trying to offer a prediction about who wrote a note as compared to simply identifying the characteristics of a handwritten note. The federal district court noted that where the proffered testimony is attempting to reach conclusions based on observations, then the proffered testimony must be based on valid science demonstrating the capability of the expert and the science to reach valid conclusions. If broadly adopted, this approach would require an assessment of the scientific validity of the proffered testimonial conclusions and thereby goes beyond the requirements of the *Daubert/Kumho* approach with their focus on the validity of the methods and procedures. Some scientists already support this new emphasis.[122]

It could be argued that this is a poor case from which to draw larger lessons because handwriting analysis is neither accepted science nor clinical practice. Yet the lessons from this case cannot be so easily dismissed. The court reasoned that without science to demonstrate the special expertise of handwriting experts in identifying who wrote a note, there is no evidence to suggest that the juror could not do it as well without expert assistance. Could not the same argument be applied to clinical opinion? To restate the court's admonition: without science to demonstrate the special expertise

---

[119] This admonition can also be applied to the FED. R. EVID. 702, 2000 Amendment Advisory Committee Note, which observes that "[t]he amendment requires that expert testimony be based on sufficient underlying 'facts or data.'" No definition is provided for the term *sufficient*, but its plain meaning is that the data relied on by the expert is adequate for the expert to reach a conclusion. But, as we have just argued, what is adequate for clinical practice is not necessarily adequate to establish the accuracy of the information offered to the court.

[120] 522 U.S. at 146.

[121] United States v. Hines, 55 F. Supp. 2d 62 (D. Mass. 1999).

[122] *See, e.g.*, William M. Grove & R. Christopher Barden, *Protecting the Integrity of the Legal System: The Admissibility of Testimony from Mental Health Experts Under* Daubert/Kumho *Analyses*, 5 PSYCHOL. PUB. POL'Y & L. 224 (1999).

of clinicians in accurately identifying disease and causation, there is no evidence to suggest that the juror could not do it as well without expert assistance. This is not to say that clinicians do not have science to support a good deal of their work, yet the study of arthroscopic surgery reported in the *New England Journal of Medicine* discussed above demonstrates that clinicians can often be wrong, even when using acceptable clinical methods and procedures, when science is not available to guide them. This is exactly the scenario for all nonscience experts under *Kumho*. The expert is opining on the basis of clinical acumen rather than scientific knowledge. To know whether the expert is offering accurate opinions and conclusions would require an assessment of the ability of the expert's methods and procedure to achieve accurate results, or the accuracy of the opinions and conclusions offered by the expert.

Truth as a Result of the Adversarial System

A second possible interpretation of Fed. R. Evid. 102's goal of truth is that it refers not to a particular result, but to the process reflected in the operation of the adversarial system. The adversary system assumes that truth is more likely to be achieved by granting the parties control over the discovery, presentation, and challenge of information and by assigning the decision on the merits to a jury panel whose collective insights and experience are greater than those of any one decision maker. The role of the judge relative to admissibility in this conceptualization of truth is to allow the litigants', lawyers', and witnesses' perceptions concerning the truth to get to the jury, which then decides where the *truth* lies. Rather than have the judge decide as a matter of admissibility which party's expert's version of the truth is correct, advancing truth as the result of the adversarial system asks the trial judge to screen out obviously unreliable expert testimony, but not to demand proof that the expert has a singular claim to truth as a condition of admissibility. From this perspective, "[w]hen a trial court . . . rules that an expert's testimony is reliable, this does not necessarily mean that contradictory expert testimony is unreliable."[123] A judge who embraces this approach may "think that an expert has good grounds to hold the opinion that he or she does even though the judge thinks that the opinion is incorrect."[124] This approach is in opposition to viewing truth as an absolute discernable state of knowledge on which the judge has a monopoly.

One important aspect of the goal of truth as a result of the adversarial system recognizes that, inherent in the adversary system, is the task of the

---

[123] FED. R. EVID. 702, 2000 Amendment Advisory Committee Note.
[124] In re Paoli R.R. Yard PCB Litigation, 35 F.3d 717, 744 (3d Cir. 1994).

parties, through their lawyers, to select the experts who will best present the foundation for admitting or challenging the admissibility or believability of an expert. Some cases may be won or lost because the lawyer for one side failed to rise to the adversarial challenge to find the expert information that would sway the judge to make the admissibility decision that would advantage their cause. For example, in *United States v. Sturman*,[125] the court refused to conduct its own review of the scientific validity of the proffered expert's methodology for reaching his opinion because the issue was not brought into question by the government: "Absent affidavit or other evidence to suggest that the methodology underlying Dr. Goldstein's diagnosis is scientifically invalid in this case—and there has been absolutely no such evidence proffered by the Government—the court concludes that Dr. Goldstein's testimony is admissible."[126]

Whatever the quality of the foundation for the expert information, the behavior of the judge in reaching an admissibility decision will also be different in the implementation of the goals of truth as accuracy and truth as the result of an adversarial system. Under the former, courts would only admit evidence that reliably advances the search for truth. Under the latter, the courts would admit evidence to permit the parties greater latitude to tell their story, relying on the jury to assess the parties' competing truths.[127]

The decisions that we reviewed above, under truth as accuracy, show that *Daubert* and its progeny have advanced both of the goals of these alternate models of truth. For example, although *Daubert* contains language that implies it adopted the goal of truth as accuracy,

> [I]n order to qualify as "scientific knowledge," an inference or assertion must be derived by the scientific method. Proposed testimony must be supported by appropriate validation—i.e., "good grounds," based on what is known. In short, the requirement that an expert's testimony pertain to "scientific knowledge" establishes a standard of evidentiary reliability.[128]

Daubert also contains language supporting the notion that it adopted the goal of truth as the result of an adversarial system:

> Respondent expresses apprehension that abandonment of "general acceptance" as the exclusive requirement for admission will result in a

---

[125] No. 96 CR. 318(BSJ) 1998 WL 126066 (S.D.N.Y., March 10, 1998).
[126] *Sturman*, 1998 WL 126066, at *6.
[127] See Christopher Slobogin, *The Admissibility of Behavioral Science Information in Criminal Trials: From Primitivitsm to Daubert to Voice*, 5 PSYCHOL. PUB. POL'Y & L. 100 (1999); Christopher Slobogin, *The Structure of Expertise in Criminal Cases*, 34 SETON HALL L. REV. 105, 118–119 (2003) (maintaining that whatever arguments for reliability exist in civil cases, process concerns grounded in the Sixth Amendment should dominate admissibility decisions in the criminal law setting.).
[128] 509 U.S. at 590.

"free-for-all" in which befuddled juries are confounded by absurd and irrational pseudoscientific assertions. In this regard respondent seems to us to be overly pessimistic about the capabilities of the jury and of the adversary system generally. Vigorous cross-examination, presentation of contrary evidence, and careful instruction on the burden of proof are the traditional and appropriate means of attacking shaky but admissible evidence.[129]

We see the same duality in some of the lower court decisions applying *Daubert*. Indeed, the 2000 Amendment Advisory Committee Note, reflecting the post-*Daubert* decisions of the lower federal courts, concludes that "*Daubert* did not work a 'seachange over federal evidence law,' and 'the trial court's role as a gatekeeper is not intended to serve as a replacement for the adversary system."[130]

The decisions that most strongly seem to advance the goal of truth as the result of an adversarial system are the post-*Kumho* cases. These cases permit clinical opinion testimony in the absence of any scientific basis for the clinician's opinion, leaving the assessment of the clinician's opinion to the fact-finder. For example, consider the case of *Cooper v. Carl A. Nelson & Co.*[131] In this case Cooper, an electrician working as a subcontractor on the construction of a new Wal-Mart store, slipped and fell while walking from the construction parking lot to the job site. Cooper sued the general contractor for the job, alleging that he was responsible for overseeing the safety of the walkway from the parking lot for the employees. Cooper unsuccessfully sought to introduce the testimony of a physician, Dr. Richardson, who in reaching his conclusion that Cooper had chronic pain syndrome resulting from this fall, primarily relied on the patient's self-reports about his pain before and after the accident. The appellate court remanded the case back to the trial court, concluding that the expert's reliance on the patient's self-report did not justify its exclusion under *Daubert*. The decision reflects a view of *Daubert* that acknowledges the adversarial nature of the presentation and decision making process. "The possibility of Mr. Cooper's CPS being attributable to a factor other than the fall is a subject quite susceptible to exploration on cross-examination by opposing counsel. Similarly, the accuracy and truthfulness of the underlying medical history is subject to meaningful exploration on cross-examination and ultimately to jury evaluation."[132]

The problem posed by truth as a result of the adversarial system is not one created by *Daubert* and its progeny, but with the tension between

---

[129] *Id.* at 595–596.
[130] FED. R. EVID. 702, 2000 Amendment Advisory Committee Note.
[131] 211 F.3d 1008 (7th Cir. 2000).
[132] *Id.* at 1021.

achieving truth as a result of the adversarial system and truth as accuracy. Each has a different goal, with each finding support in the language of *Daubert*, as noted above. To achieve truth as a result of the adversarial system requires that the parties be permitted to tell their competing stories to the jury with little interference by the trial judge. To achieve truth as accuracy requires that the parties' ability to tell their stories be limited to expert evidence that meets a rigorous threshold of evidentiary reliability. Whether these goals can be reconciled is an issue that we address in chapter 5.

Truth as a Systemwide Goal

Finally, truth also may be regarded as a systemwide goal for all trials. According to this definition, whether truth is achieved should not be judged solely on the basis of any one case. The law should be concerned with rules that inspire confidence in legal decision making across all cases. For example, in the *Daubert* case, the Supreme Court did not apply the standards it developed for the admissibility of scientific evidence, but remanded the case to the lower court for that purpose. The court of appeals chose to apply these standards without sending the case back to the trial court and found that the plaintiff's experts' testimony that Bendectin was responsible for the plaintiff's injuries did not pass muster under the new *Daubert* criteria.[133] Of course, the court of appeals did not claim that Bendectin did not cause limb reduction birth defects, only that the available epidemiological evidence did not support the conclusion that Bendectin did cause such defects. Bendectin may indeed cause limb reduction birth defects, although we may not have proof of that for some time. Yet even if the application of these criteria resulted in the wrong decision in that case, it might nonetheless encourage more accurate results in other cases if it promotes the conduct of relevant research to guide future judicial determinations and encourages courts to demand relevant research to bolster their decisions.[134] This

---

[133] This observation refers to the Ninth Circuit's application of those criteria on remand of the case.
[134] *See generally,*

In *State v. Nye,* 551 A.2d 844 (Me. 1988), we upheld the exclusion of evidence of a psychological study offered by the defense. Appearing in 2 Journal of Interpersonal Violence 27 (1987), the article entitled *Reliable and Fictitious Account of Sexual Abuse to Children* reported a clinical survey of reliable and fictitious allegations. Because the survey was uncontrolled and subject to error in the identification of reliability, the authors suggested that "the results be used as a base for further study and not as a definitive basis for proving that a case is or is not 'true.' (We are aware that our study has already been misused in court for this latter purpose.)" *See Nye,* 551 A.2d at 846.

State v. York, 564 A.2d 389, 391 (Me. 1989). *But see* William L. Anderson, Barry M. Parsons, & Drummond Rennie, *Daubert's Backwash: Litigation-Generated Science,* 34 U. Mich. J.L. Ref. 619 (2001).

development should promote confidence in our system of justice; imposing rigorous threshold scrutiny in the admissibility of expert testimony sends a systemwide signal that courts will demand reliable proof, which should persuade society that it can rely on the judicial system to adjudicate its grievances accurately.

As noted, *Daubert* may promote truth as a systemwide goal by encouraging the conduct of research relevant to the scientific or technical issues on which the case turns. But while *Daubert* has promoted the conduct of legally relevant research, that research has been criticized as litigation science conducted by partisan scientists in the employ of current or prospective litigants.[135] If *Daubert* stimulated litigation science, and if such science is not being conducted by impartial researchers, it is unlikely that *Daubert* has promoted truth as a systemwide goal.

Another assumption about the way in which *Daubert* would promote truth as a systemwide goal is by inspiring confidence in judicial decisions. Unfortunately, we do not know if this has occurred because no empirical studies have addressed this question. But we might find clues as to whether this is occurring by looking at relevant conceptual literature. Doubtful of the abilities of juries and the ethics of experts, defendants have argued that the application of these decisions has improved the evidentiary reliability of the expert testimony presented in the courts and the decisions they assist.[136] Consequentially, we would expect that if their criticisms of experts and juries are correct, and that *Daubert* and its progeny have raised the floor for the reliability of experts heard by juries, greater confidence in judicial decision making would result.

Confident in the capacity of the adversary system and the jurors that serve the system, plaintiffs have argued that *Daubert* and its progeny have been selectively applied to toxic tort and product liability claims to exclude plaintiffs' experts and so preclude jury determination of their claims.[137] Consequentially, we would expect that if their criticisms of *Daubert*'s restriction of the presentation of claims to juries are correct, less confidence in judicial decision making would result. These are interesting hypotheses about whether *Daubert* has promoted truth as a systemwide goal. But without confirmatory empirical research, these predictions remain speculative.

---

[135] William L. Anderson, Barry M. Parsons, & Drummond Rennie, Daubert's *Backwash: Litigation-Generated Science*, 34 U. Mich. J.L. Reform 619 (2001).
[136] Clifton T. Hutchinson & Danny S. Ashby, Daubert v. Merrell Dow Pharmaceuticals, Inc.: *Redefining the Bases for Admissibility of Expert Scientific Testimony*, 15 Cardozo L. Rev. 1875 (1994).
[137] Michael H. Gottesman, *From Barefoot to Daubert to Joiner: Triple Play or Double Error?*, 40 Ariz. L. Rev. 753, 775 (1998). *See also* Leslie Bender, *An Overview of Feminist Tort Scholarship*, 78 Cornell. L. Rev. 575 (1993).

JUSTICE

As noted in chapter 2, Rule 102 lists justice independent of truth or fairness as the fourth goal of the rules of evidence. ("These rules shall be construed to secure . . . [the] growth and development of the law of evidence to the end that . . . proceedings [are] justly determined.") In attempting to understand this provision, we conclude in chapter 2 that Fed. R. Evid. 102 intended to convey that justice is a value judgment about the appropriateness of an outcome both in individual trials and across cases. And to determine whether these outcomes are just, it is necessary to assess them in light of the facts, the law, and the relevant moral standards of the community. Because justice is not an objective construct, but rather a subjective view of the outcome from differing perspectives, there will always be disagreements about whether an outcome is just. *Daubert* can exacerbate this dissension.

Same Facts, Different Outcomes

When the same issue is decided differently in two cases, it may pose a problem for litigants who assess justice by comparing the outcomes in these cases. Consider, for example, the application of *Daubert* to expert testimony about recovered repressed memories. Although some courts have excluded such testimony as failing to meet *Daubert*'s threshold, preventing these claims from proceeding to trial, other courts have found that this testimony satisfies the admissibility criteria. Compare the decisions in *State v. Hungerford*,[138] in which evidence of recovered repressed memories was excluded, and *Shahzade v. Gregory*,[139] in which evidence of recovered repressed memories was admitted. *Hungerford* was a criminal prosecution based on a complaint by a woman in her twenties of memories only recently recovered in therapy of sexual abuse as a young child by her father. The father moved to dismiss the prosecution, and following a 2-week hearing in which some of the leading experts in the recovered-memory debate testified, the trial court dismissed the complaint. In an opinion that reviewed a significant amount of the extant literature, the Supreme Court of New Hampshire affirmed. *Shahzade* was a civil claim by a woman against a physician for repeated sexual touching when she was a teenager some 47 years prior to filing her claim. She claimed to have repressed these memories until her recent psychotherapy. The defendant moved to exclude the plaintiff's expert evidence on recovered repressed memories and, after an extensive presentation by the parties, the trial court overruled the defendant's motion.

---

[138] 697 A.2d 916 (N.H. 1997).
[139] 923 F. Supp. 286 (D. Mass. 1996).

Both courts had the opportunity to consider the same scientific and clinical information regarding the evidentiary reliability of recovered repressed memories in their admissibility evaluations of the proffered expert information. For these courts to reach opposite outcome-determinative admissibility decisions under a *Daubert* analysis illustrates an important problem with the application of *Daubert* and the achievement of Fed. R. Evid. 102's goal of justice.

Why might this lack of consensus occur under a *Daubert* analysis? The scientific competence of the judiciary provides a logical explanation. Some judges may have greater knowledge or aptitude in science than others, which may explain why different courts judge the admissibility of the same information differently. It is also impossible to discount the role of the judge's values and beliefs in interpreting the science, particularly where the judge's understanding of such concepts as falsifiability is equivalent to Chief Justice Rehnquist's.[140] The scrutiny that is applied to the evidence under a *Daubert* analysis could lead some courts to reject evidence that previously would have been admitted, despite the claim of the liberalness of the Federal Rules. Because *Daubert* teaches judges to critically examine the reliability of the testimony, some judges may be much more critical of the proffered evidence. Indeed, one legal commentator reports that "sixty-five percent of plaintiff and defendant counsel stated that judges are less likely to admit some types of expert testimony since Daubert."[141] Other judges will look to implement the goal of the liberal thrust of the Federal Rules of Evidence, admit the testimony, and leave it up to the jury to assess its credibility.[142] Finally, the U.S. Supreme Court's decision to allow trial courts to select different pragmatic criteria to emphasize could lead to inconsistent results.

Disparate Impact of Neutral Rules

The attainment of justice will also be challenged by *Daubert* because a shift in the admissibility standard may favor or disfavor certain social or economic interests or groups. For example, some critics of *Daubert* allege that although these rules are facially neutral, their application makes it difficult for women, minorities, indigent persons, and other groups in society

---

[140] Daubert v. Merrell Dow Pharmaceuticals, Inc., 509 U.S. 579, 600 (1993). (As Chief Justice Rehnquist observed in his concurring opinion in *Daubert*: "I defer to no one in my confidence in federal judges; but I am at a loss to know what is meant when it is said that the scientific status of a theory depends on its 'falsifiability,' and I suspect some of them will be, too.").
[141] Margaret A. Berger, *Upsetting the Balance Between Adverse Interests: The Impact of the Supreme Court's Trilogy on Expert Testimony in Toxic Tort Litigation*, 64 Law & Contemp. Probs. 289, 290 (2001). *See also* Lloyd Dixon & Brian Gill, *Changes in the Standards for Admitting Expert Evidence in Federal Civil Cases Since the* Daubert *Decision*, 8 Psychol. Pub. Pol'y & L. 251 (2002).
[142] State v. Anderson, 881 P.2d 29 (N.M. 1994).

who lack empowerment to press their claims against tortious corporate behavior (e.g., suits alleging pollution of the environment).[143] The allegation here is that Fed. R. Evid. 702 has made proving one's case more complex and costly because the threshold for admissibility is *evidentiary reliability*, which *Daubert* defines as scientific validity. Thus, to make one's argument requires experts who are likely to be more expensive than traditional opinion experts because of their need to know the scientific basis for their testimony and because of their additional preparation time. In addition, the allegation is that the science that *Daubert* demands might not prove the association between a corporation's conduct and the harm it causes until many years later, when the victims and their families may have died or the corporation may no longer exist.

Differing Levels of Advocacy

The quality of the trial court's *Daubert* analysis is dependent on the expert information that the parties provide to the court. Lawyers may do an excellent job in this role, both in selecting and presenting information and in challenging the other side's proffer of expert testimony. But there may be important differences in the quality of the advocacy or the resources available to the advocate, resulting in inconsistent *Daubert* results across cases considering the same area of expertise.[144] Although the trial court's *Daubert* analysis may be applied even handedly, differing admissibility outcomes because of the differing levels of advocacy can be outcome-determinative and create inconsistencies in the perception of justice.

Interaction of Admissibility Rules With Competence of Counsel

Daubert magnifies differences in the competence and capacity of each parties' advocate, and does so differently from *Frye*. Under *Frye*, a lawyer only had to show that the proffered information was generally accepted in its field. *Daubert*'s test is far more complex and nuanced, requiring greater sophistication on the part of lawyers and more sophisticated advocacy to satisfy its criteria. This will lead to proffers of evidence being denied admissibility under *Daubert* that would likely have been admitted under pre-*Daubert* rules.

---

[143] Michael H. Gottesman, *From Barefoot to Daubert to Joiner: Triple Play or Double Error?*, 40 Ariz. L. Rev. 753, 775 (1998). *See also* Leslie Bender, *An Overview of Feminist Tort Scholarship*, 78 Cornell L. Rev. 575 (1993).
[144] Marc Galanter, *Why the "Haves" Come Out Ahead: Speculations on the Limits of Legal Change*, 9 L. & Soc'y Rev. 95 (1974).

Interaction of Fed. R. Evid. 102's Goals

Like truth, justice is not the singular penultimate value in litigation. It may yield to one of Fed. R. Evid. 102's other goals as it applies to the operation of the courts. Consider the plight of a criminal defense lawyer representing an indigent client who wishes to challenge a prosecution expert under *Daubert*. To do so, the defense lawyer will require the assistance of a court-appointed expert. Although the defense lawyer could, in theory, mount a *Daubert* challenge without expert assistance, the case law reflects that courts are persuaded of the evidentiary unreliability of experts by other experts. As an indigent, the defendant has no resources to obtain expert assistance without court appointment, and the only specific right to a court-appointed expert that the defendant enjoys is under *Ake v. Oklahoma*.[145] The U. S. Supreme Court held in that case that an indigent defendant who makes a preliminary showing that his mental condition at the time of the offense is likely to be a significant factor at trial is entitled to a psychiatrist's assistance at state expense as a matter of due process. Despite this ruling, courts frequently find that the defendant did not make a sufficient showing to warrant the appointment of such an expert,[146] presumably because the courts seek to limit court expenditures in these appointments. The court's concern with efficiency (i.e., its financial resources) may limit the indigent defendant's ability to present an expert, which in turn will frustrate the likelihood that justice will be attained.

Variability in Admissibility Decision Making for Nonscientific Evidence

The Court's approach in *Kumho* to the admissibility of nonscientific testimony also will foster disputes about the justice of these decisions. Although *Daubert* considered the admissibility of scientific information, many expected that its pragmatic criteria would be rigorously applied to nonscientific testimony. But it was not applied this way because it would invariably deny admissibility to nonscientific testimony. For example, it is meaningless to ask if nonscientific testimony was ever scientifically tested. It is meaningless to seek the known error rate for nonscientific testimony in court. This type of testimony has never been tested, or by definition there would be science underlying it. Thus, it could not survive rigorous scrutiny under *Daubert*.[147]

---

[145] 470 U.S. 68 (1985).

[146] *See, e.g.,* Williams v. State, 795 So.2d 753 (Ala. Crim. App. 1999).

[147] Many in science would applaud such a development because it would force the evolution of clinical work along scientific grounds. This result, for example, is exactly what the clinical movement toward the empirical validation of clinical therapies is about. *See, e.g.,* EVIDENCE-BASED

For the most part, however, *Daubert* has had a minimal impact on the admissibility of clinical opinion testimony.[148] Courts may be reluctant to exclude pure, nonscientific clinical opinion testimony in fear that doing so would preclude too many litigants from having their day in court. Other courts may not exclude clinical opinion testimony because of their concern that a slippery slope would eventually lead to the exclusion of all other nonscientifically verifiable expert testimony, such as that offered by tire failure experts, plumbers, and police officers,[149] which would leave judges and juries in many cases without any expert information to help guide their decision making.[150] The assumption here is that having such experts is more helpful to the trier of fact than having no experts, with the impact on perceptions of justice being immediate. For those who believe in the importance of plaintiffs having their day in court, *Kumho* has allowed these individuals to pursue their claims and have the fact-finder decide their injury claim or defense. These proponents of the Court's opinion in *Kumho* see justice as synonymous with the concept of having their day in court. Thus, the accuracy of the expert's opinion is a decision to be made by the trier of fact. For civil defense lawyers, *Kumho* sets the standard for admissibility too low, particularly since the pronouncement of the decision in *Daubert*. How can justice be served by allowing in experts whose opinions may not be accurate, and if accuracy is in doubt, why do juries need to hear them? If *Daubert* had been applied rigorously, these so-called experts would be excluded.

Finally, what if *Daubert* had been applied rigorously in *Kumho*? The debate about whether *Kumho* promotes justice would still be heard, but in the opposite way. Plaintiffs would claim it failed to achieve justice because they are being denied their day in court, while defendants would applaud its application precisely because it would stop many cases before they began. Justice is a subjective construct.

Psychotherapies for Children and Adolescents (Alan E. Kazdin & John R. Weisz eds., 2003); Alan E. Kazdin, *Clinical Significance: Measuring Whether Interventions Make a Difference*, in Methodological Issues & Strategies in Clinical Research 691–710 (3rd ed., Alan E. Kazdin ed., 2003); Treating Adult and Juvenile Offenders With Special Needs (Jose B. Ashford, Bruce D. Sales, & William H. Reid eds., 2001).

[148] *Special Theme: Daubert's Meanings for the Admissibility of Behavioral and Social Science* (Daniel W. Shuman & Bruce D. Sales Guest Editors), 5 Psychol. Pub. Pol'y & L. 3 (1999).

[149] Daniel W. Shuman & Bruce D. Sales, *The Admissibility of Expert Testimony Based Upon Clinical Judgment and Scientific Research*, 4 Psychol. Pub. Pol'y & L. 1226, 1248 (1998).

[150] Daniel W. Shuman, *What Should We Permit Mental Health Professionals to Say About "The Best Interests of the Child"?: An Essay on Common Sense, Daubert, and the Rules of Evidence*, 31 Fam. L. Q. 551 (1997).

CONCLUSION

Our analysis of *Daubert* and its progeny's interpretation of the Fed. R. Evid. 702 suggests that few, if any, cases have advanced all four Fed. R. Evid. 102 goals of fairness, efficiency, truth, and justice. We also found ample evidence that the individual goals of Fed. R. Evid. 102 have often been thwarted. What we cannot tell from our analysis is whether in each instance of one of the goals being thwarted, another goal was achieved. To determine this would require a detailed analysis of the trial and appellate records, as well as interviews with the judge, lawyers, litigants, and experts in each case. But even with that information, we may still never find the needed proof about how each goal fared in each case. So what can we safely conclude? The goals of the Federal Rules of Evidence as applied to Fed. R. Evid. 702 under *Daubert* are not being consistently met, and often are being thwarted.

5

RECONCILING THE LAW
OF ADMISSIBILITY OF EXPERT
TESTIMONY WITH THE GOALS FOR
THE RULES OF EVIDENCE

There are two separate issues to consider when addressing why Fed. R. Evid. 102 goals have often been thwarted by the implementation of *Daubert* and its progeny. First, which we discussed in the prior chapter, is the behavior of judges and lawyers. This chapter focuses on solutions to the problems created and addresses each of Fed. R. Evid. 102's goals without compromising the others. Second is the extent to which the behavior of experts may frustrate Fed. R. Evid. 102's goals and how this problem can be remedied. This is addressed in chapter 6.

FAIRNESS

One problem in achieving fairness as consistency under Fed. R. Evid 702, as interpreted by *Daubert* and its progeny, is that judges are permitted to use *primary*, *secondary*, or *tertiary* information in their admissibility decision making.[1] The use of sources that differ in their proximity to the research

---

[1] *See* discussion *supra* in chapter 4, notes 6–7.

addressing the issue in question, and their use by judges who differ in their capacity to evaluate these different sources, can lead to inconsistent decisions across the courts, which compromises fairness. Although courts may understandably differ in their views of how high the admissibility threshold should be, there is little to be said in favor of their receipt of qualitatively different information for admissibility decisions.

If achieving fairness through consistency were the only goal with which we were concerned, the solution would be simple, although perhaps counterintuitive. Consistency in judicial decision making would likely be advanced by providing judges with information they would most likely be able to understand and apply—*tertiary* information. And to improve courts' access to this information, we recommend the development of systems to report otherwise unpublished trial court decisions on expert evidence. Yet, although comparing decisions on expert evidence across cases to increase consistency may advance the goal of fairness, it threatens other goals of the rules of evidence, most particularly truth. As we described above, tertiary sources of information about science, in which we include judicial opinions, are likely to be the least reliable sources of information about science. Thus, achieving fairness without risking truth requires that other judicial decisions serve as a starting point and not an end point in the admissibility assessment. It requires that courts consider the decisions of other courts not simply for what they decided but for understanding why they decided it. For example, what issues regarding the relevance and reliability of the science did these other courts address? What scientific studies did they identify that had not been presented in the instant case? What process did they use to assist the judge in evaluating the science (i.e., court-appointed expert)? If used thoughtfully as a starting point, these decisions may serve to improve truth and not just fairness.

But achieving fairness through consistency, under *Daubert*, without sacrificing other important goals of Fed. R. Evid. 102 implicates more than addressing the sources of information on which they may rely to answer those questions. Fairness in the implementation of *Daubert*'s commitment to judicial gatekeeping also requires a reconsideration of judicial selection, education and training, and procedures for determining admissibility.

To understand our concern with judicial selection, it is valuable to recognize that judges of courts of general jurisdiction are required to be lawyers because that provides some assurance of the necessary legal competence to serve as a judge. Just as legal competence is required of a judge, so too may scientific competence be required of a judge to decide on the admissibility of scientific evidence. It is odd that we permit judges who do not know or understand science to decide on its admissibility.

One response would be to select judges from that group of lawyers who know and understand science. Although this might produce a desirable result, its practicability is limited by several factors. Trial lawyers are not required to be scientifically proficient as a condition of practice, and trial judges are not required to have been trial lawyers. Finding lawyers who understand science and also possess other necessary judicial qualifications will not be easy. To be a judge, a lawyer must be willing to give up the potential of a lucrative private practice in exchange for a more modest governmental paycheck. Judges must also possess an appropriate judicial temperament and acceptable politics (i.e., the right political connections), to name just a few of the prerequisites for judicial selection.[2] To those, we have proposed adding scientific competence. It will be possible to find and recruit some individuals who have all of the above characteristics, but given the likely limited number of these people, the impact on the overall competence of the judiciary is likely to be small compared to the need. In addition, if we require scientific knowledge as a prerequisite to judicial selection, could not others reasonably argue for demonstration of other nonlegal competencies as well (e.g., accounting, penology, economics)? Why should scientific proficiency overshadow others?

If judicial selection incorporating a scientific competence requirement is unlikely to be a satisfactory response, an interesting incentive for judges would be pay increases for judges who acquire scientific proficiency. But this incentive is impractical. State and federal governments face serious financial constraints. And there are difficulties in justifying rewarding scientific proficiency when not rewarding other equally important aspects of judicial proficiency. Perhaps the best incentive then for judges is to make scientific programs available to them and to support their attendance at such programs. We recognize that this solution also raises cost concerns at a time when state governments are already financially overburdened.

Will there be sufficient funds to pay for the experts to develop the appropriate educational materials, provide the lectures, grade tests if they are administered after completion of the educational program, and provide appropriate feedback? For most jurisdictions the answer is no. A solution to this dilemma is to recognize that because science has no local nuances, the development and implementation of these seminars could be undertaken by a national consortium (e.g., Federal Judicial Center, National Center for State Courts, and American Judicature Society, working with the state and federal judiciaries), with the seminars conducted over the internet or through video presentations at local sites. The involvement of national organizations and experts from throughout the country, and the reliance on a uniform set of materials, should increase their quality and decrease their costs.

---

[2] Aristotle thought that four virtues were important for judges to possess: justice, temperance, prudence, and fortitude. *See generally*, ARISTOTLE, ETHICA NICOMACHEA (W. D. Ross trans. 1925).

Without denigrating other skill sets that are important components of judicial competence, the ability to rule on proffers of scientific information competently is essential given the importance of science in today's world. For judges who do not come to the bench with scientific competence, judicial education in science is necessary to gain this competence,[3] which in turn will promote consistency in decision making across trials. It is, however, beyond the scope of this book to specify which education delivery model would work best with judges and be acceptable to those who must pay for it. This will require separate analyses of the theoretical and empirical literatures identifying and evaluating education programs for professionals, the capacity of judges who lack scientific aptitude or background to achieve the necessary scientific proficiency, and the best ways of measuring whether graduates of these programs have met a threshold level of scientific competence.[4]

Beyond changing judicial selection criteria, financial incentives, or providing education to judges to bolster fairness, it is also worthwhile to consider implementing procedures that could assist judges in deciding the admissibility of expert evidence. For example, courts could use a neutral court-appointed expert[5] or special master[6] to provide the trial judge with

---

[3] See Sophia I. Gatowski et al., *Asking the Gatekeepers: A National Survey of Judges on Judging Expert Evidence in a Post-Daubert World*, 25 Law & Hum. Behav. 433 (2001) (reporting the results of a survey of state trial court judges in which a majority of respondents reported a lack of familiarity with the scientific concept of falsifiability).

[4] See, e.g., Ellen Lieberman, *Professional Responsibility and Continuing Legal Education*, 69 N.Y. St. B. J. 16 (1997).

[5]   (a) . . . The court may on its own motion or on the motion of any party enter an order to show cause why expert witnesses should not be appointed, and may request the parties to submit nominations. The court may appoint any expert witnesses agreed upon by the parties, and may appoint expert witnesses of its own selection . . . . A witness so appointed shall advise the parties of the witness' findings, if any; the witness' deposition may be taken by any party; and the witness may be called to testify by the court or any party. The witness shall be subject to cross-examination by each party, including a party calling the witness.

Fed. R. Evid. 706. *See, e.g.*, Laural L. Hooper et al., Neutral Science Panels: Two Examples of Panels of Court-Appointed Experts in the Breast Implants Product Liability Litigation (Federal Judicial Center 2001).

[6]   (a) Appointment and Compensation. The court in which any action is pending may appoint a special master therein. As used in these rules, the word "master" includes a referee, an auditor, an examiner, and an assessor. The compensation to be allowed to a master shall be fixed by the court, and shall be charged upon such of the parties or paid out of any fund or subject matter of the action, which is in the custody and control of the court as the court may direct; provided that this provision for compensation shall not apply when a United States magistrate judge is designated to serve as a master. The master shall not retain the master's report as security for the master's compensation; but when the party ordered to pay the compensation allowed by the court does not pay it after notice and within the time prescribed by the court, the master is entitled to a writ of execution against the delinquent party.

(b) Reference. A reference to a master shall be the exception and not the rule. In actions to be tried by a jury, a reference shall be made only when the issues are complicated; in actions to be tried without a jury, save in matters of account and of difficult computation of damages, a reference shall be made only upon a showing that some exceptional condition requires it. Upon the consent of the parties, a magistrate judge may be designated to serve as a special master without regard to the provisions of this subdivision.

an evaluation of the evidentiary reliability of the proffered expert evidence. Underlying these procedural changes to advance fairness is an assumption that training individuals in the relevant area of expertise should result in (a) more consistent decisions when reviewing a body of expert evidence than decisions by judges untrained in the topic and (b) more consistent decisions on the same expert evidence from case to case.

If, however, most or many of the expert admissibility questions are characterized by disputes within the expert community, the implementation of these procedures is unlikely to result in consistency unless the same or similar individuals provide assistance to courts across cases.[7] In an ideal world, we would conduct studies of the range of differences within the scientific community on issues that are of consequence in determining the admissibility of expert testimony to assess the benefits of using these procedures to advance fairness. With the results in hand, we could know for which particular topics the use of neutral experts or special masters would be most likely to improve fairness.[8] We do not have such studies readily available, unfortunately, and thus our solution must rely on surmise. Although we see many advantages for the use of these procedures for providing specialized assistance to the trial judge to advance efficiency and truth, the case for their use to advance fairness is less clear. For example, will judges, unsophisticated in science, who rely on tertiary writings (other courts' decisions) reach more consistent admissibility decisions across cases than neutral experts (if indeed such persons exist) grappling with that same testimony,

---

(c) Powers. The order of reference to the master may specify or limit the master's powers and may direct the master to report only upon particular issues or to do or perform particular acts or to receive and report evidence only and may fix the time and place for beginning and closing the hearings and for the filing of the master's report. Subject to the specifications and limitations stated in the order, the master has and shall exercise the power to regulate all proceedings in every hearing before the master and to do all acts and take all measures necessary or proper for the efficient performance of the master's duties under the order. The master may require the production before the master of evidence upon all matters embraced in the reference, including the production of all books, papers, vouchers, documents, and writings applicable thereto. The master may rule upon the admissibility of evidence unless otherwise directed by the order of reference and has the authority to put witnesses on oath and may examine them and may call the parties to the action and examine them upon oath. When a party so requests, the master shall make a record of the evidence offered and excluded in the same manner and subject to the same limitations as provided in the Federal Rules of Evidence for a court sitting without a jury. FED. R. CIV. P. 53.

[7] See, e.g., Special Theme Issue: Final Report of the American Psychological Association Working Group on Investigation of Memories of Childhood Abuse, 4 PSYCHOL. PUB. POL'Y & L. 931 (1998).

[8] But see Jensen v. Eveleth Taconite Company, 130 F.3d 1287 (1997) (expressing concern with the fairness of a special master who was clearly hostile to psychiatric and psychological clinical opinion). The record strongly suggests the Special Master foreclosed consideration of the evidence based on his own preconceived notions relating to psychiatric proof. The Special Master did not attempt to hide his hostility toward psychological evidence in sexual harassment claims, stating: "'Experts' . . . know no more than judges about what causes mental changes—which is to say that they know almost nothing." Id. at 1297.

where science has not reached a definitive conclusion? The answer is not clear.

Other aspects of procedural rules have an impact on fairness, in particular the rules for making or waiving evidentiary objections. The adversary system allocates to the parties and their lawyers the choice to present experts and raise evidentiary objections. This process can produce unfairness through an absence of consistency across courts addressing the same expert information.[9] Much as we might prefer consistency in the use of the same information across cases, it would be odd to single out a nonconstitutional concern (i.e., strategic decisions of lawyers about the admissibility of expert testimony) to justify altering the role of lawyers and the judiciary. When a litigant makes a tactical choice to waive a *Daubert* challenge and instead raises the underlying concerns on cross-examination to influence the jury's assessment of the witness' credibility, we do not suggest that judges should ordinarily intervene to preclude this choice. *Daubert* recognizes a party's right to object to the admission of expert testimony. But, like all evidentiary objections, if this objection is not asserted in a timely manner (i.e., ordinarily after it is offered but before heard by the jury), it is waived,[10] without regard to the merits of the objection that might have been made. But this tactical decision has ramifications for fairness that extend beyond the parties to this case in terms of inconsistent decisions on the same information across cases. Where does a solution lie that would protect the adversarial process while increasing fairness? When a litigant's approach to a *Daubert* challenge is tactically questionable or incompetently presented, we do not suggest that judges should ordinarily intervene to preclude this strategic choice or adversarial failing. To do otherwise would be contrary to basic tenets of the adversarial process, which does not guarantee that opposing lawyers will be equally matched or that the judge will intercede to reduce strategic errors.

Although judges do not ordinarily intervene in a party's decisions about evidentiary objections, there are circumstances where judicial intervention may be considered: cases affecting important public interests or vulnerable parties when the court has good reason to suspect that the normal operation of the adversary system has not resulted in a full presentation of the relevant expert information.[11] Under these conditions, several types of judicial intervention could be considered. When a question of admissibility has been raised but inadequately presented, for example, a judge could order the lawyers to re-brief and re-present their evidence and arguments on the

---

[9] *See* discussion *supra* in text accompanying chapter 4, note 9.
[10] Fed. R. Evid. 103.
[11] Joe S. Cecil & Thomas. E. Willging, Court-Appointed Experts: Defining the Role of Experts Appointed Under Federal Rules of Evidence 706 (Federal Judicial Center 1993).

question of admissibility. This option is rarely viable, however, because the forces that combined to result in the lawyers's presentation—lack of financial resources, inadequate scientific acumen, poor work ethic, or client limitations on lawyer actions—are unlikely to have changed during the case. A second option arises where the party's failure to advance an objection, or to respond to one appropriately, is a consequence of the absence of resources available to a lawyer representing an indigent defendant. In these situations, courts could consider expanding the application of *Ake v. Oklahoma*[12] to allow the appointment of an expert to assist counsel. Each of these approaches offers the opportunity to advance fairness as consistency in the admissibility of expert testimony without fundamentally altering the adversary system.

One lesson of the foregoing analysis is that the behavior of lawyers is an important determinant of consistency as fairness. Apart from informed tactical decisions to waive a *Daubert* objection, shortcomings in the behavior of lawyers, which fail to identify or respond adequately to *Daubert* issues, may be explained by a failure to do the work necessary in a particular case or a failure of the lawyer's education or training in science to be able to do that work. The post-*Daubert* world of expert admissibility demands more of the lawyer in understanding scientific methods. To satisfy the demands of *Daubert*, the lawyer must understand the nature of the scientific enterprise, be able to demonstrate that his expert is offering scientifically valid testimony, and be able to challenge the validity of the opposing expert's testimony. It is possible for this scientific competence to be acquired as an undergraduate, but not all law students had sufficient undergraduate science training or learned a sufficient amount of science to use it appropriately in a *Daubert* hearing. It is also possible for the needed scientific training to occur in law school, continuing education courses, or through attendance at a postgraduate training institute patterned after the National College for the State Judiciary. Although these latter three solutions sound simple, experience teaches that their implementation is and will be fraught with problems.

We could suggest that all law students take a course in scientific principles and methods. Yet, this is not a particularly practicable option for several reasons. Not all lawyers will need knowledge of scientific principles and methods. Why would law schools want to impose an additional graduation requirement when many students will not be litigators? Would the law schools then want to require it for students who are planning on being litigators? The problem with this requirement is that law students are unlikely

---

[12] 470 U.S. 68 (1985).

to know with any certainty whether litigation or a judicial appointment is in their future. In addition, courses that adequately cover scientific methods are rare in law schools. Law schools would then have to find qualified people to teach such a course, and justify using limited resources to support that course. In the face of a largely elective upper division curriculum, and competing pedagogical demands (e.g., skills courses, writing courses, breadth courses, etc.), law schools are unlikely to offer a course on scientific principles and methods, let alone make it a requirement. But even when these types of courses are taught as electives, relatively few law students enroll in such classes. Finally, it is far from clear that a law school course in scientific evidence or science and the law will leave students with a sufficient grasp of the science to assess research design and methodology.

A related option would be to require scientific education and proof of scientific proficiency as a condition to practice in the courts. Increasing the scientific proficiency of lawyers does not threaten any institutional legal values. Current standards for admission to trial and appellate practice, however, do not ensure the scientific proficiency of lawyers. Admission to practice before a state court has typically only required proof of graduation from an accredited law school and the passage of the bar examination, which is a test of a broad range of legal knowledge. The federal courts generally require proof of admission to practice in a state bar within the circuit.

Implementation of a scientific proficiency requirement would demand a systemic change in standards for admission to practice. Lawyers, like physicians and psychologists, are licensed as generalists. A lawyer who drafts wills and trusts must pass the same general legal knowledge test in the bar examination and possess the same license to practice law as a criminal prosecutor or civil personal injury defense lawyer. Would the legal system benefit from requiring scientific proficiency as a condition to try cases that present scientific evidence? We think that the answer is yes. Increasing scientific proficiency might be accomplished through board certification or requirements for admission to practice such as those required to practice before the Office Patent and Trademark Office.[13] Would the legal system require scientific proficiency for one area of practice when it has not required other nonlegal proficiency? We think the answer is no. Given that board certification in a relevant specialty (e.g., trial and appellate or personal injury) is optional and is not sought by the majority of the practicing bar, the potential impact of this option is limited.

Required continuing education for lawyers, as it now exists, does not resolve the problem. Practitioners are required by law to take a certain

---

[13] 35 U.S.C. § 32 (2004).

number of credits to maintain their licenses, but these continuing education requirements do not specify that the courses have to include training on scientific methods.[14] Moreover, there is no data addressing whether education for lawyers with no scientific aptitude or background will result in the scientific proficiency to assess the scientific issues that go to the heart of a *Daubert* challenge.

We face a serious dilemma in addressing a solution to the concerns we raise above. Altering the adversary system might elevate the consistency of decisions about the admissibility of expert testimony at the cost of fundamental values regarding the operation of the adversary system. Maintaining the adversary system in its present form might elevate the values ensconced within it at the cost of the consistency of decisions about the admissibility of expert testimony. Over the long term we believe that *Daubert* will provide an incentive for judges and lawyers to raise their scientific proficiency. In the competition encouraged by the adversary system and the marketplace, firms will seek to hire litigators with scientific proficiency to increase their appeal to clients and the odds of success at trial, and students wishing to increase their job prospects will be encouraged to develop a proficiency in science.

Another problem of consistency as fairness results because *Daubert*, *Joiner*, and *Kumho* yield a pragmatic set of criteria for trial courts to apply as they see fit in individual cases, subject to appellate court review. One trial court may apply all of these criteria in response to a particular proffer, another trial court may apply fewer than all four, with resulting inconsistency in the admissibility decisions that emerge from these differing applications. The Supreme Court explicitly endorsed this approach in *Kumho*:

> The conclusion, in our view, is that we can neither rule out, nor rule in, for all cases and for all time the applicability of the factors mentioned in *Daubert*, nor can we now do so for subsets of cases categorized by category of expert or by kind of evidence. Too much depends upon the particular circumstances of the particular case at issue.[15]

We, however, see nothing to be said in favor of different trial courts applying different criteria to the admissibility of the same scientific or technological evidence. To do so suggests that the same evidence should be evaluated differently by different courts. In addition, contrary to the Court, we do not think that context matters for determining the rigor that courts should

---

[14] *See, e.g.*, Texas M.C.L.E. Rules (Article 12, State Bar Rules), *available at* http://www.texasbar.com/Template.cfm?Section=Minimum_Continuing_Legal_Ed&CONTENTID=7490&TEMPLATE=/ContentManagement/ContentDisplay.cfm, last visited December 8, 2004.

[15] *Kumho*, 526 U. S. at 150.

apply when assessing reliability; bad science is bad science whether it is presented in a criminal, civil, family law, or probate case.[16] Thus, we encourage appellate courts to provide guidance across cases about the application of the *Daubert* criteria.

Of what should that guidance consist? To answer that question, we have to return to the lessons of *Daubert*, *Joiner*, and *Kumho*. It might be argued that *Daubert*'s emphasis on assessing the scientific validity of the proffered information as the measure of evidentiary reliability was unchanged by *Kumho*. Under this view, despite the Court's statements in *Daubert* and *Kumho*, courts should consider all of the *Daubert* criteria in each and every case addressing scientific experts, and any other criteria that are necessary to help them determine whether expert evidence is scientifically valid.[17] Failure to apply all of the criteria in every case could inadvertently lead to inconsistent and unfair procedures, as well as an incorrect admissibility decision.

Whereas *Daubert* responded to an offer of scientific information, *Kumho* addressed nonscientific evidence, whose validity is unknown. Thus the Court couched its opinion in terms of the reliability of the proffered information without defining what that means. The dilemma the Court faced was that although nonscientific evidence can include some scientific information, it can also be based solely on personal experience and opinion that is unvalidated. Rather than explicitly addressing this conundrum, the *Kumho* Court simply observed that the judge's gatekeeping task centers on reliability, and that the court has "the same broad latitude when it decides *how* to determine reliability as it enjoys in respect to its ultimate reliability determination."[18]

---

[16] This does not mean that context is irrelevant in terms of admissibility decision making. For example, although the hallmarks of good science cut across topical domains, valid research for one question may be invalid for other questions. Thus, courts must evaluate evidentiary reliability in terms of the special question or questions that the expert information is offered to address. *See* Daniel A. Krauss & Bruce D. Sales, *The Problem of "Helpfulness" in Applying* Daubert *to Expert Testimony: Child Custody Determinations in Family Law as an Exemplar*, 5 PSYCHOL. PUB. POL'Y & L. 78 (1999) and Daniel A. Krauss & Bruce D. Sales, *Legal Standards, Expertise, and Experts in the Resolution of Contested Child Custody Cases*, 6 PSYCHOL. PUB. POL'Y & L. 843 (2000).

[17] *See, e.g.*, United States v. Cordoba, 991 F. Supp. 1199 (C.D. Cal. 1998). Some may argue that this recommendation will not improve consistency and fairness. The proponents of this argument would wonder what weight each criterion would carry when there are conflicting outcomes based on the different criteria? For example, would proof of publication supersede a rigorous *de novo* analysis of the scientific methods? This argument misses the mark. The issue is not one of weighting, but rather a question of whether any of the criteria support the scientific validity of the proffered information. If not, then the evidence is denied admissibility. If the answer is yes, then the judge needs to determine if any of the criteria demonstrate invalidity. Once these two questions are answered, the *Daubert* questions are resolved.

This solution raises the opportunity for the scientific and judicial communities to support each other. We would hope that over time scientists will evaluate in learned journals the validity of different types of proffered scientific information, and that courts will be able to incorporate their analysis in future legal decision making. *See* discussion in text accompanying chapter 6, note 18 *infra*.

[18] Kumho Tire Co. v. Carmichael, 526 U.S. 137, 142 (1999).

This discretion, combined with the Court's admonition that expert testimony should be based on methods that correspond to practice outside the courtroom,[19] might be read to yield a best available or most reliable evidence approach. Yet, the Court is clear that there are limits to this approach, noting that

> the presence of *Daubert's* general acceptance factor [does not] help show that an expert's testimony is reliable where the discipline itself lacks reliability, as, for example, [the] . . . theories grounded in any so-called generally accepted principles of astrology or necromancy.[20]

The Court does not provide any further guidance to assist in distinguishing astrology or necromancy from other schools of thought or fields of study, apparently leaving this to the sound discretion of trial courts applying the *Daubert* criteria flexibly. Nor does the Court justify the logic of this approach, although it appears grounded in problems of practicability. Courts are faced with the practical necessity of deciding disputes before them on the best information that is available at the time. It is not practicable to wait for new scientific or professional developments before deciding a case, or to force litigants to wait to file a case until newer information is available.

Courts face the following dilemma. *Kumho* admonishes judges to admit only reliable expert information, but its lack of guidance to trial judges leaves room for other factors, such as alternative sources of proof available to the parties and the interests at stake in the litigation, to play a significant role in their discretionary judgments. This invites inconsistency and unfairness across trials. For example, returning to the court's decision in *United States v. Hankey*,[21] the judge was faced with the choice of admitting the police expert who based his testimony on personal experience and opinion, or denying admission and leaving the prosecution with no alternative source of expert information to prove its case. Given this court's assessment of the importance of stopping illegal drug use in this country and the involvement of gangs in the illegal enterprise, the court used its discretion to admit the testimony. Not all courts will necessarily view this balance similarly, which bodes ill for consistency in admissibility decisions across cases.

There are two responses to this inconsistency. It might be argued that an absence of consistency is not problematic so long as cases are decided appropriately on the facts presented. Besides the dilemma of defining appropriately in this context, this approach flaunts Rule 102's goal of fairness. Thus, we reject it. Courts also could recognize that *Kumho* fails to offer

---

[19] *Id.* at 152 ("It is to make certain that an expert, whether basing testimony upon professional studies or personal experience, employs in the courtroom the same level of intellectual rigor that characterizes the practice of an expert in the relevant field.").
[20] *Id.* at 151.
[21] 203 F.3d 1160 (9th Cir. 2000).

guidance on how to assess the evidentiary validity of nonscientific informa-tion in the same manner that *Daubert* offered guidance to courts on how to assess the evidentiary validity of scientific information. *Daubert*'s instruc-tion that evidentiary reliability is synonymous with scientific validity is not helpful in judging the evidentiary reliability of nonscientific information. And the pragmatic consideration of scientific testing/falsification and error rate will not be helpful to courts in assessing the evidentiary reliability of nonscientific information. Leaving courts with the impression that the only relevant *Daubert* criteria to assess the admissibility of nonscientific informa-tion are general acceptance and peer review discourages the creative testing of accuracy of nonscientific methods. What we propose is for the courts to develop more detailed guidance to define evidentiary reliability and constrain admissibility decisions for nonscientific expert testimony. It is that approach which we find most sensible. We do not consider the specifics here of what such guidance would entail because we consider this issue below under "Truth."

Finally, one reading of *Kumho* is that its flexible treatment of the *Daubert* criteria exacerbates their flexibility when applied to both scientific and nonscientific evidence. Indeed, this observation is not inconsistent with *Daubert*'s assertion that its pragmatic considerations ought to be applied flexibly. But this reading of *Kumho* could modify *Daubert*'s reliance on scientific validity as the measure of evidentiary reliability for scientific infor-mation. The *Kumho* Court used broad, unrestrictive language to describe the flexibility and discretion that trial judges enjoy in their approach to assessing the reliability of expert testimony. "[A] trial court should consider the specific factors identified in Daubert where they are reasonable measures of the reliability of expert testimony."[22] What a court should consider reason-able was left undefined. This could be problematic because although *Daubert* is careful to note that its use of the term *evidentiary reliability* is intended to correlate with scientific validity, *Kumho* makes no such effort to do so.

Is it possible that *Kumho* then could presage courts solely relying on nonscientific criteria to judge science? Although a literal interpretation of the *Kumho* language might leave the impression that courts are free to abandon the *Daubert* criteria in its entirety when assessing scientific evi-dence, we conclude that this interpretation is unlikely. For example, the 2000 Advisory Committee comments to the amendments to Fed. R. Evid. 702 list additional considerations that courts have applied to assess eviden-tiary reliability. These criteria were used to supplement and not supplant the *Daubert* considerations. Our analysis suggests that this interpretation of

---

[22] 526 U.S. at 152.

Kumho's application to *Daubert* will not raise new problems in consistency and fairness in judicial discretion, and thus requires no further discussion.

EFFICIENCY

Although there are no empirical studies to prove or disprove our conceptual analysis, *Daubert* and its progeny appear to demand that lawyers and judges devote more time and effort to the admission process for scientific evidence than prior to the enactment of the Federal Rules of Evidence, or subsequent to their enactment but before *Daubert*. The same picture appears to emerge in the case of nonscientific expert evidence. Where courts have attempted to increase the rigor of the analysis of the expert's reliability, efficiency in the admission of evidence appears to have decreased. However, where courts have been no more rigorous in their scrutiny of admissibility, efficiency has not been affected.

If *Daubert* decreases efficiency, perhaps it can be justified if its overall impact is to increase the fairness, truth, or justice of the judicial process. Although there is an appeal to this response, the problem with it is that it requires that we treat some of Rule 102's goals as subordinate to the others. As discussed in chapter 2, Rule 102 neither renders some of its goals as subordinate to others, nor provides a basis for ranking their importance. To take the opposite view would give rise to much mischief; the discretion to subordinate efficiency to the goals of fairness, truth, and justice is the discretion to prioritize efficiency to the goals of fairness, truth, and justice. This type of idiosyncratic decision making gives rise to a new form of inconsistency in judicial decision making in admissibility decisions that thwarts Fed. R. Evid. 102's goal of fairness. In addition, without a principled approach to decision making, how can we know the appropriateness of a judge's conclusion in a case that one goal should supersede all of the others?

One approach to increasing efficiency is to increase judges' and lawyers' scientific proficiency. If judges and lawyers understand science, they should need to spend less time in case preparation or in reaching admissibility decisions regarding scientific evidence. Because we have discussed this issue under fairness, and the same arguments apply to efficiency, we simply reiter-ate our conclusions. Over time *Daubert* will likely provide an incentive for judges and lawyers to increase their scientific proficiency. In the interim, continuing education for judges and lawyers holds the best potential to aid this transition.

A second approach to increase efficiency is to make better use of the judges' and lawyers' time by delegating these decisions to others. For example, the court could appoint an expert to evaluate the testimony presented in a *Daubert* hearing, and provide the court with an analysis of the information's evidentiary reliability.[23] Or, the court could appoint a special master to hear evidence and make a recommendation to the trial judge regarding admissibility.[24] The approach must be analyzed both in terms of its costs for other goals such as justice, as well as its actual benefit for efficiency. In regard to justice, the trial process is shaped by constitutional, statutory, and customary considerations. Even if modifying this process is legally permissible[25] and achieves greater efficiency, changing it comes at a cost—the corresponding impact on the values that underlie the trial process.[26] Is that worth the cost? The answer to this question is likely to vary from state to state, just as states have varied in their willingness to permit other innovations that change the trial process, such as jury note taking.[27]

Will delegating a part of the decision making process to others achieve greater efficiency? It can increase efficiency because a person with expertise in the evidentiary reliability of the proffered information will likely take less time to analyze it than a judge who is not knowledgeable about the topic. But, it may also create inefficiency if it results in pursuing issues that the judge or parties would not otherwise have addressed.

Apart from the impact of delegating part of the decision making process' actual time to an expert, there are the administrative costs. Using the services of someone to assist the court in making admissibility determinations may lower efficiency because of the financial costs that will have to be borne by the parties or the taxpayers. Creating another layer of decision making also creates another set of issues about which to litigate—who may serve to assist the court; what process should govern their appointment; can they be deposed regarding their decision; can their finances or politics be discovered to reveal biases or prejudices, etc?[28] In the absence of empirical data, it is unknowable whether these costs will offset the efficiency gained elsewhere in the admissibility determinations.

---

[23] Soldo v. Sandoz Pharms. Corp., 244 F. Supp. 2d 434, 442 (W.D. Pa. 2003) ("[T]he Court appointed three medical experts who were directed to opine as to whether the methodology or technique employed by the plaintiff's medical experts in [generating information] is scientifically reliable.").

[24] FED. R. CIV. P. 53.

[25] Ellen E. Deason, *Managing the Managerial Expert*, 1998 U. ILL. L. REV. 341 (1998) (examining the myriad uses of nontestifying court-appointed experts and questioning the authority for that practice under existing law).

[26] These values include such matters as a decision on matters of law made by a judge selected by the process prescribed by state or federal law; a decision on matters of fact made by a jury according to the process prescribed by state law; and all of these decisions informed by information provided by the parties according to the adversary process.

[27] Tom M. Dees, III, *Juries: On the Verge of Distinction? A Discussion of Jury Reform*, 54. SMU L. REV. 1755 (2001).

[28] Laurens Walker & John Monahan, *Scientific Authority: The Breast Implant Litigation and Beyond*, 86 VA. L. REV. 801 (2000).

Another approach to improving efficiency is to change the procedural rules that surround the implementation of *Daubert* and its progeny. For example, the courts could address rules that govern the procedure for an admissibility challenge (i.e., when the *Daubert* challenge must be made). Although it may not always be possible where discovery is limited, as in criminal cases, to anticipate *Daubert* objections prior to trial, it is arguably more efficient to require litigants to raise admissibility objections during pretrial proceedings. As in the *Daubert* case, resolving the admissibility issue predetermined the plaintiff's ability to make out a *prima facie* case and obviated the necessity to impanel a jury and commence the trial process. Even when there is no jury, pretrial resolution of expert admissibility may result in an increase in efficiency. If the result of the pretrial hearing is an exclusion of the testimony necessary to make out a *prima facie* case, it will not be necessary to assemble the judge and the court personnel, lawyers and witnesses, as well as the courtroom, which is not then available for the trial of other cases.

There is, of course, a potential problem in this solution. Where the party proffering the expert has done its homework and presented the expert with the best chance of surviving a *Daubert* challenge, the argument we made above about efficiency seems sound. However, where the party proffering the expert has not done its homework well, excluding the expert prior to trial may provide that party with a second chance to find an expert who can present science to survive a *Daubert* challenge. Although no concept of preclusion prohibits a court from considering the evidentiary reliability of another proffered expert, any rule that seeks to mandate pretrial *Daubert* challenges would have to limit expert supplementation if it is to achieve efficiency.

The rules that govern the impact of decisions in different cases on each other could also be used to improve efficiency. The abuse of discretion standard for appellate court review articulated in *Joiner* tolerates disparate decisions from trial court to trial court on the same issue of evidentiary reliability. Apart from the fairness (i.e., consistency) implications of this approach, there also are efficiency concerns. This standard encourages re-litigation of the same issue in a multitude of courts because affirmation of the admissibility determination means only that the trial court did not abuse its discretion. The opposite decision in another trial might also not be regarded as an abuse of discretion. This approach invites mischief. Although it is unlikely that the United States Supreme Court would overturn its decision in *Joiner*, which reflects a long-standing deference to trial court evidentiary rulings on efficiency as well as fairness grounds, appellate courts should provide greater guidance to trial courts in how a particular category of evidence should be handled in future cases under this standard.

Decisions like those of the *en banc* panel[29] in *Moore v. Ashland Chemical, Inc.* provide a good example of the guidance we seek. One of the issues in the case was the use of temporal proximity to prove causation in a toxic tort case. The *en banc* panel decision, which concluded that the trial court did not abuse its discretion in excluding causation testimony relying on temporal proximity, provides guidance to federal district courts about the propriety of this mode of proof that is likely to be helpful in achieving efficiency as well as consistency from case to case.

> The district court was also correct in viewing with skepticism Dr. Jenkins's reliance on the temporal proximity between the exposure and injury. *Cavallo v. Star Enter* . . . contains a helpful discussion of this issue. In that case, the plaintiff alleged that she suffered respiratory illness as a result of exposure to aviation jet fuel vapors. The proffered expert relied substantially on the temporal proximity between exposure and symptoms. The court concluded that this reliance was "not supported by appropriate validation" as required by *Daubert*, and was "ultimately unreliable." . . . The court observed that although "there may be instances where the temporal connection between exposure to a given chemical and subsequent injury is so compelling as to dispense with the need for reliance on standard methods of toxicology," this was not such a case . . . The court pointed out that the plaintiff in Cavallo was not doused with jet fuel and that there was no mass exposure of jet fuel to many people who in turn suffered similar symptoms. In the absence of an established scientific connection between exposure and illness, or compelling circumstances such as those discussed in *Cavallo*, the temporal connection between exposure to chemicals and an onset of symptoms, standing alone, is entitled to little weight in determining causation.[30]

TRUTH

As discussed throughout this book, there are three notions of truth implicit in Fed. R. Evid. 102: (a) truth referring to accuracy of the testimony

---

[29] *En banc* refers to the entire panel of the federal court of appeals. Most federal court of appeals decisions are made by panels composed of three judges. A majority of the judges may vote to hear a case *en banc* because it brings to the attention of the panel an error of great public importance or a conflict with a prior decision of the Supreme Court, court of appeals, or state law. *See, e.g.*, U.S.C.S. Ct. App. 5th Cir., Loc. R. 35 (2004).

[30] Moore v. Ashland Chemical, Inc., 151 F.3d 269, 278 (5th Cir. 1998). In Cavallo v. Star Enter., 892 F. Supp. 756 (E.D. Va. 1995), *aff'd. in part*, 100 F.3d 1150 (4th Cir. 1996), the plaintiff, Ardith Cavallo, dined at a restaurant 500 feet from the defendant's petroleum distribution, mixing, and transfer terminal, which had earlier experienced an overflow from its 34,000 gallon jet fuel storage tank. The disputed expert testimony concerned the accuracy of the plaintiff's air modeling expert's calculations, which addressed the concentrations of jet fuel vapors to which Mrs. Cavallo was exposed.

conveyed in court; (b) truth referring to an outcome that culminates after the adversarial process occurs, rather than an absolute discernable state of knowledge; and (c) truth referring to a systemwide goal for all trials without regard to whether that goal is achieved in any one case. Because these three facets of the problem of achieving truth in the admission of expert testimony are interrelated, we offer an integrated solution.

In chapter 4 we identified numerous problems that the courts will experience in seeking truth when applying *Daubert* and its progeny. One important problem is caused by the experts. Under the best of circumstances, expert testimony using science to assist courts in achieving truth as accuracy is inherently limited by the ability of scientists to ascertain truth or accuracy, even when scientists agree about a body of research. This is exacerbated when scientists disagree about research. The dilemma will be further exacerbated in the case of nonscientific professionals who do not have validation of their knowledge. We do not see this as a problem requiring a legal solution, however. If scientists cannot agree on the facts because of the inherent limitations of current scientific knowledge and techniques, it would be arrogant to believe that the law can remedy this dilemma. If nonscientific experts disagree, courts must be cognizant of their inability to discover truth as accuracy. If the experts cannot measure the scientific validity of their testimony, the courts are not going to solve that problem.

Another important problem in seeking truth is caused by the behavior of the legal actors in the adversary system. As we have noted, *Daubert*'s implementation requires lawyers and judges to have scientific proficiency that neither current legal education nor judicial selection assure. Although the free market and the adversary system provide incentives that will, we believe, over time raise the scientific proficiency of these legal actors, it still leaves some unspecified interim period of transition in which the goal of truth as accuracy and confidence in legal outcomes, within and across cases, is at risk. The suggestions that we discussed earlier in this chapter under "Fairness" and "Efficiency" to increase scientific proficiency of the bench and bar pertain with equal weight here.

Not only does a scientific proficiency deficit have an impact on truth as accuracy because judges may not understand the science on which an admissibility determination turns, it also risks a more subtle but equally troubling problem. Judges are lawyers trained in the adversary system that seeks to lay bare the biases and prejudices of the actors. Decisions by judges who lack education and training in science are more likely to default to other decision making strategies, some of which will reflect personal biases. Admissibility decisions purporting to apply scientific principles, by judges who lack a firm grasp of these principles, risks cloaking judicial biases under the veil of science. This absence of transparency risks not only truth as accuracy but also confidence in decision making across the adversary system.

This point further highlights the importance of judicial education and training.

Our earlier discussions of the use of court-appointed experts and special masters, and modifying the adversary system to increase fairness and efficiency, pertain with equal weight to truth as accuracy. Just as consistency from case to case (i.e., fairness) might be increased by modifying the adversary system such that judges assumed a responsibility to challenge questionable expert testimony even when the parties did not, so truth as accuracy might be increased if judges assumed a responsibility to challenge questionable expert testimony even when the parties did not. But earlier, under our discussion of "Fairness," we rejected wholesale modification of the adversary system, concluding that it would be inappropriate to do so to achieve consistency. We suggested that one way to address the underlying problem of fairness that did not threaten the fundamentals of the adversary system was for courts to provide funding for an expert when the lawyer's client could not afford one. Here, we recommend a similar outcome. We encourage judges to assist lawyers in making the adversary system work more effectively without fundamentally altering the adversary process. This assistance might take the form of scrutinizing the experience of appointed counsel for indigent criminal defendants relative to the issues that might be raised in the case, and providing adequate funding to retain competent experts to assist in raising and responding to *Daubert* objections.

We cannot recommend that judges play a more active role in raising *Daubert* objections not raised by counsel. *Daubert*, *Joiner*, and *Kumho* do not modify the fundamental relationships among judges and lawyers reflected in Fed. R. Evid. 103 (i.e., that a party enjoys the right to object to inadmissible evidence, in this case expert evidence lacking evidentiary reliability, but is not required to do so). A final decision in a case is valid and enforceable, even when that decision is based on expert evidence that could have been successfully objected to under *Daubert* but was not. Evidentiary reliability as defined by *Daubert* describes a litigant's right to object to the admissibility of expert evidence; when the opposing lawyer does not object to the expert's testimony, there will be no consideration of the admissibility of the testimony, and it will be heard by the trier of fact. *Daubert* does not address the sufficiency of evidence necessary to support a judge or jury verdict.

From the standpoint of science, we recognize that this aspect of the adversary system is lacking in logic. In science, there is no concept of waiver of objections to the validity of research, nor should there be. But legal battles are governed by other concerns, which we have discussed throughout this book, including the right of the parties to advance the arguments that they choose and not to advance others. This argument is ultimately dispositive because the arena in which the issue arises is legal, and the values of the legal system are controlling. Although some might wish to abandon the adversary system in favor of a different mode of dispute resolution, it is unlikely that *Daubert* and its progeny can or will produce this result and less likely that it should.

More troubling, however, is the case in which the lawyer raises a *Daubert* challenge, or seeks to respond to one, ineptly. Although it is more difficult to defend the values of the adversary system in this setting, we think that the judge's behavior must be limited to ensuring that the adversary system works well. This assistance can take the form of the court assisting counsel by providing expert assistance at court expense in criminal cases, and by assuring that appointed defense counsel are competent. The judge might improve the likelihood of achieving truth as accuracy by intervening when counsel fails to object or makes an artless objection or response, but what guidance might be provided to distinguish sound strategic decisions unknown and unknowable to the judge from ineptitude? Only in hindsight is it possible to begin to assess these questions and, even then, the practical problems of doing so are often insurmountable. Thus, we conclude that, except in cases of great public importance or vulnerable persons, the judge should be limited to attempting to see that the adversary system works well, rather than altering it by playing a role in objecting to expert evidence to achieve truth as accuracy.

Although we do not think that it is possible to define with precision when judicial concern with public importance or vulnerable persons is present, there has always been an understanding that some boundaries exist for the protection of transcendent concerns. Just as the rules governing settlement of class actions require judicial approval to ensure that the class representatives have adequately represented the interests of those bound by the judgment who have not participated in the proceedings,[31] so courts understand that they may have an obligation to third persons who will effectively be bound by the consequences of the admissibility determination.

One of the problems in achieving truth as accuracy that we noted in chapter 4 was the flexibility allowed in the use of *Daubert*'s criteria. Insofar as scientific evidence is concerned, not only does this risk fairness, but it also risks truth as accuracy and truth as a systemwide goal. The logic of *Daubert*'s criteria for scrutinizing evidentiary reliability is based on an interdependent set of assessment criteria. Hypothesis testing, error, publication, and peer review are not independently good ideas, because each without the other fails to provide a complete analysis of the validity of the science. For example, hypothesis testing is critical for followers of Popper, but without knowing more, we cannot conclude that the methods are valid. In a similar

---

[31] FED. R. CIV. P. 23 (e) ("A class action shall not be dismissed or compromised without the approval of the court, and notice of the proposed dismissal or compromise shall be given to all members of the class in such manner as the court directs.").

way, publication suggests peer review and the validity of the research reported in the article, but in some situations does not guarantee it. What becomes critical then for courts to achieve truth in and across trials is that criteria are applied in such a way as to be able to determine if the proffered expert information is valid. Perhaps the best way that we know of is for courts to apply all criteria, and any others that can help in this determination. Depending on the expert information, these additional criteria may involve a consideration of the sampling methods, the research design, and the statistical analyses used in the research. Any one of these additional factors may lead a court, and a scientist, to conclude that the research was not valid. But conversely, a positive evaluation of one of these criteria would not guarantee the validity of the research without a consideration of the rest of the criteria. Thus we urge trial courts to engage in a comprehensive analysis of the *Daubert* criteria as well as other relevant criteria that can help assess the scientific validity of the expert information, and for appellate courts not to be tolerant of trial courts that fail to do so.

For proffers of nonscientific expert testimony, our analysis of the problem and the potential solution, of necessity, differs. Trying to adapt the *Daubert* criteria to nonscientific expert evidence under *Kumho* creates two dilemmas. First, the *Daubert* criteria are premised on judging science. To apply these criteria to judging nonscientific information stretches their application beyond reason. For example, as noted earlier, nonscientific information by definition has not been tested, nor will there be a known error rate for it. Second, whereas *Daubert* selected scientific validity as the measure of evidentiary reliability, *Kumho* explicitly avoided setting the goal of scientific validity for nonscientific information. Indeed, it would be logically impossible to do so. Given that nonscientific information cannot be judged by its scientific validity, how can we achieve Fed. R. Evid. 102's goal of truth as accuracy and truth as a systemwide goal when considering the admissibility of nonscientific information?

The assumption that most courts and commentators have made is that for judgments about the admissibility of nonscientific expert information we can and should only apply *Daubert*'s final criteria—*Frye*'s resurrected general acceptance standard. As we have noted, this provides some assurance of reliability, but does not address validity. The question then becomes, is there a way to go beyond scientific reliability and come closer to assessing the accuracy of the evidence? Courts should not be so quick to abandon this possibility.

There are examples that reveal the ingenuity of courts and experts in conducting tests of accuracy outside of the field of science. When assessing the admissibility of a drug tracking dog's "identification" of the defendant, courts have little difficulty examining the success of the dog's past tracking efforts or requiring simple tests of the dog's ability to identify drugs (e.g., testing drug sniffing dog's false negative rate).[32] Although it would be pretentious to call that a test of scientific validity, it reflects a sensible implementation of *Daubert*'s underlying demand for proof of why we should believe that the expert will present accurate testimony. Another example, provided by clinical practice, would be to ask whether psychotherapists have followed up on treatment outcomes with their patients.[33] In a personal injury case, where the issue is how long a person would require therapy, why should the court admit the testimony of a therapist who cannot show reasonable accuracy in predicting outcomes with past patients.

To meet the demands of *Daubert* and its progeny, courts should presumptively demand proof of the accuracy of the nonscientific expert's methods, excusing this proof of its accuracy or validation only when the proponent of the expert can demonstrate that testing of the method is not possible. This encourages experts and the lawyers who offer their testimony to develop innovative techniques to test the expert's claims beyond the expert's claims to reliability. It implements *Daubert*'s demand that courts independently assess evidentiary reliability as a condition of admission and encourages confidence in decision making in and across cases, while acknowledging the practical necessity of courts to decide disputes before them without undue delay.

Some scientists might object to this procedural approach, arguing that the lack of a rigorous scientific study should preclude a court from concluding that any expert's testimony is admissible. To this argument we respond that Fed. R. Evid. 702 teaches that nonscientific expert testimony is admissible. It would be illogical to argue that although nonscientific experts are admissible, they must prove the impossible, the scientific validity of the methods and principles underlying their testimony.

JUSTICE

Justice is the most subjective of Rule 102's goals and certainly the most difficult to quantify or measure, because it reflects a value judgment about the outcome of cases. Although we cannot provide a rule for implementing Fed. R. Evid. 702 that will result in outcomes always being regarded as just, we can identify problems that result in case outcomes being perceived as unjust and seek to implement solutions that avoid these problems.

---

[32] United States v. Elgin, 57 Fed. Appx. 659 (6th Cir. 2003).
[33] Michael J. Lambert et al., *Is It Time for Clinicians to Routinely Track Patient Outcomes? A Meta-Analysis*, 10 CLIN. PSYCHOL. SCI. PRAC. 288 (2003).

One concern under the category of justice that stands out is that rigorous *Daubert* scrutiny has been selectively applied to favor or disfavor certain classes of litigants. The appropriate response to this concern is that differential scrutiny of expert testimony cannot be justified. Neither *Daubert* and its progeny nor the Federal Rules of Evidence recognize a different threshold for admissibility according to the type of case or litigants. Yet intolerable differences in the level of threshold scrutiny abound.[34] For example, consider two decisions of the United States Court of Appeals for the Fifth Circuit. In one, *Moore v. Ashland*,[35] the court issued an *en banc* decision, which we pointed to earlier as an example of careful scrutiny of the evidentiary reliability of differential diagnosis, that appropriately responded to the U.S. Supreme Court's decisions in *Kumho* and *Daubert*. In another decision, *Johnson v. Cockrell*,[36] the Fifth Circuit appears to ignore the need for the rigorous scrutiny that they deemed necessary in *Moore v. Ashland* under a *Kumho/Daubert* analysis. In *Johnson*, during the punishment phase of a capital murder case, the defense lawyer failed to object to the government psychiatrist's opinion testimony about the defendant's future dangerousness. The Fifth Circuit Court of Appeals rejected the defendant's federal *habeas corpus* attack, which claimed ineffective assistance of counsel for failure to object to the psychiatrist's clinical predication of future dangerousness. The court concluded that the objection would have been regarded as frivolous under the Court's pre-*Daubert* decision in *Barefoot v. Estelle*[37] that applied a simple relevance threshold to admissibility of such clinical opinion testimony in the face of much scientific criticism of its validity. Although pre-*Daubert*, the clinical opinion that the Fifth Circuit rejected in *Moore v. Ashland* would likely have not evoked much dispute over admissibility, *Daubert* changed that, and justice demands that the change be reflected in all classes of cases affecting all classes of litigants.

Another significant justice concern is raised by courts reaching opposite admissibility decisions when faced with identical offers of expert testimony. Perceptions of justice may be diminished when society legitimately perceives that outcome-determinative judicial admissibility decisions turn on the judge who is hearing the case. As noted in chapter 4, these outcome differences likely have multiple causes: differences in judicial competence, pragmatic criteria used, and policy; and differences in lawyer competence and strategizing. We discussed earlier in this chapter our thinking on how the courts ought to respond to differences in judicial competence and the use of selected *Daubert* criteria. Thus, we need not repeat our arguments here.

---

[34] Daniel W. Shuman, *Science, Law, and Mental Health Policy*, 29 Ohio N.U. L. Rev. 587 (2004).
[35] Moore v. Ashland Chemical, Inc., 126 F.3d 679 (5th Cir. 1997), *on reh'g* 151 F.3d 269 (5th Cir. 1998), *cert. denied* 526 U.S. 1064 (1999).
[36] 306 F.3d 249 (5th Cir. 2002).
[37] 463 U.S. 880 (1983).

The third possible cause for differences in admissibility decision making that may result in outcomes being regarded as unjust is judicial beliefs about what policy the Federal Rules of Evidence, and the Supreme Court decisions interpreting them, are intended to foster. Although some judges' application of the rules is colored by an understanding that the rules, as interpreted by the Court, are intended to liberalize the admissibility of expert evidence that would have been excluded under *Frye*, others see the mandates of *Daubert* and *Kumho* as requiring more rigorous scrutiny of expert evidence. Both groups cite authority that supports their position. Our solution is straightforward. We strongly urge the Supreme Court or the Advisory Committee for the Federal Rules of Evidence to clarify the goals that should guide the trial court's exercise of their discretion in the application of the rules governing the admissibility of expert evidence.

A fourth possible cause for a perception of injustice, arising out of differences in admissibility of the same expert evidence from case to case, is the difference in resources available to the parties. As we noted, although financial differences resulting in different legal resources available to the parties always plays a role in the perception of justice, *Daubert* exacerbates these concerns because it increases the cost of offering or challenging expert evidence. Particularly in the case of indigent criminal defendants, justice would appear to demand that the court play a role in providing expert assistance to the defendant at state expense, not just in the limited circumstances required by *Ake v. Oklahoma*. This conclusion is consistent with our recommendation under fairness.

Yet, this suggestion has important implications for other Rule 102 goals, specifically efficiency. Promoting fairness and justice may increase the financial cost of the financial and temporal inefficiency of a trial. Although avoiding this problem of injustice may result in decreased efficiency in a single trial, it may result in an increase in efficiency across cases. If decisions about admissibility reached fairly and justly (and more accurately) are more likely to be accorded precedential value by other courts because they appear more deserving, this will lead to less litigation over the issue across the legal system, with the result that fairness, justice, and efficiency will also be served. Judges are less inclined to accord cases precedential value when they perceive that it will not produce a just result.[38]

Finally, perceptions of justice can be affected by how trial courts interpret *Kumho*'s decision to grant them discretion to apply *Daubert*'s or other criteria to nonscientific expert evidence. When *Kumho* has been

---

[38] *See* Liang Kan, *A Theory of Justice Souter*, 45 Emory L. J. 1373, 1375 (1996). *See also* Ronald Dworkin, Taking Rights Seriously 113 (1977) ("The gravitational force of precedent may be explained by appeal, not to the wisdom of enforcing enactments, but to the fairness of treating like cases alike.").

interpreted liberally, admitting evidence and leaving it to the jury to decide its credibility, some perceive that justice is served (e.g., plaintiffs lawyers who need expert testimony to establish their case). Conversely, when the courts interpret *Kumho* to require scrutinizing nonscientific expert testimony more rigorously, others perceive that justice is served because the risk of the jury deciding the case on inaccurate information will be reduced (e.g., defense lawyers in civil suits). So where does a neutral solution to these differing perceptions of justice in implementing *Kumho* lie?

We believe that the answer to these competing visions of justice in the admissibility of nonscientific experts can be found in our prior critical analysis of judicial attempts to apply more rigorous scrutiny. When science is available to address the accuracy of the methods or procedures on which the expert testimony relies, perceptions of justice will be enhanced by judging its admissibility with regard to that science. But nonscientific information, by definition, does not have science to prove the accuracy of the expert information. In this situation, justice is best served by imposing the realistic test for the accuracy of nonscientific expert evidence that we suggested above. Perceptions of justice will be enhanced when courts presumptively require indicators of the accuracy of the expert's methods and procedures, where it is feasible to do so, even when those indicators may not meet all of the hallmarks of rigorous laboratory experimentation. When the expert fails to provide such indicators, the testimony should be excluded. Admitting expert testimony without indicators of its accuracy risks decreasing people's faith in the justice of the proceeding.[39]

But what if such demonstrations of accuracy are impossible to provide to the court, beyond evidence of the expert's qualifications and general acceptance of the expert's methods and procedures? Perceptions of justice should still be enhanced by admitting the best expert information available at the time. Courts and the lay public believe that admitting the best available sources of expert information maximizes the opportunity to reach the right result. Scientists believe admitting expert evidence solely because it is the best available source of expert information will increase the jury's confidence in their decision without any proof that it will increase its accuracy. But absent the ability to prove the accuracy or inaccuracy of the expert information, the practical necessities to make timely decisions faced by legal decision makers demand that courts not discard the best available sources of expert information. This approach to implementing *Kumho* will best serve justice.

---

[39] As decision making science progresses, its findings may be able to supplement or even supplant demonstrations. In time, this science might be able to specify the level of accuracy for the different clinical methods. *See, e.g.*, John A. Swets, Robyn M. Dawes, and John Monahan, *Psychological Science Can Improve Diagnostic Decisions*, 1 PSYCHOL. SCI. PUB. INT. 1 (2000).

CONCLUSION

Fed. R. Evid. 102 does not suggest a hierarchy for the goals of the rules it identified, and neither should any proposed set of solutions that is faithful to the rule. Thus, proposed solutions that we identify under each of Fed. R. Evid. 102's goals attempt to solve problems that *Daubert* and its progeny have created for the admissibility of experts, while not denigrating the other three goals. Our list of solutions considered, rejected, or endorsed is lengthy. Rather than review our analysis of solutions under each goal, we take this opportunity to synthesize them across Rule 102's goals.

Daubert and its progeny create much room for trial courts to differ in their decisions because of broad discretion granted in applying pragmatic criteria laid out in those cases. There is little to be said for broad differences across courts in admitting the same expert evidence. One solution is for trial and appellate courts to explain their decisional logic in sufficient detail so that judges in future cases will fully appreciate not just what prior courts decided and why, but how similar cases should be decided. Over time, these decisions will define what offers of proof the courts should accept for particular categories of evidence.

Daubert and its progeny also serve as a stimulus for trial courts to differ in their decisions about the admissibility of expert evidence because judges can rely on different decisional rules. The goals would be enhanced by having courts apply all of the criteria that are relevant to a category of evidence when reaching an admissibility decision. This approach will increase the likelihood that courts will be demanding consumers of the evidentiary reliability of the proffered expertise. Although context matters in terms of assessing its relevance, it should not matter in terms of the rigor of assessing its reliability.

Although the teachings of *Daubert* argue for the rigorous scientific assessment of the accuracy of the principles and methods underlying proffers of scientific information, courts and commentators suggest that we either apply a similar standard to nonscientific expert testimony or that we apply no standard beyond the qualifications of the expert. The former solution will exclude much if not all nonscientific testimony, whereas the latter will allow almost all nonscientific expert test testimony to be admitted. We believe that the proper solution lies in between. We suggest that courts ought to require an indicator of accuracy (e.g., a scientific demonstration) in the case of nonscientific testimony where such an indicator is possible. Fairness and justice dictate that if it would be impossible to provide such an indicator, then courts should reach their admissibility judgments by relying on the best available sources of expert evidence.

Implementation of *Daubert* and its progeny can be no better than the lawyers and judges who must apply their teachings. We think the marketplace will ultimately assign sufficient importance to scientific and technical sophistication that legal employers will demand and therefore lawyers will seek, and law schools and providers of continuing legal education will supply, needed education. In the interim, we strongly encourage law schools and continuing education programs to develop courses that teach lawyers and judges how to appropriately evaluate expert information.

Part of the dilemma in guiding judicial discretion under the Fed. R. Evid. 702, as implemented by *Daubert* and its progeny, is that this body of law does not address the ambiguity posed when attempting to apply the liberal thrust of the Federal Rules. The dilemma is only slightly less problematic under *Kumho* than it is under *Daubert*. Although we would be surprised if the U.S. Supreme Court were to address this issue in a future opinion, it is an issue worthy of further consideration and clarification by the Advisory Committee for the Federal Rules of Evidence.

Finally, we consider a number of procedural innovations that offer the potential to improve the implementation of *Daubert* and its progeny (e.g., court-appointed experts or special masters, pretrial resolution of admissibility determinations). Although we see much to be said in their favor, we see limitations to their solving many of the core problems we have identified. For example, where, as is often the case, genuine disputes exist in the expert communities, the use of a court-appointed expert or special master is not a panacea. Similarly, if indigent criminal defendants are not provided with funds to retain expert assistance in raising and responding to *Daubert* objections, procedural innovations will have a limited or skewed impact. For this reason, we made some additional recommendations. For example, in criminal cases we suggest that indigent defendants be afforded the use of experts to advance their claims or refute opposing experts. Similarly, in cases in which the rights of vulnerable third parties are at issue, courts should be proactive in taking steps to ensure that the expert information needs are adequately represented.

Even with modification in the way the law is implemented to achieve the Fed. R. Evid. 102 goals, there may still be problems in the manner in which the goals are implemented. Experts make choices when engaging in their court related responsibilities, which can affect the achievement of the 102 goals. We address this issue in the next chapter.

6

RECONCILING THE BEHAVIOR OF EXPERTS WITH THE GOALS FOR THE RULES OF EVIDENCE

Fed. R. Evid. 102 describes a neutral set of laudable goals that frame the approach of the rules of evidence and its use of experts, with which it is difficult to quarrel. Experts, however, are frequently heard to complain about how the law uses or misuses their services. Thus, our analysis of whether Fed. R. Evid. 702, as interpreted by *Daubert* and its progeny, has advanced the goals of the rules of evidence would be incomplete if we did not look at the behavior of experts in light of these goals.

Have lawyers and the courts denied admission of expert testimony that frustrated the goals of Fed. R. Evid. 102? If so, we would expect to find a body of case law reflecting the rejection of substandard expert testimony in the post-*Daubert* era. However, "the caselaw after *Daubert* shows that the rejection of expert testimony is the exception rather than the rule."[1]

If lawyers and courts fail to protect against this behavior, it is important to consider how the behavior of experts can either frustrate or facilitate Fed. R. Evid. 102 goals[2] and what solutions would ameliorate the problems.

---

[1] FED. R. EVID. 702, 2000 Amendment Advisory Committee Note.
[2] *See* Mike Redmayne, *Expert Evidence and Scientific Disagreement*, 30 U.C. DAVIS L. REV. 1027, 1067 (1997). ("The experts who appear during a trial will obviously not be a random selection from the relevant scientific community. They will be specifically chosen by each party because they support

This chapter undertakes this task. It directly considers experts and their behavior, focusing on how and when experts further or frustrate the four goals of the rules of evidence (i.e., fairness, efficiency, truth, and justice) in the resolution of legal disputes, and the potential solutions to problems they create.

FAIRNESS

In an opinion recognizing the right of indigent criminal defendants to have an expert appointed by the court to assist in their defense when mental status is an issue, the Supreme Court eloquently identified the importance of experts, particularly mental health experts, in furthering the goal of fairness in the adversary system.

> We recognized long ago that mere access to the courthouse doors does not by itself assure a proper functioning of the adversary process, and that a criminal trial is fundamentally unfair if the State proceeds against an indigent defendant without making certain that he has access to the raw materials integral to the building of an effective defense. . . . [3] The foregoing leads inexorably to the conclusion that, without the assistance of a psychiatrist to conduct a professional examination on issues relevant to the defense, to help determine whether the insanity defense is viable, to present testimony, and to assist in preparing the cross-examination of a State's psychiatric witnesses, the risk of an inaccurate resolution of sanity issues is extremely high. With such assistance, the defendant is fairly able to present at least enough information to the jury, in a meaningful manner, as to permit it to make a sensible determination. [4]

Ake speaks to fairness and the correlative rights that criminal defendants should enjoy, but its logic illustrates the way in which experts can contribute to fairness in both civil and criminal cases by making themselves available to assist litigants presenting their case. Several aspects of experts' behavior affect their availability.

Expert Accessibility

By *expert accessibility* we mean individuals who fit the particular issue(s) presented in the case engaging in conduct that will make them more easily

---

that party's case. This does not mean that those experts do not believe the propositions to which they are testifying, merely that they are an unrepresentative sample.").
[3] Ake v. Oklahoma, 470 U.S. 68, 77 (1985).
[4] *Id*. at 82.

identifiable to lawyers as experts. Because the necessity for expertise is contextual and not merely categorical, an expert's ability to provide relevant assistance is case specific. To select an appropriate expert, a lawyer must be able to sort through the issues and identify an expert with the relevant expertise. Success in this effort obviously turns on the capacity of the lawyer, but it also depends on the information that experts provide about their expertise to assist lawyers in this decision.

Many experts would argue that accessibility is achieved if lawyers look at the most accurate measure of their relevant expertise—what they have published in the scholarly literature. For some lawyers, these scholarly publications will be adequate to identify appropriate experts. For other lawyers who do not or cannot successfully navigate scholarly literature, more will be necessary to identify appropriate experts. For this reason, some experts list themselves in professional directories of persons available for hire in litigation; present talks at local, regional, and national bar meetings; and write brief articles for publication in bar journals and related publications (e.g., *Trial* magazine), with the intent of facilitating accessibility. Finally, lawyers can also rely on their prior experience in either using or cross-examining the expert in other litigation.

All of these methods of obtaining accessibility have drawbacks. Although these latter approaches (e.g., publication in bar journals) can identify someone who is interested in working for the lawyer, they may not result in the identification of an expert whose expertise is adequate for the current litigation. The decision to publish an article in a scientific journal will be made by professional peers; however, the decision to publish a scientific article in a legal journal will not be similarly vetted, thereby potentially frustrating fairness by not assisting litigants in accessing appropriate expertise. The result is that a litigant may access the most visible expert even though the individual's knowledge may not adequately fit the question that he or she will need to address. Directories of potential experts have a similar problem. They may use self-identification of expertise. If accessibility is the only goal, then on balance, the above approaches will best advance it and fairness. We recognize, however, that this solution may compromise truth as accuracy.

Experts' Economic Availability

By experts' *economic availability* we refer to setting fair rates and occasionally offering to serve *pro bono*. What are the consequences to the goal of fairness when experts do not make themselves readily available? When experts charge unreasonably high rates, they leave some litigants with the choice of hiring a low cost expert or none at all. We recognize that the rate an expert charges is not a proxy for his or her expertise. But when the expert's fee for service is too high, it dissuades a litigant from even interviewing an expert to determine whether that person would better represent the litigant's interest in the case than some lower cost expert.

Whereas for many litigants and experts market forces will determine a solution to this problem, for indigent litigants it will not. The solution to address this class of litigants is for experts to provide some of their time *pro bono*, or to charge lower rates to clients who cannot afford to pay more. This recommendation is consistent with Principle D of the American Psychological Association's ethical principles. It states: "Psychologists recognize that fairness and justice entitle all persons to access to and benefit from the contributions of psychology and to equal quality in the processes, procedures, and services being conducted by psychologists."[5] Although this principle is aspirational and not enforceable, it states a goal that is worthy of the discipline. The Principles of Medical Ethics also note that a "A physician shall recognize a responsibility to participate in activities contributing to an improved community," and the first annotation of the American Psychiatric Association to this principle states that "Psychiatrists are encouraged to serve society by advising and consulting with the executive, legislative, and judiciary branches of the government . . . ."[6] Although this language does not go so far as to state that physicians and psychiatrists should provide some of their services *pro bono* or at a reduced rate where appropriate, it is a socially responsible interpretation of this principle. But some experts might argue that it is unfair to ask experts to provide services *pro bono* or at a reduced rate if the same is not being asked of lawyers. In response, we note that lawyers are increasingly required to provide *pro bono* services. For example, as a condition of practicing law in Pennsylvania, "[a] lawyer should render public interest legal services . . . by providing professional services at no fee or a reduced fee to persons of limited means. . . . "[7]

We do not advocate that all individuals with expert knowledge participate as expert witnesses when asked. There are professional activities that are as important as being an expert witness (e.g., providing *pro bono* services to clients in a battered women's shelter). Although we think it is appropriate to leave questions of priorities and temperament to individual choice, we urge that an important consideration be the risk that courts are provided with less than reliable information because only a limited group of competent experts chooses to participate as expert witnesses.

---

[5] AM. PSYCHOLOGICAL ASS'N, ETHICAL PRINCIPLES OF PSYCHOLOGISTS AND CODE OF CONDUCT (2002), http://www.apa.org/ethics/ (last visited October 7, 2003).

[6] AM. PSYCHIATRIC ASS'N, THE PRINCIPLES OF MEDICAL ETHICS WITH ANNOTATIONS ESPECIALLY APPLICABLE TO PSYCHIATRY, (2001), http://www.psych.org/psych_pract/ethics/ethics.cfm, last visited December 8, 2004.

[7] 204 Pa. Code Rule 6.1 Pro Bono Publico Service, http://www.pacode.com/secure/data/204/chapter81/s6.1.html, (last visited October 7, 2003).

Numerosity of Experts

As already noted, for the expert to contribute to the fairness of the proceeding, he or she must be willing to testify, with this need becoming acute when there are few appropriate experts available on the issue. Even when compensation is adequate, some experts may be unwilling to testify because of competing professional demands or the stress of the adversary system. For example, scientists working on the development of new knowledge may view the additional compensation that they can earn from serving as an expert as inadequate to leave, even temporarily, what they consider critical professional or scholarly work. For other potential experts, the confrontational, noncooperative aspects of the adversarial process are unacceptably stressful. In many instances these counterweights result in a natural selection process of only some experts willing to participate in the adversary process. However, when they choose not to participate, and a litigant is unable to obtain an appropriate expert, the fairness of the proceeding may be compromised.

The solution to this dilemma is similar to that posed just above. Experts should donate some time *pro bono* to serve the public good and encourage those whose abilities and temperament permit to do so as expert witnesses. Although we are aware of no reliable surveys of the need for experts to testify on behalf of indigent litigants, we are optimistic this *pro bono* service as an expert witness will go a long way in addressing fairness by increasing expert availability.

Expert Competence

For fairness to be achieved in the adversary system, each party must be able to present its best case to the fact finder. Although it is obvious that many factors may contribute to or frustrate the realization of this goal, the expert's competence in his or her area of expertise is an important one. When one party's expert is not competent in the issue at hand, a litigant's case is compromised and the goals of the process are subverted.[8] Thus, an expert's competence is critical to realizing Fed. R. Evid. 102's goal of fairness.

An expert's lack of competence can be an obstacle in achieving fairness in three ways: (a) when the expert lacks expertise on the specific question in issue, (b) when the expert's behavior on the witness stand is below her or his actual expertise on the issue, and (c) when the expert's lack of

---

[8] How often there is a disparity in the competence of the parties' experts is unclear. Shirley A. Dobbin et al., *Applying* Daubert: *How Well Do Judges Understand Science and Scientific Method?*, 85 JUDICATURE 244 (2002) (reporting that a study of trial judges did not find this to be a common problem).

understanding of the substantive and procedural rules that govern legal conflict resolution compromise the advice and information she or he provides to the lawyer. As to the first concern, when an expert lacks expertise on the specific question in issue but still agrees to serve, the decision puts the party at a disadvantage and compromises the fairness of the system. For example, although the research literature on the accuracy of eyewitness identifications has been almost exclusively written by cognitive psychologists and some social psychologists,[9] some clinical psychologists agree to serve as expert witnesses on this issue.[10] Clinical training typically involves minimal study in visual perception. Thus, in general, it does not provide the desirable competence for achieving fairness on the issue of the accuracy of eyewitness testimony. It is certainly possible that some clinical psychologists will have gained a great mastery of the subject through self-study, but our system of education is built on the assumption that specialized education and training provides the best assurance of specialized professional competence.

The problem of an expert's attempt to go beyond his or her competence on the witness stand was recognized by the court in *Smith v. Rasmussen*.[11] In that case, John Smith sued the Iowa director of the Department of Human Services, challenging his denial of Medicaid benefits for sex reassignment surgery. The state sought to introduce the testimony of Dr. Kavalier, a psychiatrist, on the effectiveness of sexual reassignment surgery. The court denied admissibility because he did not have sufficient training or experience with the topic he was asked to testify about.

> The basis for Smith's motion was that Dr. Kavalier had been involved in only one instance of treatment of one patient with a similar, but not identical, diagnosis to that claimed by Smith, eight years earlier, and treatment of that individual occurred only over a very short period. Thus, Dr. Kavalier's opinions rested primarily on a literature review, but not on any connection between his practice and his opinions in this case, and consequently he had no specialized knowledge, education, experience, or training to bring to bear upon the issues in the case.[12]

The court agreed with the plaintiff and excluded the testimony, finding that although Dr. Kavalier possessed adequate qualifications to testify on general psychiatric principles, he lacked the qualifications specific to treating gender identity disorder.

The solution to this problem is explicitly or implicitly accepted by every expert community. Experts should not offer services outside of their

---

[9] *See, e.g.*, Elizabeth F. Loftus, Eyewitness Testimony (1976); Brian L. Cutler & Steven D. Penrod, Mistaken Identification: The Eyewitness, Psychology and the Law (1995).
[10] Russell Contreras, *More Courts Let Experts Debunk Witness Accounts*, The Wall Street Journal, August 10, 2001, at B, P1.
[11] 57 F. Supp. 2d 736 (N.D. Iowa 1999).
[12] *Id.* at 764.

expertise. For example, the American Psychological Association's *Ethical Principles of Psychologists and Code Of Conduct: 2002* states that "Psychologists provide services . . . only within the boundaries of their competence . . . "[13] If experts comply, then fairness within and across trials will be enhanced. When experts avoid their responsibility, in addition to the courts' denying admissibility, there are other approaches to addressing such lapses: published commentary on the expert's testimony; disciplining of the expert by the expert's learned society[14] or state licensure board;[15] and a professional negligence or breach of contract action against the expert.[16] There have been calls in the past to create journals or magazines that republish portions of expert testimony followed by peer commentary on the quality of that testimony. Such public vetting can inform the courts, lawyers, and experts what other members of the discipline think about the expert testimony and its limitations.[17] Over time such visibility may encourage lawyers and judges to be more discerning of whether experts are adequately addressing the relevant issues and may encourage experts to confine their testimony to their existing expertise. Sanctioning of experts for testimony that violates the norms of the discipline recognizes that incompetent expert testimony not only jeopardizes the fairness of legal proceedings, but also casts a visible pall over the profession. This is not to argue that experts cannot disagree, but when the professional deviancy cannot be explained or justified by legitimate professional reasoning, then the need for sanctioning becomes appropriate.

As to the second way an expert's lack of competence can diminish fairness (i.e., where the expert's behavior on the stand is below his or her actual expertise on the issue), consider the following example. Jane Patel, PhD, a professor of sociology at the local university, is asked to testify on a topic on which she conducted research some years ago. For Dr. Patel to bring her full level of competence to bear on the witness stand, she would need to carefully review this research and update her knowledge to ensure that she is familiar with the most recent work on the topic. Because facts

---

[13] Am. Psychological Ass'n, Ethical Principles of Psychologists and Code of Conduct (2002) § 2.01, http://www.apa.org/ethics/ (last visited October 7, 2003).
[14] Austin v. American Ass'n. of Neurological Surgeons, 253 F.3d 967 (7th Cir. 2001), *cert. denied* 534 U.S. 1078 (2002) (affirming discipline by a voluntary professional organization for offering expert testimony that was not supported by the sources on which the expert relied).
[15] Deatherage v. Examining Board of Psychology, 948 P.2d 828 (Wash. 1997); Huhta v. State Board of Medicine, 706 A.2d 1275 (Pa. Commw. Ct. 1998), *appeal denied* 727 A.2d 1124 (Pa. 1998).
[16] Daniel W. Shuman and Stuart A. Greenberg, *The Expert Witness, The Adversary System, and The Voice of Reason: Reconciling Impartiality and Advocacy.* 34 Prof. Psychol.: Rsch. & Prac. 219 (2003).
[17] *See generally* Bruce D. Sales & Leonore Simon, *Institutional Constraints on the Ethics of Expert Testimony,* 3 Ethics & Behav. 231 (1993); Richard A. Posner, Economic Analysis of Law (5th ed. 1998); Am. Med. Ass'n, Report of the Board of Trustees (1998) http://www.truthinjustice.org/amareport.htm (last visited October 8, 2003).

on which the experts base their opinions are often in dispute in litigation, competent practice would require that Dr. Patel be able to identify which facts she relied on in reaching an opinion, the evidentiary grounding for such facts, and how that opinion would change if different facts prevailed in the opinion of the fact finder.[18] It is unfortunate that because of competing demands Dr. Patel may not do all of that. This may occur because other professional or personal matters compete with the demands placed on her by the adversary system and because the reimbursement structure does not result in her giving their witnessing responsibilities high priority. Whatever the cause,[19] the impact of her failure to devote sufficient time and attention to the case, to permit her full expertise to be brought to bear, will result in the fairness of the adversary system being compromised.

The solution here is in some regard provided by the adversary system and in some regard must come from the expert herself. The expert in our example is competent in her field of expertise and, except for an unwillingness to spend some preparation time, would be competent on the witness stand. The rigors of cross-examination and the embarrassment of having been revealed to be inadequately prepared should provide a powerful incentive for her to prepare. Likewise, professional peer review of her testimony should provide an added incentive for adequate preparation. Yet, because the vast majority of cases will settle without trial, but be influenced by pretrial expert opinion reports, ultimately experts must recognize that the final responsibility for adequate preparation lies with them.

The third way that an expert's advice and testimony can affect the attainment of fairness is when the expert's lack of understanding of the substantive and procedural rules that govern trials compromise his work. Being a good expert and being a good expert witness are not synonymous; expert witnesses are required to comply with a different set of rules than apply to experts in their professional work outside the courtroom. For example, relying on hearsay as the basis for an opinion where it is forbidden to do so,[20] using a test that fails to satisfy the legal standard for admissibility in that jurisdiction,[21] or expressing an ultimate opinion where that is forbidden by the applicable evidence code[22] will result in all or a portion of the

---

[18] FED. R. EVID. 702, 2000 Amendment Advisory Committee Note does not demand as much of experts: "When facts are in dispute, experts sometimes reach different conclusions based on competing versions of the facts. The emphasis in the amendment on 'sufficient facts or data' is not intended to authorize a trial court to exclude an expert's testimony on the grounds that the court believes one version of the facts and not the other."

[19] Bruce D. Sales & Leonore M. J. Simon, *Institutional Constraints on the Ethics of Expert Testimony*, 3 ETHICS & BEHAV. 231 (1993).

[20] People v. Angelo, 666 N.E.2d 1333 (N.Y. 1996).

[21] In re CDK, 64 S.W.3d 679 (Tex. App. 2002).

[22] FED. R. EVID. 704(b).

expert's opinion not being received into evidence.[23] Having an expert's testimony or portion thereof struck because of avoidable evidentiary errors compromises the fairness of the adversary system.

The solution here is for experts to become apprised of the procedural rules that govern their giving of testimony. For the occasional expert witness, this may entail careful preparation and instruction by the lawyer who has retained the expert. For the experts who serve regularly as expert witnesses, this entails forensic education and training.[24] Experts should not assume that their willingness to testify will result in their immunity from the rigors of the adversarial process.

EFFICIENCY

Experts can affect whether the goal of efficiency is met through their availability at the time of trial, their expense, and the time it takes to provide their services effectively. Although it might be thought that retained or appointed experts would be available when needed in court because they are being paid for their services, judges report that this is not always the case, that this problem delays trials, and that this is one of the problems experts pose most frequently for the courts.[25] Availability is affected by the administration of the courts in scheduling cases and in communications between lawyers and experts about that scheduling. These issues are made more complex for the expert who mixes a clinical and forensic practice requiring that patients be rescheduled, often on short notice.

It would be unreasonable to ask that experts always prioritize the efficiency needs of the court over their research or practice. But it is reasonable to ask that experts be as sensitive to the needs of the lawyers who hire them and the needs of the court as they are to the needs of their clients or research participants.[26] Experts should also take on the responsibility of communicating effectively with the lawyer who retains them about their scheduling needs and difficulties.

Expense also affects efficiency. There is, as a matter of efficiency, a point where fair compensation for the expert meets fiscal responsibility for

---

[23] See generally DANIEL W. SHUMAN, PSYCHIATRIC AND PSYCHOLOGICAL EVIDENCE (2nd ed. 1994).
[24] Committee on Ethical Guidelines for Forensic Psychologists, *Specialty Guidelines for Forensic Psychologists*, 15 LAW & HUM. BEHAV. 655 (1991).
[25] Shirley A. Dobbin et al., *Applying* Daubert: *How Well Do Judges Understand Science and Scientific Method?*, 85 JUDICATURE 244 (2002).
[26] There is an interesting empirical question about whether experts who regularly testify create fewer problems for the courts in this regard because of their familiarity with the needs of the system or because they see their annual compensation as being substantially affected by their satisfying those needs.

the courts. From a judicial marketplace perspective, efficiency refers to an optimal level of compensation that, by definition, meets the economic interests of experts as well as the courts. Unreasonably high fees create inefficiency in the judicial process. For example, when court-appointed experts charge unreasonable fees, it will affect the ability of courts with finite fiscal resources to appoint experts in other deserving cases, resulting in a less than optimal allocation of judicial resources from case to case.

The fees that retained experts charge litigants will have an impact on the ability of litigants with finite fiscal resources to pay for other costs in conjunction with the litigation. In addition, unreasonably high expert fees[27] will unnecessarily inflate the cost of the trial. When the expert has developed a niche as a leading expert for a particular topic, this inflation will be multiplied across trials. Finally, where the expert agrees to serve but is not compensated adequately from the expert's point of view, efficiency may be affected by altering the priority that the expert will give to the forensic role. Delays in writing reports, for example, because of competing demands of better paid or higher priority activities threaten the efficiency of the judicial process.

There is not always a mutually satisfactory solution to dilemmas of financial efficiency. When deciding whether to serve as an expert for clients who can afford to pay for services, experts should have the right to charge what the market will bear. However, the fee provided court-appointed experts is usually fixed in advance and is almost always below market rates for privately retained experts. The concern that experts will delay work while providing services to other clients to compensate for the lower fees, is best addressed by reminding experts that such behavior unacceptably compromises their professional responsibilities and social obligations. If the expert will not perform competently, then the expert should not agree to provide the service. Once experts agree to serve, the quality of their service should not be affected by the fee arrangement.

The time that experts take to provide their services also affects efficiency. When experts are efficient, as we use that term here, they spend the optimal amount of time necessary to reach an opinion competently. When experts are inefficient, they spend too much time in preparation for a case, posing efficiency problems both within the case and across the judicial system. For example, if a court-appointed expert administers and bills for tests that add no incremental validity to their opinions and conclusions, it will unnecessarily add to the costs associated with the case, thereby contribut-

---

[27] Shirley A. Dobbin et al., *Applying* Daubert: *How Well Do Judges Understand Science and Scientific Method?*, 85 JUDICATURE 244, 246 (2002) (reporting that one of the most frequent problems judges perceive with experts is their "excessive expense").

ing to judicial inefficiency both in the current case and the court's ability to pay for experts in other cases.

When decreased efficiency results from differences in human abilities, there is no solution to the efficiency concerns noted above. Although it would be wonderful if all professionals performed at an optimal level, we know that they do not. Expert witnesses are no different, and should be held to no higher a standard. But when efficiency is compromised because experts intentionally try to create more work to increase their fees, when they agree to testify on an issue that is outside their area of expertise, or when they slow their work because of competing priorities, they are performing incompetently and should be held accountable.

Finally, matters of efficiency will also affect other goals of Fed. R. Evid. 102. For example, efficiency can affect fairness. The cost of retaining experts can limit the number of experts retained, providing an incentive for lawyers to use experts in multiple and inconsistent roles. If, for instance, one expert is retained to serve both as a trial consultant, whose work product is not discoverable, and as an expert witness, whose work product is discoverable, there is a risk of exposing otherwise undiscoverable information.[28] This threatens the fairness of the trial by limiting a litigant's effective assistance of counsel. Concerns with efficiency may similarly result in lawyers seeking to use treating psychologists in the conflicting role of forensic experts.[29] This threatens the fairness of the trial process through a litigant's use of an expert whose competence is compromised by serving in dual roles. For example, because of a positive therapeutic relationship with the patient-litigant, the psychologist may be biased, and consequentially not credible in providing expert testimony on behalf of the litigant.

The solution to these concerns is straightforward. Even where the lawyer fails to see the potential conflicts, the expert must refuse to serve in multiple and inconsistent roles.[30]

---

[28] Trial consultants who are not intended to be called as witnesses are not discoverable by an opponent, but proposed witnesses are discoverable. The possibility that a deposition of a proposed expert may result in the revelation of conversations between the lawyer and the expert that reveal trial strategy is created by the use of a single person to perform both roles.

[29] Stuart A. Greenberg & Daniel W. Shuman, *Irreconcilable Conflict Between Therapeutic and Forensic Roles*, 28 PROF. PSYCH.: RES. & PRAC. 50 (1997).

[30] (a) A multiple relationship occurs when a psychologist is in a professional role with a person and (1) at the same time is in another role with the same person, (2) at the same time is in a relationship with a person closely associated with or related to the person with whom the psychologist has the professional relationship, or (3) promises to enter into another relationship in the future with the person or a person closely associated with or related to the person.

A psychologist refrains from entering into a multiple relationship if the multiple relationship could reasonably be expected to impair the psychologist's objectivity, competence, or

Perhaps the most obvious goal of the rules of evidence on which experts may have an impact is truth as accuracy. Providing accurate, reliable information enhances the likelihood that truth as accuracy will be ascertained, while providing inaccurate, unreliable expert information decreases the likelihood that truth as accuracy will be achieved. But what specific behaviors of experts enhances or frustrates this goal? We suggest that the answer is competence in one's field of knowledge, competence on the witness stand, and choice of roles as an expert.

Under state licensure laws, mental health professionals can address the full panoply of their patients' clinically presented problems, using the full spectrum of clinical therapies and interventions. But this recognition of generic expertise can present a problem for expert witnesses in achieving the goal of truth as accuracy. An expert must have appropriate training and sufficient knowledge of the scientific and professional literatures and practices to present an accurate representation of the knowledge that is relevant to the specific questions being asked. Furthermore, competence on the witness stand requires that the expert comprehend the factual nuances of the case that she will be addressing, become familiar with the opposing parties explanations for the topics being addressed, understand the strengths and weaknesses of those explanations, and appreciate how the law will affect the types of information she will likely be asked to present and defend during cross-examination. Having a degree and a license to practice does not demonstrate that the expert is competent to fulfill these responsibilities. For example, a review of the scientific literature demonstrates that at any given point in time some questions are unanswerable.[31] In addition, an

---

effectiveness in performing his or her functions as a psychologist, or otherwise risks exploitation or harm to the person with whom the professional relationship exists.

Multiple relationships that would not reasonably be expected to cause impairment or risk exploitation or harm are not unethical.

(b) If a psychologist finds that, due to unforeseen factors, a potentially harmful multiple relationship has arisen, the psychologist takes reasonable steps to resolve it with due regard for the best interests of the affected person and maximal compliance with the Ethics Code.

(c) When psychologists are required by law, institutional policy, or extraordinary circumstances to serve in more than one role in judicial or administrative proceedings, at the outset they clarify role expectations and the extent of confidentiality and thereafter as changes occur. (See also Standards 3.04, Avoiding Harm, and 3.07, Third-Party Requests for Services.)

See, e.g., Am. Psychological Ass'n, Ethical Principles of Psychologists and Code Of Conduct, § 3.05, http://www.apa.org/ethics/ (last visited October 7, 2003).

[31] *See, e.g.,* Daniel A. Krauss & Bruce D. Sales, *Legal Standards, Expertise, and Experts in the Resolution of Contested Child Custody Cases,* 6 Psychol. Pub. Pol'y & L. 843 (2000) (discussing the fact that research has not yet answered what is in the best interests of a child for purposes of deciding custody disputes even though credentialed experts regularly testify as to this issue. Because science is iterative, there will always be unanswered questions at any given point in time).

expert's response to answerable questions may be inaccurate unless the expert keeps abreast of the relevant scholarly literature on that topic.

A different perspective on the competence of experts comes from asking how much expertise is required to be an expert witness. Many courts, as just noted, accept entry level credentials (e.g., a degree, a state license to practice, or experience in one's field) as sufficient proof of expert qualification.[32] Other courts, however, explicitly reject entry level credentials as sufficient to establish competence, and look instead for specialized knowledge associated with what the practice and scientific communities would call experts.[33] These determinations are committed to the sound discretion of the trial court and are unlikely to be disturbed on appeal. Therefore, the use of the term *expert* as in expert witness may mean different things for the law and for the disciplines or professions. The dilemma for achieving the goal of truth as accuracy is that some witnesses who want to serve as experts may be admitted even though their testimony may compromise the attainment of truth.

Can a solution be found by asking what mastery entails within the scientific and professional communities? In some circumstances, the standard is clear. For instance, where learned and professional associations, federal agencies, or task forces of associations or federal agencies have published detailed scholarly reviews or practice guidelines,[34] the person being offered as an expert witness should be fully conversant with the contents of these

---

[32] Rule 702's liberal policy of admissibility extends to the substantive as well as the formal qualification of experts. We have eschewed imposing overly rigorous requirements of expertise and have been satisfied with more generalized qualifications. See Hammond v. International Harvester Co., 691 F.2d 646, 652–653 (3d Cir. 1982) (holding that an engineer, whose only qualifications were sales experience in the field of automotive and agricultural equipment and teaching high school automobile repair, nevertheless could testify in a products liability action involving tractors) . . .
In re Paoli R.R. PCB Yard Litigation, 35 F.3d 717 (3d Cir. 1994).

[33] Daubert did not include the expert's qualifications in its list of pertinent considerations. Daubert, however, did not intend to set forth "a rigid or exclusive list." See United States v. Hall, 93 F.3d 1337, 1341 (7th Cir. 1996). And we have no doubt that an expert's qualifications bear upon the scientific validity of his testimony. In United States v. Benson, 941 F.2d 598 (7th Cir. 1991), we stated, "An expert's opinion is helpful only to the extent the expert draws on some special skill, knowledge, or experience to formulate that opinion; the opinion must be an expert opinion (that is, an opinion informed by the witness' expertise) rather than simply an opinion broached by a purported expert." Id. at 604. Because an expert's qualifications bear upon whether he can offer special knowledge to the jury, the Daubert framework permits—indeed, encourages—a district judge to consider the qualifications of a witness. Cf. Braun v. Lorillard Inc., 84 F.3d 230, 234–235 (7th Cir. 1996) (determining that jury could not hear testimony that plaintiff's lung tissue contained asbestos fibers, when purported expert was not experienced in the testing of human tissue and spent 99.9 percent of his time engaged in administrative and marketing activities for his consulting firm).
United States v. Vitek Supply Corp., 144 F.3d 476, 486 (7th Cir. 1998).

[34] See, e.g., Special Theme Issue: Final Report of the American Psychological Association Working Group on Investigation of Memories of Childhood Abuse, 4 PSYCHOL. PUB. POL'Y & L. 931 (1998); The Agency for Health Care Research and Quality Clinical Practice Guidelines, http://www.ahcpr.gov/clinic/cpgsix.htm (last visited November 4, 2003).

writings and the references within them. But in most situations, these types of reviews and pronouncements do not exist.

Where these reviews or pronouncements do exist, the problem for the expert is to master the relevant literature. The proliferation of scholarly and professional periodicals and the increase in the number of pages published imposes a heavy burden on both practitioners and researchers to remain current in their field. Generalists in any field are unlikely to be able to find the time to keep current with this burgeoning knowledge across their field of practice. Even where a professional seeks to keep up with the literature, it is expanding so rapidly that it will be impossible to do so other than in a few select topics. And where the attempt is made to keep up with the scholarly literature on any given topic, the ability to do so accurately may be limited. The years spent in receiving education and training in one's field only allows trainees to become knowledgeable about some of the research methods, statistical techniques, and professional skills. As new substantive literatures develop based on methods, techniques, and skills that practitioners never studied in school, it is often impossible for practitioners to understand what this new literature proves and teaches without additional formal training or study.[35]

Do proffered witnesses expend such effort? It is unfortunate that there are no direct empirical data to answer this question.[36] In addition, even where experts attempt to read and master these literatures, mastery requires that they understand the limits of that knowledge and what any body of research or professional opinion actually proves.

> [T]he testing of theories and methodologies is almost always partial. Those theories that survive testing still have components that have never been tested, contain subjective elements, and require that reasonable inferences be made if they are to be used in real world examples. Scientific theories, including those that are extremely useful, are imperfect. It follows that scientific knowledge itself must be imperfect. As a result, the underlying theories and "knowledge" on which experts rely in testimony almost always have imperfections.[37]

There are a variety of factors that may impede an expert's ability to perceive those limits and provide accurate information in court.

---

[35] See, e.g., Susan K. Mikulith et al., Relating the Classical Covariance Adjustment Techniques of Multivariate Growth Curve Models to Modern Mixed Effects Models, 55 BIOMETRICS 957 (1999).

[36] A survey of judges found that judges did not perceive lack of preparation as a significant problem for the experts who testify in their courtrooms, but it is unclear whether judges have the capacity to perceive gaps in the preparation and knowledge of these experts. Shirley A. Dobbin et al., Applying Daubert: How Well Do Judges Understand Science and Scientific Method?, 85 JUDICATURE 244, 246 (2002).

[37] Jan Beyea & Daniel Berger, Complex Litigation at the Millennium: Scientific Misconceptions Among Daubert Gatekeepers: The Need for Reform of Expert Review Procedures, 64 LAW & CONTEMP. PROB. 327, 337 (2001).

Relevant Professional Experience

To understand the literature, scientists or practitioners should also have practice experience or have done research in the area. But when the individual has a doctoral degree, or relevant training, or relevant experience, many courts, as noted, will admit the testimony and leave it to the jury to decide the expert's credibility. The result is that the expert's opinions will be deemed competent by the court but not by colleagues, compromising attainment of the goal of truth.

This concern is attenuated by the U.S. Supreme Court's decision in *General Electric Co. v. Joiner*.[38] As discussed in chapter 3, *Joiner* set the threshold for review of admissibility decisions by trial courts to be the abuse of discretion. This standard is intended to grant trial courts a wide range of latitude in their conduct of trials. Short of decisions that are clearly erroneous, appellate courts are unlikely to overturn lower courts on admissibility determinations. Thus, experts cannot expect that trial judges will be consistent from issue to issue, with some judges tolerating unreliability on the part of experts that others would not. This places an additional responsibility on experts and the community of experts to ensure that their testimony will be expert.

Pecuniary Interest

Pecuniary interests reflected in funding of the research by the litigant (such as a funding research by a tobacco company to assess the risks from smoking)[39] can limit one's perspective and ability to be objective and expert. Such work will not necessarily be invalid, but the potential for bias for financial reasons is clearly present and should be considered by the court as well as the proffered witness before presenting information to the court.[40]

> One very significant fact to be considered is whether the experts are proposing to testify about matters growing naturally and directly out of research they have conducted independent of the litigation, or whether they have developed their opinions expressly for purposes of testifying.

---

[38] 522 U.S. 136 (1997).

[39] Tobacco industry documents indicate both that the industry's criteria for research projects discouraged those that might have shown risks from smoking, see Diana Henriques, Tobacco Lawyers' Role Is Questioned, N.Y. TIMES, Apr. 23, 1998, at A18, and that the industry suppressed the results of studies that did detect health risks, see Milo Geyelin, R.J. Reynolds' 60s Data Removal Cited, WALL ST. J., Apr. 15, 1998, at B15; Milo Geyelin, Tobacco Papers Show Lawyers' Control of Data, WALL ST. J., Apr. 22, 1998, at A3.
Mark R. Patterson, *Conflicts of Interest in Scientific Expert Testimony*, 40 WM. & MARY L. REV. 1313, 1314 n.1 (1999).

[40] William L. Anderson, Barry M. Parsons, & Drummond Rennie, *Daubert's Backwash: Litigation-Generated Science*, 34 U. MICH. J.L. REFORM 619 (2001).

... [I]n determining whether proposed expert testimony amounts to good science, we may not ignore the fact that a scientist's normal workplace is the lab or the field, not the courtroom or the lawyer's office. [41]

An extreme example of this type of interest is presented by the expert who works for a contingent fee.[42] Indeed, some courts explicitly consider whether the expert is a "hired gun" when evaluating the reliability of expert testimony, and examine whether the expert's assessment of the data arose independent of the litigation.[43] But courts should also be concerned about whether financial interests will indirectly affect expert testimony. Biases in human decision making are well known and may render testimony less than accurate.[44]

Adequate Preparation

As we argued earlier in our discussion of fairness, some scientists and professionals will fall short of that necessary to achieve the goal of truth as accuracy because they will not expend the necessary preparation time because they have received what they perceive as inadequate compensation, competing professional priorities, or lack of interest.

Political or Moral Interests

Political or moral interests may also affect the accuracy of the testimony. For example, consider the Seventh Circuit Court of Appeals opinion in *Gacy v. Welborn*,[45] an appeal of a serial murder conviction. The defendant, John Wayne Gacy, offered expert testimony by a professor at the University of Chicago. The state argued that the potential bias may have infected the research and the testimony: "Finally, the state reminds us that Prof. [Hans] Zeisel['s] ... study was conducted under the auspices of the MacArthur Justice Center, an organization devoted to the defense of capital litigation, which may have influenced the findings no matter how careful the principal investigator sought to be."

---

[41] *Id.* at 1317.

[42] Committee on Ethical Guidelines for Forensic Psychologists, *Specialty Guidelines for Forensic Psychologists*, 15 Law & Hum. Behav. 655, 659 (1991) ("Forensic psychologists do not provide professional services to parties to a legal proceeding on the basis of 'contingent fees,' when those services involve the offering of expert testimony ...").

[43] *See, e.g.,* Ambrosini v. Labarraque, 101 F.3d 129, 139 (D.C. Cir. 1996): "That Dr. Goldman testified to his opinion of general causation in a public hearing, without any connection to the Ambrosinis' litigation, reduces concerns that Dr. Goldman is simply 'a gun for hire'."

[44] *See, e.g.,* D. Michael Risinger et al., *The Daubert/Kumho Implications of Observer Effects in Forensic Science: Hidden Problems of Expectation and Suggestion*, 90 Calif. L. Rev. 1 (2002).

[45] 994 F.2d 305, 310 (7th Cir. 1993).

Choice of Roles

There is also the matter of the witness' choice of roles. Competence and expertise operate in the context of the adversary system, in which most experts are retained, not court-appointed. Lawyers retain experts to assist them in presenting their case favorably and portraying the weaknesses of their opponent's case. Insofar as experts are concerned, therefore, achieving truth has much to do with how they fulfill their role as retained experts. Detached neutrality may advance the pursuit of truth but not reemployment, whereas overzealous advocacy may advance the expert's employment prospects but not the pursuit of truth as accuracy.[46] For example, overzealous advocacy may result in an expert's selective presentation of the science underlying an opinion, leaving out its limitations necessary to further the pursuit of truth as accuracy. Experts may have difficulty balancing these roles because of the seductiveness of the litigant, the litigants' case, or the lawyer who asks for assistance, or because they see their role as advocate for the client rather than for scientific and professional knowledge.[47]

Moreover, part of being competent is recognizing the boundaries of one's expertise both in terms of one's knowledge and in terms of one's willingness to use that knowledge to present truth as accuracy. When the expert is lacking in either component, he or she should turn down offers to testify. Potential expert witnesses have both a legal and ethical obligation "[to] provide services . . . only within the boundaries of their competence, based on their education, training, supervised experience, consultation, study, or professional experience."[48] And in defining what is their boundary for competence, expert witnesses will not aid in the achievement of truth as accuracy in the courtroom unless they are willing to be unbiased and appropriately prepared to answer the specific questions they are asked to address. The solution to these problems focuses on the expert (e.g., self-vigilance), the professional community (e.g., public vetting of the expert testimony and peer commentary on it; professional sanctioning), and the

---

[46] Daniel W. Shuman & Stuart A. Greenberg, the Expert Witness, *The Adversary System and the Voice of Reason: Reconciling Impartiality and Advocacy*, 34 PROF. PSYCHOL.: RES. & PRAC. 219 (2003).
[47] Bernard Diamond, The Fallacy of the Impartial Expert, 3 ARCH. CRIM. PSYCHODYNAMICS 221 (1959); PETER W. HUBER, GALILEO'S REVENGE: JUNK SCIENCE IN THE COURTROOM 206–209 (1991). A recent survey of judges shows that they perceive experts abandoning objectivity and becoming advocates for their side as one of the most frequent problems they encounter with experts. Shirley A. Dobbin et al., *Applying Daubert: How Well Do Judges Understand Science and Scientific Method?*, 85 JUDICATURE 244 (2002).
[48] AM. PSYCHOLOGICAL ASS'N, ETHICAL PRINCIPLES OF PSYCHOLOGISTS AND CODE OF CONDUCT: 2002, § 2.01(a) Boundaries of Competence, http://www.apa.org/ethics/ (last visited October 7, 2003; ("Psychologists undertake ongoing efforts to develop and maintain their competence.") *Id.* at § 2.03 Maintaining Competence, http://www.apa.org/ethics/ (last visited October 7, 2003); ("Psychologists' work is based upon established scientific and professional knowledge of the discipline."). *Id.* at § 2.04 Bases for Scientific and Professional Judgments.

litigants to the lawsuit that gave rise to the expert testimony (e.g., malpractice and breach of contract lawsuits).

Evaluating the Validity of Nonscientific Opinions

A different problem with attaining truth as accuracy derives from the fact that nonscientific experts do not have any way of determining if their assumptions, opinions, and conclusions are accurate. Practical experience in a clinical setting cannot substitute for rigorous or scientific feedback on the success of one's work. Yet, the work of nonscientific professionals is almost never subjected to such scrutiny. This concern was also raised in the prior chapter. The solution that we provided earlier was to require experts to develop innovative methods to test the accuracy of their conclusions. We offered by way of example the use of simple tests of false-positive identifications by a drug sniffing dog and clinicians' following up patient outcomes. The same recommendation applies with equal force here.

Accuracy When Truth Is a Systemwide Goal

In addition to the goal of truth as accuracy in an individual case in which an expert testifies, truth as accuracy can also be considered as a systemwide goal, which experts may hinder or facilitate in three ways. First, research conducted for nonforensic purposes can influence litigation. For example, research on decision making addressing the phenomenon of hindsight bias has been appropriately used in negligence cases to address claims of failure to predict violence.[49] But nonlitigation research can also be misused in litigation. Consider Roland Summit's work on the child sexual abuse accommodation syndrome, done to provide clinicians with a common vocabulary and to facilitate treatment.[50] This work has been inappropriately used as a forensic tool to identify children who have been abused:

> Some professionals conflated the reactions described by Summit, which are not probative of abuse, with behaviors that are probative of abuse. This combination of behaviors was then denominated a syndrome, the presence of which was supposedly probative of abuse. The defect of this "syndrome" is that some of its components are probative of abuse and

---

[49] Higgins v. Salt Lake County, 855 P.2d 231, 236 (Utah 1993) ("Second, in part because the proposed duty is incompatible with the real world environment in which patients and health care professionals coexist, this ill-defined, amorphous duty would invite jury hindsight bias. *See* Robert F. Schopp & David B. Wexler, *Shooting Yourself in the Foot with Due Care: Psychotherapists and Crystallized Standards of Tort Liability*, J. Psychiatry & L. 163, 165 (Summer 1989)").
[50] Roland C. Summit, *The Child Sexual Abuse Accommodation Syndrome*, 7 CHILD ABUSE & NEGLECT 177 (1983); Roland C. Summit, *Abuse of the Child Sexual Abuse Accommodation Syndrome*, 1 JOURNAL OF CHILD SEXUAL ABUSE 153 (1992). *See also*, Kathleen C. Faller, *Criteria for Judging the Credibility of Children's Statements About Their Sexual Abuse*, 67 CHILD WELFARE 389 (1988).

others are not. Opinions based on such a "syndrome" are of dubious reliability.[51]

Second, scientists may read of cases and decide to conduct original research that will affect future cases raising identical issues. For example, based partially on the testimony of a child witness, a defendant was convicted of murder and sentenced to death.[52] Several years later, the child recanted her testimony, explaining that her mother had on numerous occasions spoke negatively about the defendant, and that she was trying to please the adults interviewing her. After learning of these events, two scientists decided to study the effect of providing negative stereotypic information prior to an event, and suggestive questioning by interviewers after the event, and demonstrated the powerful effect that the two variables in combination had on the accuracy of children's reports for an event. This research was appropriately relied on in other cases.[53] Just as the potential to benefit truth as a systemwide goal may be geometrically advanced by social scientists who identify relevant issues in the forensic setting and conduct sound research to address those issues, so too the potential for harm may be geometrically advanced by flawed research or research conducted to advance an ulterior agenda.

Third, a scientist may conduct research at the request of a lawyer and present the results in the case, with the research also being used in subsequent cases that raise similar factual issues.[54] We have already discussed how adversarial-driven research can affect truth as accuracy in the original litigation, so we will not repeat our arguments here. But if this research is being used in subsequent litigation as well, it also can affect truth as a systemwide goal. In some situations, the researcher may not be aware that the research performed in one case will be used in other litigation. Thus, the researcher may be unaware that he or she is affecting truth as a systemwide goal. In other situations, a researcher may know that the lawyer plans to use the research in more than one case.[55]

In summary, experts teach courts and lawyers lessons when they research and publish that research, and when they testify, which has important implications within any given case and systemwide. The logical implication

---

[51] John E. B. Myers et al., *Expert Testimony in Child Sexual Abuse Litigation*, 68 Neb. L. Rev. 1, 67–69 (1989).

[52] Michelle D. Leichtman & Stephen J. Ceci, *The Effects of Stereotypes and Suggestions on Preschoolers' Reports*, 31 Developmental Psychol. 568, 370 (1995).

[53] See, e.g., State v. Michaels, 642 A.2d 1372 (N.J. 1994); Stephen J. Ceci & Maggie Bruck, *Amicus Brief for the Case of State of New Jersey v. Margaret Kelly Michaels Presented by Committee of Concerned Social Scientists*, 1 Psychol. Pub. Pol'y & L. 272 (1995).

[54] See Witherspoon v. Illinois, 391 U.S. 510 (1968) and Lockhart v. McCree, 476 U.S. 162 (1986) (citing to research relevant to jury death qualification in capital cases).

[55] See, e.g., Peter W. English & Bruce D. Sales, More Than the Law: Behavioral and Social Facts in Legal Decision Making (2005) (discussing McCleskey v. Kemp, 481 U.S. 279 (1987)).

of this conclusion is that we should be concerned with protecting against experts' failing to meet minimum standards of competence both within and across cases. As previously noted, to help achieve such competence, publication and peer commentary of the work of experts ought to be encouraged. In addition, expert witnesses should be subject to disciplinary proceedings, and contract or tort actions, when they fail to act competently or misrepresent their work in litigation. But perhaps the most important solution is for experts to recognize that they should adhere to the principles that guide their learned society when pursuing knowledge and offering services.

JUSTICE

Experts may do more than contribute to or frustrate the goals of fairness, efficiency, and truth. They can also play a significant role in the promotion of justice. Case outcomes affect not only litigants but also have a broader impact on society at large. As Tom Tyler notes in his book, *Why People Obey the Law*,[56] people abide by legal rules in some large measure because of judgments they make about the legitimacy of the system. Beyond the way in which public perceptions of justice affect compliance with legal rules, these perceptions affect our reliance on societal institutions.

Experts can help shape perceptions of the justness of case outcomes in a variety of ways. Scientists' decisions about the subject matter of their research may affect the truthfulness as well as the justness of case outcomes. Absent research on confessions, for example, the impact of certain police interrogation tactics and of the suspect's mental condition on the voluntariness of confessions might never be brought to light. In *United States v. Hall*,[57] the defendant, Larry Hall, was suspected of kidnapping and murdering a teenage girl. After multiple police interrogations by multiple officers, Hall confessed. The defense offered testimony by an expert on false confessions, Richard Ofshe,[58] who would have testified that Hall had a mental condition (attention seeking behavior and high level of suggestibility), which in conjunction with the highly suggestive interrogation style used by the police, could easily result in Hall's giving the response sought by the interrogator. The trial court excluded the proffered testimony on the basis of its belief that it would usurp the province of the jury in deciding whether to believe the confession. The appellate court disagreed, pointing out that "This ruling

---

[56] Tom R. Tyler, Why People Obey the Law (1990).
[57] United States v. Hall, 93 F.3d 1337 (7th Cir. 1996).
[58] Richard J. Ofshe & Richard A. Leo, The Social Psychology of Police Interrogation: The Theory and Classification of True and False Confessions (1997).

overlooked the utility of valid social science. Even though the jury may have had beliefs about the subject, the question is whether those beliefs were correct. Properly conducted social science research often shows that commonly held beliefs are in error."[59] Research that gives voice to a segment of the population whose perspective about the behavior of the police and its impact is often silenced can contribute to a vision of justice for all.

Although there is a compelling logic to the notion that scientists should have an obligation to conduct research that contributes to a more just society, that notion has not yet been recognized in professional codes. Nonetheless, given the importance of litigation-relevant research to justice, society ought to encourage the conduct of such work by neutral scientists. Although the government typically eschews funding applied research, we believe that this policy ought to be reconsidered, particularly where the research can improve justice in the courts.

Of course, expert opinions like those offered in *Hall* can also compromise justice. The appellate court in *Hall*, which reversed the exclusion of Dr. Ofshe's testimony, never engaged in a review of the scientific research on which the expert's conclusions were based. What if the research was flawed?[60] Reliance on the flawed research would result in an injustice to the crime victim in *Hall*. To the extent that the public became aware that faulty science was admitted in court,[61] it should diminish the public's perception of justice.

It follows that if experts are to further the goals of justice, it is important not only that they conduct forensically relevant research, but also that they do it right. To the extent that a scientist fails to act competently in the conduct of research, the traditional scientific mechanisms of peer review and other types of professional vetting are the appropriate ways to encourage competence. When the scientist provides incompetent expert testimony, the solutions we offered above in our discussion of the goal of truth, namely publication and professional peer commentary on the testimony and professional discipline and civil actions seeking to hold the expert accountable, should also be applied here.

The way in which retained experts are used also contributes to the perception of justice. Although lawyers and the experts they retain contribute to a sense of justice in which everyone has an opportunity to tell his or her story, there is another side to this tale. The way experts are used

---

[59] 93 F.3d. at 1345.

[60] *See, e.g.*, Paul G. Cassell, *Balanced Approaches to the False Confession Problem: A Brief Comment on Ofshe, Leo, and Alshuler*, 74 DENV. U. L. REV. 1123 (1997), in which a law professor who had studied the impact of *Miranda* offered a critique of Ofshe's research, claiming that he failed to provide empirical proof that police behavior of the type claimed had actually resulted in false confessions.

[61] *See, e.g.*, PETER W. HUBER, GALILEO'S REVENGE: JUNK SCIENCE IN THE COURTROOM (1991).

also contributes to public perceptions of a battle of the experts, in which there is no objectively correct scientific truth, only partisan witnesses and the lawyers who retain them.[62]

To reconcile this tension between retained experts helping litigants to find their voice and contributing to a perception that there are experts who are willing to say just about anything for the right price, requires the retained expert to be and be perceived to be impartial. This impartiality increases the likelihood that the information provided to the retaining lawyer will be accurate for strategical decision making and that the fact finder will perceive the expert to be credible.[63]

As noted in our discussion of fairness, the fees experts charge often preclude litigants from retaining their services, which in turn affects perceptions of justice. When fees are very high, less well off litigants will be precluded from hiring those experts. Even when fees are very low, indigent defendants will still be precluded from hiring the expert. When expert testimony is critical to the success of a case, justice turns on a litigant's fiscal resources. Although the lack of an expert affects the basic ability of the defendant to present his defense effectively and hence the fairness of the trial, it also teaches the public that indigent defendants do not receive the same treatment under the law as nonindigent defendants. This will affect the perception of justice. The solution to this lack of access to experts appears above in our discussion of fairness, and thus will not be repeated here.

The willingness of experts to testify for unpopular parties or politically unattractive causes can play an important role in attaining justice for all. The American Film Institute recently voted Atticus Finch, the lawyer played by Gregory Peck in the film based on Harper Lee's novel, *To Kill A Mockingbird*,[64] as the number one movie hero of all time.[65] Although Mr. Finch's client is convicted in the face of overwhelming evidence of his innocence, Finch's unpopular defense of a black man in a small southern town during the Depression evokes a notion of justice in which a lawyer is willing to take an unpopular case in an effort to see that the system works for all.

This aspect of justice has implications for expert witnesses. As cases become increasingly complex, and as science offers more relevant evidence for particular cases, the willingness of experts to stand up in the face of popular opinion is an important aspect of justice. One example of social

---

[62] *See, e.g.*, Mike Kataoka, *Expert Witnesses See Big Money: Scientific Evidence Creates Opportunity*, PRESS ENTERPRISE (RIVERSIDE, CA), (June 16, 1997), at B01.

[63] Daniel W. Shuman & Stuart A. Greenberg, *The Expert Witness, The Adversary System and the Voice of Reason: Reconciling Impartiality and Advocacy*, 34 PROF. PSYCHOL.: RES. & PRAC. 219 (2003).

[64] HARPER LEE, TO KILL A MOCKINGBIRD (1960).

[65] *American Film Institute's 100 Years of Heroes and Villains*, available at http://www.afi.com/docs/tvevents/pdf/handv100.pdf (last visited June 25, 2003).

scientists' participating in an unpopular case, which contributed to a perception of justice being served, was their involvement in the John Demjanjuk case. Demjanjuk, a Cleveland factory worker, was thought to have been Ivan the Terrible, the sadistic operator of the gas chamber at Treblinka, Poland, where over 850,000 Jews were murdered during the Second World War. Both the United States and Israel wanted to identify Demjanjuk as Ivan and punish him accordingly, which required denaturalizing and deporting him to Israel for trial on war crimes. Once in Israel, he was convicted and sentenced to death. Social scientists involved in this case identified flaws in the methods by which the few living concentration camp survivors were questioned about Demjanjuk's identity.[66] Partially based on this information and other contradictory eyewitness testimony, the Israel Supreme Court concluded that Ivan the Terrible was another man. His denaturalization was ultimately reversed as fatally flawed.[67]

Ultimately, it is important for scientists and other experts to acknowledge that the justness of the resolution of some legal disputes turns on their decision to come forward to address relevant issues. When this involves helping an appealing victim of wrongdoing, or a child or a person with a disability, it is often relatively easy to persuade experts to come forward. When the person at risk of injustice is less appealing (e.g., a suspected concentration camp guard), the matter is more troubling for many. These unappealing victims of injustice raise more fundamental questions about the purpose of science. If the goal of science is to gain knowledge that can ultimately improve the condition of man, one way to do so is to provide knowledge that will result in more just outcomes in legal proceedings.

---

[66] WILLEM WAGENAAR, IDENTIFYING IVAN: A CASE STUDY IN LEGAL PSYCHOLOGY (1988).
[67] Demjanjuk v. Petrovsky, 10 F.3d 338 (6th Cir. 1993).

7

EPILOGUE: LOOKING TO THE FUTURE

Having identified our proposed solutions to the problems created by *Daubert* and its progeny, it is important to step back and ask, How can we know if our analysis is correct, how we can improve on it, and how we can implement our proposed solutions most effectively? The answers lie with the construction of an empirical research program designed to address the three major components of our analysis: the goals of the Federal Rules of Evidence, the problems caused by *Daubert* and its progeny in implementing these goals, and our proposed solutions to these problems. This chapter begins the discussion of what such a program of research might consider.

THE GOALS OF FED. R. EVID. 102

Our epistemological approach to evaluating Fed. R. Evid. 702, and its interpretation under *Daubert* and its progeny, highlights the importance of Fed. R. Evid. 102 and its goals of fairness, efficiency, truth, and justice. We have proceeded in this book on the assumption that the goals articulated in Fed. R. Evid. 102 are commonly understood and shared by the trial court judiciary, but we have not examined this assumption further, because we know of no empirical work on the topic.

A logical next step in the inquiry we have begun is an empirical examination of the understanding and the conduct of trial judges relevant to the goals of the Federal Rules of Evidence. For example, do trial judges have a common understanding of the rules' meaning? Do trial judges share an understanding of their importance? Do they have additional goals that they use to supplement or supplant the goals of the rules? Do they prioritize some goals over others? Do trial judges consider and seek to balance the goals within or across cases? Do they prioritize some goals in particular classes of cases and minimize other goals in particular classes of cases? Are trial judges consistent across cases in their attention to these goals? If the Fed. R. Evid. 102 goals are important to understanding the implementation of the Federal Rules of Evidence, then seeking a precise understanding of what they mean to trial judges and how judges try to embody them in their decision making will be critical to improving the implementation of Fed. R. Evid. 702.

THE PROBLEMS GENERATED BY *DAUBERT* AND ITS PROGENY

Once we understand how Fed. R. Evid. 102's goals are applied, it is next important to reexamine *Daubert*'s impact on each of these goals. Our conceptual analysis of this issue throughout the book proceeded on the assumption that reported decisions accurately reflected trial court practice. It is important to ascertain whether the picture presented by reported opinions is an accurate representation of trial court practice. A study of legal decisions about the admissibility of expert testimony, like all attempts to study legal decision making, is limited by the fact that only appellate decisions are regularly reported. Because most cases are settled and the majority of the remaining cases that are tried are never appealed, appellate opinions are a precarious basis for speculating about trial court conduct on any issue, including the admission of expert testimony.

What is necessary to examine *Daubert*'s impact on Fed. R. Evid. 102's goals more extensively is better information that includes data sets containing all offers and responses to offers of expert testimony. We need to know what experts are offered and how frequently, when objections are made, including why they are made and why they are not made, the substance of those objections and responses to them, and how judges rule on those objections and their reasoning for so doing. Correlatively, we need to know about the experts who are offered and the basis for their claims of expertise, their conduct as experts, and how their work as experts might be assessed by other members of their professions. Relying on reported appellate cases to assess the impact of *Daubert* and its progeny leaves too much of day-to-day trial court conduct unexamined.

OUR PROPOSED SOLUTIONS TO THE *DAUBERT* PROBLEMS

The empirical information sought above is important to understand the way experts are used in trials and how we can improve this part of the adversarial process. Once this information is available, it is likely to lead to a refinement of our proposed solutions to the problems *Daubert* has created. For example, knowing that judges do not agree on the definitions of the Fed. R. Evid. 102 goals will lead to the expansion of their education to include training on the meaning and appropriate implementation of the goals.

If we are correct in our logic, then it is important that we concurrently seek empirical information on the most effective ways to implement our proposed solutions. For example, we know little about what is possible and what is necessary to mount effective education programs for law students, lawyers, and judges in science. There is theoretical and empirical literature on education in other fields that should be critically scrutinized for ideas about how to best implement our education proposals. Once reviewed, it should be followed up with empirical studies to determine the most effective means to carry out these educational programs with lawyers and judges.

Another one of our solutions to the dilemma posed by *Kumho* was to have the court seek demonstrations of the accuracy of the nonscientific expert testimony and not simply rely on scientific reliability. Demonstrations of accuracy have long been recognized as of value in science and even in law. A next step in implementing the solutions we propose is to survey science and law to collect more instances of these demonstrations to ascertain what can be learned about how to improve their quality and expand their application to assess the admissibility of nonscientific expert testimony.

Our solutions also included recommendations about how the *Daubert* criteria ought to be applied. For example, we recommended that the criteria be applied with equal rigor across all categories of cases, and that all criteria be applied in every case prior to a judge's reaching an admissibility decision. These are solutions that would benefit from decision making research into the effect of these recommendations on process and outcomes in simulated decision making tasks.

As we noted in chapter 5, trial court judges may also benefit from appellate decisions that elaborate on the criteria and how they should be applied to various types of expert information. Whether this would be helpful to trial court judges, and how helpful it would be, could also benefit from empirical scrutiny in simulated settings. Such research could also explore whether our recommendation that there be better reporting of admissibility decisions and supporting analysis would help subsequent decision makers reach better decisions.

Although research into the epidemiology of proffers of expert information (e.g., when it is offered, how often it is offered) was discussed in the prior section, our recommendations would also benefit from empirical scrutiny of two other issues. First, it would be helpful to understand the judgment and decision making of experts in their roles in the adversarial process. For example, when and why are they likely to act less competently or impartially? What peer review process is best able to bring the judgment of the expert's professional peers to bear on assessing the competence of the expert's opinions? If an effective system of peer review of expert testimony is implemented, what impact would that have on the competence of expert witnesses in that profession? What is the deterrent effect of professional disciplinary proceedings, state licensure actions, and civil actions on the behavior of experts? Second, it is important to gather information on how many cases should qualify for the appointment of court-appointed experts and how financially capable are the courts of paying for these experts. Stated a slightly different way, what has been the impact of fiscal constraints on the appointment of experts? Have some judicial systems developed approaches to appointment notwithstanding fiscal constraints from which others might learn?

Finally, it is important to gather empirical information on how our proposed solutions would impact on Fed. R. Evid. 102's goals of fairness, efficiency, truth, and justice. For example, if judges were required to apply all possible *Daubert* criteria in each case, would it change our evaluations of the likelihood that truth as accuracy in admissibility decisions would be achieved? Would better reporting of admissibility decisions, and their supporting analyses, increase truth as accuracy?

CONCLUSION

The importance of empirical research to validate our analysis and refine our proposals cannot be overstated. However, *Daubert*, *Kumho*, and *Joiner* are being implemented every day in the courts in this country. As the courts cannot place litigation on hold, waiting for research to be conducted that is relevant to a contested issue in the case, neither should the recognition of the problems that we identified or the solutions that we proposed be put on hold until our recommended program of research has yielded its findings. We have provided a framework to reconcile the law with scientific and other expert knowledge that should be vigorously discussed and implemented in the near future.

TABLE OF AUTHORITY

INDEX

competence of, 92
educating, 103–105, 109
for indigent defendants, 115
responsibility of, 4, 46
scientific knowledge of, 51–52
Lay witnesses/testimony, 4–6, 27
Lee, Harper, 144

MacArthur Justice Center, 138
Macro-level notions of efficiency, 18–19
Mancuso v. Consolidated Edison Co., 71
Medical history, 81
Medical literature, 82–83
Memories, recovered repressed, 90–91
Mental health professionals (MHPs), 7–9
    competence of, as expert witnesses,
        134–135
    criticisms of use of, 8–9
    general acceptance standard used
        for, 75
    qualifications of, 29
Mental states, 8
Methodology
    accuracy of, 120
    focus on, 84–85
Methodology, validity of, 36
MHPs. See Mental health professionals
Micro-level notions of efficiency, 18
Moore v. Ashland Chemical Inc., 53
Moral interests, 138
Moral standards, 25
Multiple relationships, 133–134n.30

National College for the State Judiciary,
    103
National Research Council, 57, 62–64,
    67
Neutral experts, 100–103
Neutral rules, disparate impact of, 91–92
New England Journal of Medicine, 83, 85
New Hampshire Supreme Court, 90
New Mexico Court of Appeals, 59, 60
Ninth Circuit Court of Appeals, 47–48,
    78–79
Nonscientific evidence and testimony,
    8n.18
    and efficiency, 52–53
    evaluation problem with, 73–84, 140
    and Kumho, 38–40, 106–109

and perceptions of justice, 119–120
and truth, 116–117
variability in admissibility decision
    making for, 93–94
Novel science, 29–30, 33–35

Objections to expert witnesses
    adversarial model of justice, 102
    litigant's right to raise, 114–115
    responsibility of lawyers, 46
Observations
    clarity of, 57–60
    opinions as personal, 74
    order/weighting of, 60
Ofshe, Richard, 142, 143
Opinions. See also Expert opinion
    facts vs., 27
    of lay witnesses, 4
Order of general observations, 60
Orthopedic surgery, 83

PCBs. See Polychlorinated biphenyls
Pecuniary interests, 137–138
Peer review, 36, 58–60, 64, 65, 143
Perception of justice, 25, 119–120, 144
Personal examination, 80–81
Personal knowledge, 40
Physicians' criteria for life–death
        decisions, 80–83
Physicians' training, 83
Police testimony, 47–48, 53
Policy choices of judges, 69–70
Political interests, 138
Polychlorinated biphenyls (PCBs), 41,
        57, 71
Popper, Karl, 36, 56
Popular opinion, standing up to, 144–145
Precedents, 68–69, 98
Preparation of expert witnesses, 138
Primary scientific literature, 45, 64–66
Principle D (APA ethical principles),
    126
Principles of Medical Ethics, 126
Private interest litigation, 55
Privilege, 13n.3
Pro bono service, 125, 127
Procedural rules, 111, 131
Product liability claims, 38
Professional standards, 66

ABOUT THE AUTHORS

Bruce D. Sales, PhD, JD, is a professor of psychology, sociology, psychiatry, and law at the University of Arizona, where he is also director of its Psychology, Policy, and Law Program. Among his other works are: *More Than the Law: Behavioral and Social Facts in Legal Decision Making* (with P. English; in press); *Laws Affecting Clinical Practice* (with M. Miller & S. Hall; in press); *Courtroom Modifications for Child Witnesses: Forensic Evaluation* (with S. Hall; in press); *Family Mediation: Facts, Myths, and Future Prospects* (with C. Beck); *Treating Adult and Juvenile Offenders With Special Needs* (coedited with J. Ashford & W. Reid); *Ethics in Research With Human Participants* (coedited with Susan Folkman); *Law, Mental Health, and Mental Disorder* (coedited with D. Shuman); and *Mental Health and Law: Research, Policy, and Services* (coedited with S. Shah). Professor Sales, the first editor of the journals *Law and Human Behavior* and *Psychology, Public Policy, and Law,* is a fellow of the American Psychological Association and the American Psychological Society, an elected member of the American Law Institute, and recipient of the Award for Distinguished Professional Contributions to Public Service from the American Psychological Association, the Award for Distinguished Contributions to Psychology and Law from the American Psychology–Law Society, and an honorary doctor of science degree from the City University of New York for being the "founding father of forensic psychology as an academic discipline."

Daniel W. Shuman, JD, is a professor of law at Southern Methodist University School of Law in Dallas, Texas. He received his JD in 1972 from the University of Arizona. His other works include *Psychiatric and Psychological*

Evidence (winner of the American Psychiatric Association's Manfred S. Guttmacher Award in 1988); *Conducting Insanity Defense Evaluations* (with R. Rogers); *Predicting the Past: The Retrospective Assessment of Mental States in Civil and Criminal Litigation* (coedited with R. Simon); *Justice and the Prosecution of Old Crimes: Balancing Legal, Psychological, and Moral Considerations* (with A. McCall Smith); *The Psychotherapist–Patient Privilege: A Critical Examination* (with M. Weiner); *Law and Mental Heath Professionals: Texas*; *Doing Legal Research: A Guide for Social Scientists and Mental Health Professionals* (with R. Morris and B. Sales); and *Law, Mental Health, and Mental Disorder* (coedited with B. Sales). He has also authored more than 70 articles and book chapters. He is a member of the American Law Institute and former chair of the Association of American Law Schools sections on Law and Mental Disability and Law and Medicine. His main areas of interest are in the field of law and mental health.